HOPE
FOUND

When life isn't all you hoped it would be.
God is.

Jim and Ginger Ravella

WESTBOW
P R E S S®
A DIVISION OF THOMAS NELSON
& ZONDERVAN

WestBow Press books may be ordered through booksellers or by contacting:

WestBow Press
A Division of Thomas Nelson & Zondervan
1663 Liberty Drive
Bloomington, IN 47403
www.westbowpress.com
1 (866) 928-1240

ISBN: 978-1-5127-7787-1 (sc)
ISBN: 978-1-5127-7788-8 (hc)
ISBN: 978-1-5127-7786-4 (e)

Library of Congress Control Number: 2017903591

Print information available on the last page.

WestBow Press rev. date: 10/25/2018

Dedication

Hope Found is dedicated to Andrea June Ravella and Troy Lee Gilbert, both well-loved warriors of the faith. So much of who we are is because of what we learned from the two of you. *Hope Found* is a memoir of the stories that make up our family, so it is also dedicated to our seven children, Nicholas, Anthony, Boston, Greyson, Isabella, Aspen, and Annalise, who have endured much at a young age and have done it with grace. May God always be the center of your lives, and may you never forget the examples set forth by Andrea and Troy. Their stories of authentic strength through Christ help us all find hope along life's broken roads.

> Precious in the sight of the Lord is the death of his faithful servants. (Psalm 116:15 NIV)

Contents

Acknowledgments

Hope Found was written with a tremendous amount of reflection, many tears, and—with seven children and two full-time jobs—a lot of interruptions. It took almost five years to finish a story that is constantly being written as the Lord teaches us how to trust Him more. He put it on our hearts after the success of our blog—not success in terms of "look how great we are" but success in terms of "look how great God is!" Obedience to Him and a desire to help someone find hope have been the two driving factors behind writing *Hope Found*. But there is a time when you know you simply must finish something because something bigger is happening. That season is now. The world needs Jesus more than ever.

We would first like to thank our kids, Nic, Anthony, Boston, Greyson, Bella, Aspen, and Annalise, who have endured great amounts of heartache far too early in life. They have not only stood up under the weight of loss but also have each supported our hectic lifestyle of writing and speaking so that others may be helped. It's selfless to give up time with a parent, no matter the reason. We are very proud of each of our children!

We could not have told the long and complicated story of not just one but essentially three different families—Jim and Andrea's, Troy and Ginger's, and the Gilbert–Ravella blended family—without the wonderful editing help of Ginger's father, Dr. Jay Gurley, and our friends Amy Henrichsen and McKenzie Cranford. The tireless efforts of all of these people to help us weave together the many different elements into a common theme have been invaluable. Cover, jacket, and some family photos are all courtesy of Jennifer Denton, an amazing photographer friend in San Antonio, Texas.

We are thankful for every family member and friend who selflessly contributed to building us back up when our worlds were falling apart. There are too many to name here, but we hope they know that the fingerprints they left on our souls will forever remain.

Most of all, we thank the Lord Jesus Christ, from where our help comes.

> The Lord says, "I will rescue those who love me. I will protect those who trust in my name. When they call on me, I will answer; I will be with them in trouble. I will rescue and honor them. I will reward them with a long life and give them my salvation." (Psalm 91:14–16 NLT)

Introduction

We are not sure where you are in life as you pick up *Hope Found*. Whether you find yourself in a time of joy or pain, or possibly transitioning between the two, our heartfelt prayer is that you are pointed toward hope as you read these pages. Our deepest desire is that the truth of God's promises in your journey to healing will remain as a lasting source of encouragement. In our story, you will be reminded that God is far bigger than the box in which we tend to confine Him. If you are gifting this to someone as they struggle to remain afloat in the deep waters of sorrow, remember to pray for them long after the book leaves your hands.

Is your relationship with God built on a foundation of what He does for you? Or, even more so, what He prevents in your life? Are all the testimonies you hear only about answered prayers? Will your faith in God change if He allows suffering in your life? What price is too high for God to ask you to pay? What do you secretly hope God will not ask of you? These are the difficult questions we don't want to ask ourselves.

Most of us come to God when we hit rock bottom and realize we can't fix a problem alone. Realizing our inadequacy, we fall at His feet in times of great desperation. God in His faithfulness lifts us from the pit of despair. When the imminent danger is removed, we tend to go back to our former ways, until the next disaster hits. It becomes a never-ending process of seeking our independence, all the while searching for a way to "get through" the hard parts. We measure His goodness or unfairness according to our own devices, because our view of God is often skewed by limited perspective or fleeting emotions.

However, without our God, we wander this earth facing an eternity apart from all that is holy. If He saves us from pain or suffering in this life, we rejoice, but we must not turn our back on Him if our prayers aren't answered in the way we wish. He already paid the ultimate price and showed us the greatest love ever known by laying down His life on the cross.

Hope Found is about two Christian military families and their stories, including the good and the bad, as they faced the ultimate tests of their faith. Herein are the stories of two men, faithful husbands and caring fathers living out their boyhood dreams to become United States Air Force fighter pilots, and of two women, loving mothers and dedicated military wives following their college sweethearts and loving every minute of it. Andrea and Jim Ravella fought cancer. Troy and Ginger Gilbert fought the war on terror. After the battle was over, there were some casualties, many tearful good-byes, and countless broken hearts. Andrea and Troy received their crowns of victory as they met Jesus face-to-face. Andrea, having suffered a four-year fight with breast cancer, died at the age of forty-five. Troy was killed flying a combat mission in Iraq. He died at the age of thirty-four. Between the two families, seven children were left without one of their parents. Two widowed spouses, Jim and Ginger, were left to pick up the pieces.

It is we, those spouses left behind, who pen *Hope Found*. Seemingly, God had not fulfilled His promises. Why would He allow such destruction to wreak havoc in the lives of those faithfully loving and serving Him? Did He change in an instant? Or were we, those left behind, the ones who needed to change? Our faith was based on our plans, instead of our plans being based on our faith.

Our lives were shaken by drastic events caused by death. We never intended to live a shallow Christian life, and outwardly we looked "faithful." We went to church every week, attended small groups, and served in our respective churches' ministries. We believed that Christians are meant to be the light of the world—and what better light is there than being set apart through blessings? Sound familiar? It certainly does for many of us as part of the affluent Christian church in the Unites States. Our focus more often falls on family happiness, creature comforts, financial security, and physical safety more than on resting in God's will, trusting His sovereignty, choosing joy through sorrow, and furthering His kingdom on earth, even when life has seriously let us down.

Our writings were never intended to be a book. We certainly don't have "author" on either of our resumes. The pages of *Hope Found* were initially simply the lamentations of our hearts on our blog. One day we realized, much to our surprise, that we had thousands of followers. It appeared we weren't the only ones who wanted to find reconciliation between the God we loved and the life we lived.

We remember well what it's like to face the fog that makes focusing on any task a serious challenge. So, we wrote this with that in mind. Our hope is that *Hope Found* is easy to read and provides a simple way to find some truths amid all the confusion of life. Each chapter has one common message, but from two different perspectives. Lessons learned along the way as we found God's silence and seemingly unanswered prayers. They became moments mingled with His mercies. Some things were learned after considerable reflection and years of searching. There are corresponding biblical scriptures highlighted throughout. In the beginning chapters, you will find the foundation and history of our two families. You will meet two great heroes of faith, Troy Gilbert and Andrea Ravella. We are honored to share our journeys as grieving widow and widower, single parents, sojourners of Jesus, and now husband and wife. Our journeys of loss were very different. One was slow and painfully drawn out; the other, tragically instant. While the losses may be very different from yours, the struggles, questions, and principles expressed herein can easily be applied to any loss—not just the loss of a person, but also perhaps the loss of a dream, of an expectation, or even of your faith.

Most of all, *Hope Found* is a story of God's faithfulness to us and how His love always wins. There are times in our lives when He teaches us how to say, "Not my will, but Yours, Lord." He loves us too much to let life's complacency and comforts keep us from having an authentic relationship with Him. We may walk away from God in anger, frustration, and bitter disappointment, yet He not only waits for us but also meets us in the darkest valleys. If we open our eyes, the light will eventually break forth.

Dear friends, do not be surprised at the fiery ordeal that has come on you to test you, as though something strange were happening to you. But rejoice in as much as you participate in the sufferings of Christ, so that you may be overjoyed when His glory is revealed. (1 Peter 4:12–13, 19 NIV)

C. S. Lewis wrote a book titled *The Problem of Pain*. He reminds us that even though none of us enjoy pain, we all know it serves a purpose—to alert us to the fact that something is wrong so we can take the measures to cure the ailment. Deep pain, especially deep emotional pain, has no quick fix. But it doesn't have to leave us hopelessly stranded on the side of life's roads. If we cling to Christ, hold fast to the truth, and lean on others who have gone before, beauty will rise from ashes. Don't give up as you walk the long, broken roads of this life on earth. There is a path that leads to peace and healing. You may not see it right now, but hope can be found.

Ginger and Jim Ravella
June 2016

Chapter 1

Troy

I am comforted to know that regardless of the outcome, God is in control.

—Major Troy Gilbert (e-mail to home from Iraq, October 5, 2006)

I have fought the good fight. I have finished the race. I have kept the faith.

—2 Timothy 4:7 (NIV)

The righteous will be remembered forever.

—Psalm 112:6 (NASB)

Ginger

There are few people we meet in life who demonstrate the true meaning of devotion. Most of us struggle with authentic devotion because it requires total focus on something or someone else. Motherhood does a lot to stretch a woman (and I don't just mean literally). It's a huge step to put us on the path of real selflessness and maturity; to make us put ourselves last. Thankfully most of that comes naturally and begins the moment you know you are responsible for the life growing inside of you. I teach my children the mantra, "I am third." Jesus is first, others are second, and we come last. I know there are still many moments when I focus more on myself than on those around me. I consider myself unworthy to have known someone very early in my life who modeled how to put others first in everything. That person was Troy.

He was only seventeen years old when we met, but even then I knew he was different. He was handsome, kind, fun, and all the things a college girl wanted. There was a genuine deepness about the way Troy loved. It was selfless. It was all-encompassing. If Troy cared about you or believed in something, he never wavered in his loyalty. He possessed a rare passion for his convictions and a rare compassion for people. Troy uniquely captured the essence of both. As I recognized early on, and as many others would later learn, if he was devoted to you, then he was devoted to you until the day he died.

Major Troy "Trojan" Gilbert, was born in Bossier City, Louisiana on February 19, 1972. Troy and his sister, Rhonda, were only eighteen months apart. Soon after Rhonda was born, Troy's military family moved to Texas. His father, Ron, served active duty and civil service in the US Air Force for a total of forty years; his mother, Kaye, was in the Air Force Civilian Service for twenty years.

Troy began his education in an Air Force Academy preschool and completed high school in Germany at a Department of Defense Dependents School (DoDDS) on Bitburg Air Force Base. He was the definition of an Air Force brat. A life deeply rooted in the military helped him learn how to adapt to new people and different environments with grace and ease.

Even at a young age, Troy was a rare combination of all-boy rambunctiousness and thoughtful sensitivity. He was known for his kindness and a selfless attitude.

His mother recalls that he never missed someone's birthday, a holiday, or Mother's Day. She loves to tell a story of how once, when Troy was in second grade in Germany, he climbed into a Dumpster to retrieve a discarded plaster-of-paris flamingo plaque. He thought that it was pretty and that his mom would love it. Even without money, he always found a way to give gifts. That plaque is still hanging in her kitchen today.

Throughout Troy's childhood, his family was assigned to many different military bases around the globe. Troy attributed his appreciation for different kinds of people and the ability to make new friends easily to this nomadic lifestyle. He was always a go-getter and readily got involved in whatever sports team or activities he had access to. From participating in Little League baseball, competitive swimming, and soccer, to exploring the great outdoors, he was always active. When he was young, his family was stationed in Colorado and would go camping nearly every weekend. His parents recall Troy and his sister wading into the Colorado streams seeking adventure. They caught fish, cooked them on an open fire, and sat around the campfire telling stories. His dad took him on his first deer-hunting expedition when he was in high school, during which time he shot his first big buck. Troy would later become a skilled hunter and outdoorsman. Our firstborn, Boston, shares his father's love of soccer, and our second son, Greyson, shares his love of the great outdoors. All our children are friendly and kind and genuinely love people—traits that reflect much of who their dad was.

While Troy had many interests, he had one passion: flying airplanes. Many who knew him say he was born to be a pilot.

His mom remembers he always loved aviation. As a boy, he watched the planes take off and land on the base runways. He was always mesmerized and fascinated by the phenomenon of flight. He would ride his bike as close to the flight line as possible just to get a better look.

Troy loved his little sister, but he always found a way to make everything a competition with her. So she was never surprised that he worked hard to be the best at whatever he set out to do. She recalls that he was "the Energizer bunny of the family," always active, always doing something for others. Rhonda remembers, "He was a great older brother who went out of his way to take care of all of us."

Troy and his sister, Rhonda, at his Pilot Training
Graduation, Sheppard AFB TX, December 1999

Handsome by anyone's standards, Troy had an all-American clean-cut look that drew attention wherever he went. He was also a sharp student blessed with little need to study. After he graduated from high school at Spangdahlem Air Base, Germany, he returned to the States without his family. Troy first attended college in Texas at Angelo State University and later graduated from Texas Tech University at the age of twenty-one with a degree in international economics. Soon afterward, he joined the US Air Force with the goal of becoming an F-16 fighter pilot.

Troy and Ginger's wedding day May 22, 1993

I met Troy at Angelo State, where the story of our life began. He was a freshman and I was a sophomore. I was smitten from the first day I spotted him in the cafeteria. He was a good southern gentleman, yet quite cosmopolitan and mysterious with all his world travels. He was dashing, confident, and more mature than young men his age. Yet I quickly realized he was also authentic and sincere. He treated me like a queen. And something about him made me know that he could handle anything, most of all his strong-willed girlfriend: me. We married in 1993, one week after college graduation. A year later, Troy was accepted to Officer Training School at Maxwell AFB, Alabama. We were officially grown-ups and felt ready to take on the world together.

Troy Gilbert becomes a Second Lieutenant in the USAF 1995

Like most young military families, we had little money in the early days and were constantly moving to follow assignments, including an overseas tour at RAF Lakenheath in England. During the three-year assignment there, Troy and I both rededicated our lives to the Lord. We joined a Bible study full of young Christian military families. The experience of being so far from home and all that was familiar really solidified who we were as a couple. It helped us establish not only our commitment to walking closer with Christ but also our commitment to one another. While stationed there, we once attended a "marriage encounter" weekend for couples. These retreat weekends were pretty popular in the States. I'm not sure if the idea had caught on yet in Britain. Unlike Americans, who tend to be more touchy-feely, the Brits are generally more proper and stoic. I recall how Troy and I stood out from the group. He and I were the only Americans, and we ended up giggling the whole time about how uncomfortable the English couples appeared at this overtly Americanized open approach to communication, love, and marriage enrichment.

Troy wasn't one to journal a lot, but that weekend in the English countryside, he did. I still treasure the little blue notebook in which he told me why we should always remain a couple, facing whatever the future threw at us. Following is an excerpt from Troy's journal.

I remember the day we moved into our first apartment after we were married. I was so proud, happy, and ecstatic to be your husband. After graduation from Officer Training School (having been away from you for three months), and after being so busy, focused, and alone, seeing you was an incredible breath of fresh air in the Montgomery Alabama, sky. I am excited about us, our love for one another, and the things we can and will accomplish together.

The Lord blessed me when He brought us together. He gave me the most incredible woman in the world—a woman who has pledged her life with mine and meant it. I know it's been hard to follow my choice of an Air Force officer career. You will never know how much I thank God for your support, your love, and your friendship.

—Troy

Here are some of my written words to him from my own journal:

I belong with you. We're like a chain of paper dolls that, when cut in half, are still connected. One without the other is not complete. A part of me would be missing without you.

—Ginger

After he was accepted to pilot training and obtained his wings, Troy logged more than a thousand flying hours. He was given the call sign "Trojan," a reference to his given name, but also meaning "great warrior." Later, I would see that it was prophetically fitting. On a fast track within the military ranks, he served as a protocol officer, an executive aide, a command pilot, a flight instructor, and a squadron assistant director of operations. He worked on advance logistics for President George W. Bush's Air Force One and was selected for the Army Command and General Staff College in Kansas.

At heart, he was first and foremost a family man: husband and father to our five children, all under the age of eight when he deployed to Iraq. He was a man whose love and respect for God, family, and country spoke volumes as to how he lived his life. One of the permanent images of Troy etched in my mind is of him kneeling down gently while explaining things to our children or lovingly disciplining them. He never yelled or lost his temper. It was evident—he was not only born to fly; he was also born to be a dad.

Troy and Greyson – just a couple of cowboys, Aviano AB 2001

Among his military colleagues, Troy was known as a model pilot who never failed to put his best effort forward and who could always be counted on to help others. Trojan could also be assertive, strong-willed, and opinionated—traits shared by many fighter pilots who prefer action to words.

The constant relocations, our lack of finances, and our growing houseful of kids, though challenging, never tore us apart as it did some couples. As long as we were together, we didn't mind where we went or what we didn't have. We both wanted a big family and were happy when our two boys, Boston and Greyson, came along so quickly.

Our first daughter, Isabella, was born while we were stationed at Aviano Air Base, Italy. Twin girls, Annalise and Aspen, were born later at Luke AFB Arizona, six months before Troy left for Iraq. Those twin girlies completed our family. Troy and I were tired, but proud parents of a full quiver of kids. He spent every spare moment he had with them before deploying to Iraq. I prepared for his absence once again, this time with five young children and the fear of sending him off to war for the first time.

We had faced eleven moves, spent countless months apart during deployments, lived in two foreign countries, and had five children in our thirteen years of marriage. In our hearts, we knew that a four-month combat deployment might be one of our toughest challenges yet.

Despite all of his obligations with combat training, instructing younger pilots, and readying our lives for his deployment, Troy's parting gift to his parents, grandmothers, and family was a road trip to Texas. He not only wanted to visit family and friends, but also unselfishly committed to help take care of things they might need done while he was away.

He was a man on a mission, determined to lay a ceramic floor in his parents' kitchen. Once finished with that, he drove a couple of hours to his grandmother's house to mow her grass. Afterward, he went to his other grandmother's house, where he bought and installed a window air conditioner. He did all of this in spite of the sweltering 110-degree Texas summer heat. With the spirit of a true servant, Troy gave his eldest family members his most precious gift—his time.

Phoenix had been our home for two years. Troy and I certainly embraced the ease of living back in the States after being overseas. He and I marveled at the sense of community we felt there, especially from our church. It felt like we had lived there forever, an experience we hadn't had at any other assignment. I never could have imagined how much I would come to lean on this family of believers in the months ahead.

Troy by his F-16, Prague 2002

My best friend, Amy, lived in Dallas, but she promised to help me while Troy was in Iraq, especially getting through the holidays. She and I had weathered many of life's trials via a long-distance friendship. One of the beautiful things about our friendship had always been unconditional love through the hard days and the ugly moments. She promised to come for a visit during Thanksgiving, three months into Troy's four-and-a-half-month deployment. I eagerly waited for that day to arrive. Once Amy was with me, she and I drove from Phoenix to San Diego to take the children to Sea World and the beach. She was trying to help us pass the time on Thanksgiving and ease the sadness while Daddy was at war during the holidays.

There, along the beautiful beaches of San Diego, my cell phone rang. We were overjoyed to see it was a call from Troy. Holidays apart are one of the most difficult parts of deployments. He missed us as much as we missed him. He told me he worked such long hours the day prior that the meager Thanksgiving dinner was long over by the time he made it down to the chow hall. I told him of our day at Sea World with the kids. We talked of Christmas plans. He told me he had just mailed us a special Christmas box containing a video he had made especially for our kids. The kids and I never imagined that this would be the last time we would ever hear his voice.

The next day, the kids and I arrived back home in Phoenix. Amy flew back to Texas, not knowing she would be returning to Phoenix in less than forty-eight hours. When I think about the two days between my return from California and the devastating knock on my door on Monday, I look back and hope I enjoyed the last "normal" days of my life. I doubt I did. It's always in retrospect that you wish you had the perspective of what differentiates a good day from a bad one. There was unpacking, laundry, church, and lunch with friends. I also recall sitting in the morning church service weary of the single-parenting gig and tired of being alone. It seemed like Troy had been gone forever at that point. Now, years later, that seems absurd. The lifetime apart hadn't even begun.

Ginger and her best friend Amy Henrichsen, Central Park NY 2016

11

During the sermon, I stumbled across this verse in my Bible: "He who watches over you will not slumber" (Psalm 121:3 NIV). (In my own handwriting next to it is written, "Hang onto this right now, 11/26/06.") I knew it would remind me that God would help me through the next six weeks until Troy returned. Weeks later when I found that verse, I knew it was a promise that I wasn't alone. Even now, I still remember that I worship a God who never sleeps and who never fails at keeping His promises. He is ever alert, never taken by surprise. On that particular Sunday, I realized the value of clinging to the comfort of the Lord's words reassuring me that I would not be alone in my parenting while Troy was away.

I got an email from Troy that Sunday night. He was counting the days until he would be home with us again, especially with Christmas fast approaching. After New Year's Day, he'd be just weeks away from his return. His spirits were high. He had gotten some good sleep and changed his office to a better location with a window. There was not much to look at, but at least there was some natural light. He was excited about flying the next day. Flying missions were what he lived for over there. He typed "good night" and said he would call soon. It would be his last message to us.

That Sunday evening, my good friend Tracy came over. She is one of those rare people who genuinely cares about what is going on with you and truly listens to your answers more than she talks about herself. She instinctively knew when and how to love me in the way I needed.

My "need" on that Sunday night, November 26, was help with getting lights on the Christmas tree. I can get obsessed with putting Christmas decorations out (the year of the three Christmas trees comes to mind). Troy's big job had always been stringing the lights on the tree and hanging the lights outside. I did the rest. Tracy knew that and probably sensed I was lonely and wanting some adult company. She faithfully showed up, like she would in the months to follow. I tucked the kids in bed and promised them that the next day, November 27, the lights would be up and we would decorate the tree as a family like we always did.

I don't remember the details of what Tracy and I talked about that night, but I am certain she was making me laugh while encouraging me to persevere through the next six weeks. We finished our tree trimming, plugged in the lights, and *poof!*—they all went out simultaneously.

Tracy said, "Let's take them all off and put more on. We're getting this tree ready for those kids!" We were both more than a little tired. She helped me see the project through and then left my house at midnight. As I said good-bye to her, I knew once again that she was a true-blue friend. She hadn't even mentioned putting up her own decorations. Instead, she simply showed up and helped with what she knew was important to me. That is, she helped me as I strived to keep things normal for my kids while my husband was defending our nation.

Little did I know that at almost the same moment as I lay my head down on my pillow that night, Troy was embarking on the most dangerous combat mission known in the history of Operation Iraqi Freedom. November 27, 2006, at Balad Air Base in Iraq began as just another day on the job for Troy. As an experienced Air Force F-16 fighter pilot, he was always mission-ready, whether it be for training, instructing, or actually engaging in combat. On that particular day, he was in combat, deeply engaged in our nation's mission to fight world terrorism. He and his wingman had breakfast in the chow hall at 5:00 a.m. after Troy gave the blessing, asking God to grant them safety and to care for their families back home.

That day Troy would fly over the desolate desert fields about twenty miles northwest of Baghdad. The ground below lay broken and torn apart from war. He was on a routine surveillance mission when an army special operations unit began frantically calling for assistance from anyone in the vicinity. They requested close air support and were in desperate need of Troy's help. After an army helicopter had made a crash landing, insurgents had unleashed heavy machine guns, rocket-propelled grenades, small-arms fire, and mortars, all designed to attack the coalition troops and capture US intelligence equipment. Engaging the enemy meant certain danger for Troy as he singlehandedly launched a counterattack.

For me, that day began as any normal Monday. When I awoke to two hungry baby girls, it was a sunny November morning in the

West Valley of Phoenix. A good cup of coffee and the organized chaos of young motherhood was just par for the course. I got my two older boys, Boston (nine years old) and Greyson (six years old), off to school. I returned home from elementary carpool and put Aspen and Annalise (nine months old) down for a quick morning nap. Isabella (three years old) was rambunctious and happy. I heard a knock at the door. It was my dear friend Christy, who was also a fighter pilot's wife. For most military spouses, deployments and running our homes as single moms was not enjoyable but was commonplace. She arrived with Starbucks coffee in hand. We took her little one and my Bella to the backyard to jump on the trampoline while we chatted and figured out a plan for the day's laundry, dishes, baby-related tasks, and errands. I was happy to have her help, company, and friendship that day. She had faithfully come over every Monday since Troy's deployment began.

From the backyard, I heard another knock at the front door. I walked to the door thinking it was strange to have unannounced company so early in the morning. Christy was the only one I had been expecting. When I looked through our screen door, I remember seeing the color blue, the exact same shade as the military uniform that hung in our closet—dress blues. There were three men standing at attention, along with our commander's wife, whose face was tearstained.

I noticed right away their aversion to making eye contact with me. Usually this sight brings military wives to their knees, assuming something must be wrong. But I had recently heard about a situation where uniformed staff came to the door in need of paperwork to be signed. For one second, the thought crossed my mind that this could be the case. But why would anyone look so horror-stricken if all they had to deliver was paperwork? I looked down and saw my sweet toddler Bella hanging onto my leg. It was then that the visitors asked if they could come in and if my friend Christy, who had just walked up behind me, would please take the children away.

I remember walking down the hallway to Bella's bedroom with the uniformed men following me and then shutting the door behind them. They told me in very measured words that there had been an accident and my husband's plane had gone down.

I rattled off rapid-fire questions, desperate for details, but they gave me very few answers. How and where had this happened? It was somewhere in the desert of a war-torn country. Suddenly Troy felt farther away from me than he ever had. That's all I remember. My college sweetheart, the love of my life, the father of our five children, had been involved in a combat-related crash. They told me the ground fighting was so fierce that they couldn't send search-and-rescue teams immediately to the crash site. I was horrified to think Troy was hurt and needed help or, much worse, that he was dead and lying there alone.

I just kept repeating, "This can't happen; we have five children. This can't happen; we have five children," like a mantra to reverse the words they'd told me. If I said it enough, surely everything would be right again, back to the way it was supposed to be.

Later I would learn the details of Troy's mission and the horror of what happened afterward. Yet at that moment, all I knew was that his aircraft had hit the sunbaked earth and they believed the impact had been swift. But before that happened, Troy saved an entire special operations unit, twenty-two soldiers who walked away and eventually went back to their families. That was the only thing they told me that made sense. Troy rescued someone. Of course he did. That was who he was. Then black smoke billowed into a clear blue Iraqi sky.

The minutes turned to hours as I waited for more news. I wept so fiercely that I thought I would vomit. I still remember sitting at our kitchen table, my head in my hands, unsure of what to do next. Wasn't this the same table the kids sat at eating breakfast as Troy went around to each of them to tell them good-bye just a few months earlier. How had the world changed so quickly? Friends and family started pouring in to help. None of us knew what to do, so we all began cleaning. I know that sounds odd, but the house was a mess and no one could sit still. My priorities had always been family first, housework later, so the house looked a little neglected. Not that day. I picked up a broom and started sweeping like a madwoman—like Troy's life depended on it

Before I knew it, there were literally dozens of friends scattered about in every room. They reminded me of worker ants scurrying to stay busy. I remember watching some girlfriends, ones who were former teachers, sitting on the floor alphabetizing the kids' books. Others were taking my children's outgrown clothes from their closets. These things certainly didn't matter, but they made the time pass. Everyone worked in silence or spoke in hushed whispers.

Men in uniforms came and went. Some I knew like brothers. Others I had never laid eyes on. They showed up and gave me their condolences and/or their latest information. That evening, eight hours after my official notification of the crash, the team knocked on my door for a second time with even more devastating news. I learned that once the search-and-rescue teams were able to get to the crash site and survey the wreckage, they were unable to find Troy's body.

It was explained that the force of the jet colliding with the ground would have propelled Troy out of his seat still attached to his parachute and harnesses. The parachute never deployed. Slowly, my mind began to understand what they were saying. The unimaginable consequence of him being left alone those minutes and hours before rescue teams arrived could mean only one thing: my beloved husband's body had been taken, stolen. Overhead footage filmed the insurgents. The enemy watched Troy's plane crash and almost immediately ran to the crash site and unharnessed his body from his jet seat, carrying him off. Speculative reports followed. There was video showing what was believed to be his remains wrapped in a rug being loaded in the back of an insurgents' vehicle. According to Islamic culture, Troy would be buried within twenty-four hours, but every theory was speculative at best. All I knew was every branch of our nation's military was teaming up on a manhunt for Troy, knocking down doors, chasing leads, doing whatever it took. Back home, we prayed for a miracle. But that miracle would be something we would have to wait for, in God's perfect timing.

Later, I would have to come to terms with what this meant. There was no body to bury, no wedding ring or dog tags to keep and cherish. But mostly it meant that I would have to learn to forgive someone for an unthinkable act, one that showed hatred and disrespect for the person I loved most in the world. It was the bad dream that followed the nightmare.

Only a small portion of critical DNA evidence from skull fragments was left behind. These fragments contained just enough traces that allowed authorities to cross-match Troy's DNA on file in Bethesda, Maryland. For five hellish days, we all waited for the confirmation. On Friday, the DNA was found to be a match. Science and the mercies of the Lord confirmed that it was Troy and that he had been killed upon impact. I remember feeling relief that he was not a POW, alive yet dying at the hands of the enemy. Once the DNA was confirmed, Troy's status changed from "Duty Status Whereabouts Unknown" to "Killed in Action" (KIA). I had the first glimpse of thankfulness I could muster. Though we at home were suffering, Troy was not. Insurance was able to release proceeds to us so that I could support our children. We now had some closure, devastating though it was, that many families from past conflicts never received. My heart aches for their lifetime of unanswered questions.

During that week of waiting, I did many seemingly impossible tasks. The most difficult one, the hardest thing I believe I will ever be asked to do in this lifetime, was telling our precious innocent children that their daddy had died and gone to heaven to be with Jesus and would never be coming home to us.

I don't remember it well or how I found the exact words to use. Friends and family told me later that I was strong and loving with the children. I will always refer to that moment as God-orchestrated and proof that the Holy Spirit can work in, through, and despite our weaknesses. I think the Lord spoke and I just moved my mouth. We were surrounded by God's love, and only with His strength did I find the words to say.

Afterward, as odd as it seemed to all of us, Greyson was completely fixated on decorating that Christmas tree, as we had planned to do the day before. We often tease him about his laser-lock approach to everything. He likes to stick with the plan, but I think in this case, it was the only thing that seemed within his six-year-old control. After delivering the crushing news to my babies, we decorated that beautifully lit tree. It was like standing in the middle of your house after it's been blown to bits by a tornado and trying to put it all back together with some glue and silver tinsel.

Later, as I sat on the sofa with the kids, surrounded by my parents, close friends, and pastor, it was the first time I truly understood and believed the verse in the Bible I knew so well:

> I can do all things through Christ who strengthens me.
> (Philippians 4:13 NIV)

I know it was only Christ's strength in me that got me through that day. I had no previous experience with real loss other than losing both my grandmothers. Losing Troy was vastly different—nothing short of monumental. Since then, I have seen that God specializes in working on monumental tasks in our lives.

After the local news broke, police and television crews began swarming the house to interview us and capture photos of our family. To protect the children from the media, it was decided to move them elsewhere for a couple of days. I had the twins at home with me, along with an onslaught of family and friends.

As more information began to flow, I learned that Troy's efforts that day were of epically heroic proportions as he singlehandedly (his wingman was refueling miles away) saved the twenty-two soldiers, who were heavily outnumbered. He flew at extremely low levels—200 feet above the ground at 500 mph, taking out an enemy vehicle and targeting the second insurgents' truck while taking enemy fire. Given the insurgents' close proximity to our own troops (less than one mile away), Troy had to use the Gatling gun on his F-16. Dropping a bomb would have meant disaster for our own soldiers. On his second pass he came in lower and steeper, not taking his eyes off the enemy. The tail of his jet impacted the ground on his ascension. He was within feet and seconds of making it. The second enemy truck turned and sped off. Both his heroic acts of selfless bravery and his stolen body soon became national news.

Suddenly, our private pain became very public. News crews, local and national, had already camped in front of our house waiting for a snapshot of the devastated widow and her young children. We also had Luke AFB personnel, Troy's fellow pilot friends, and policemen at our door around the clock, keeping people—most of whom were well-meaning—away from us. An extremely unusual cold snap blew in. I remember those fighter pilot brothers huddled around outdoor heaters on the front porch, standing guard all day and night. It was a touching scene among the chaos. I still have the makeshift schedule, a yellow legal pad with shift times and fighter pilot call signs. Some of the pilots I personally knew, but many I did not. Years later I would bump into one of them at a speaking engagement. His wife told me he always refers to those nights sitting guard on my porch as his finest hours of Air Force service. That's how deeply pilots feel about their uncommon brotherhood.

The phone rang off the hook. Political leaders at state and national levels left messages. I was too overwhelmed to reply. Suddenly, I felt as if I had stepped onto center stage for a play for which I had never rehearsed.

I ached for Troy's mother, father, and sister back in Texas. I knew they were devastated and hurting too. According to Troy's last wishes in his military will, it was now my job not only to care for all of our precious, confused, and scared children, but also to plan a funeral, burial and take charge of all our affairs. The press wanted statements. The military paperwork demanded my attention. I had to oversee the rubble that was left of our family life. Paperwork, bills, letters, and e-mails poured in. Thankfully my amazing parents, affectionately known to their grandchildren as Juju and Boppa, wrapped their parental arms around me tight. Amy returned to my home, after having just been there, and didn't leave my side for weeks. Countless others like our Pastor Steve and his wife, Tami, who is my friend, linked arms with my support network and dove in. For every task at hand, God never once left me to deal with it alone. When I look back, I see how the Lord provided for us moment by moment just like He did for the Israelites when He sent them manna, their daily bread, on the dew of each morning.

Troy's gravesite Arlington National Cemetery

My only break from the insanity was to go in my room, shut the door, lie on the floor, and fall apart. Then I would get up, wipe the running mascara from my face, and get back to work at the hardest job on earth—grieving and caring for all six of us. At thirty-six years of age, knowing I still might have forty or fifty more years to live, I couldn't imagine the thought of spending each of those years feeling like this.

Home now became a command and control center. A place I used to love filled with the laughter of children, art projects, warm yummy meals, lit candles—in one word, comfort—my home now felt and looked very foreign to me. "Home" to me always meant Troy, the kids, and me together—a unit, even when we weren't under the same roof. Now I wandered through each room lost, alone and afraid during many sleepless nights. I was a military wife, and that meant that wherever you, your husband, and your children are is home. Simple military housing, a long-term hotel room, a mansion in the Italian countryside—it mattered little as long as we were all together. This was the first house we had ever bought. Each corner had our own personal touch. Now it felt more like four walls about to crumble under the weight of our sorrow.

The days were a blur. When I went to buy something to wear for the memorial service, I walked up and down the aisles of the department store looking at the racks of black dresses. A saleswoman asked, "What is the occasion?" I replied, "The occasion is to bury my soul mate." No response. There is no proper clothing for that.

The night before the memorial service, I was sorting through Troy's neckties with Greyson because he had told me, "Mom, tomorrow for Dad's funeral, I want to wear one of his ties." It was said with confidence, eloquence, and determination. He selected a pale yellow one. To Greyson, wearing his dad's tie was a way to honor him. The pain was almost unbearable.

I don't recall who knotted the necktie for Greyson that December morning, but I do remember seeing him in his little blue dress shirt, a smaller version of one just like Troy's, and a too-big tie to offset it. He wore it proudly. He wanted to be like his Dad. It all made sense. Why hadn't I thought of it myself? He wore the tie the rest of the day, until I made him take it off.

More than eighteen hundred people attended the memorial service in Phoenix on December 6. It was full of warm words, touching stories, music, an emotional slideshow, and a gripping call to invite others to believe, to serve and worship the Lord, just like my husband had done. In fact, more than thirty people accepted Christ as their Savior that day, and numerous others were moved to rededication or service in their own walks of faith. I remember the peace that washed over me each moment of that service. I requested that some friends who sang at our church sing a song they had performed one Sunday morning when I was especially missing Troy back in October—back when I thought I knew what missing him felt like. This time, the lyrics brought a different kind of peace to my soul:

> When the night is falling and the day is done, I can hear You calling, Come. When the night surrounds me and my dreams come undone, when the night would hide my way, I will listen until I hear You say, How I love you, child, how

I love you. When this life is over and the race is run, I will hear You calling, Come.[1]

Five days after Troy's memorial service in Arizona, Greyson packed the same tie to wear again at his father's burial in Arlington National Cemetery. Later that month, photos of the service flashed across the *Air Force Times* website. I'm sure anyone who saw it had to know that the little boy standing by the casket was wearing his dad's oversized necktie. The trip to Washington, DC, for Troy's burial was brutal. Air travel with five little ones, even on a dream vacation, holds certain challenges. But we were headed to bury the small portion of remains of a beloved husband and daddy. Everyone had been weakened by the stomach flu. The twins were nine months old and none too happy to travel almost six hours on an airplane. Only Boston truly understood the gravity of where we were headed.

---

[1] Dennis Jernigan, "When the Night is Falling," 1998, Shepherd's Heart Music.

Greyson wearing his Dad's tie, Arlington National Cemetery, Dec 11, 2006

The flight back was equally horrible. I hand-carried the flag, folded in the beautiful triangular wooden box, and felt oddly unlike any other passenger as I stowed it away in the overhead compartment with carry-on bags from other people. If this shifted in flight, my soul shifted with it. My carry-on was attached to my heart. And my heart belonged to Troy.

As my children, Amy, my parents and I boarded the aircraft home, we realized none of our seats were together. The airline was unwilling or unable to mend the situation, so we would have to rely on the goodness of strangers to swap seats. Amy asked a gentleman if he would move for us. He said no; he didn't want to give up his window seat. I was angered and bewildered that this man did not understand my situation. I assume he did not take the time to see the folded United States flag in my arms, the confused kids who had just buried their father, or my tearstained cheeks. I guess we all can, at times, get caught up in our own world and miss the look of pain on another's face. I'm sure there are many times I have crossed paths with someone facing a trial and never noticed the person. One of the changes in me as a result of going through this suffering is that that I am much more aware of the hurting people around me. I do hope I have learned to take the time to look beyond my own agenda or problems and be open to the opportunities God might be providing me with to meet and help someone in their grief.

Three hundred people came to Troy's burial in Arlington National Cemetery. Another five hundred were at his memorial service in Iraq. People everywhere wanted to pay their respects. At the stateside services, the Patriot Guard Riders were there in red, white, and blue to honor a fallen hero. I had never witnessed such an outpouring of love and support. The Patriot Guard Riders are a nonprofit group of volunteer motorcycle riders who ensure dignity and respect at memorial services honoring fallen heroes or first responders. Many of them are Vietnam veterans who are assuring this generation of heroes that they will have the proper welcome home that they themselves never received.

Troy's remains, weighing no more than a handful of paper clips, had a traditional full-casket military burial. Our situation was anything but traditional. All we had to bury would have easily fit inside something more the size of a shoebox, yet I couldn't have the children find out what had really happened to their father's body. They were too young, too innocent. We all walked behind the caisson, which carried the almost completely empty flag-draped casket. Knowing that Troy's body was still missing was an ongoing source of tremendous sadness and pain for not just us, his family, but also for the nation.

Yet, strangely, I had never felt such peace from the Lord as I did on the days of the memorial service and funeral. I felt not like everything was okay, but like another saint had been welcomed into heaven. While earth mourned, heaven rejoiced. I knew that Troy was safely in the arms of Jesus. He received the gift of salvation he had accepted as a boy and the rewards he had earned as a man. I knew that angels were celebrating his arrival. I also, for the first time, really felt the solidity of the beliefs I'd always had—that there is so much more out there beyond the skies than we can see.

Bella picking flowers to place on her Daddy's coffin,
Arlington National Cemetery, Dec 11, 2006

I have no doubt God was in the cockpit with Troy that fateful day. He loved and cared for Troy more than I ever possibly could have. He was with him until the moment He took him home. And I know Troy must have prayed to Him, seeking His help as warfare became chaotic—maybe a simple "Lord, help me," just as I have done many times since then.

The army special operations commander in charge of the unit Troy saved (whose name is not revealed for security reasons) wrote to me soon after Troy's death. The letter expressed both gratitude and praise for Troy's actions:

> I feel that it is important that you know what Troy did to save us from almost certain disaster on that day. My men and I are part of a small special operations element that became outnumbered and outgunned in the Iraqi desert west of Taji. The pending attack would have been absolutely disastrous for us. Troy, however, stopped that from happening. His amazing display of bravery and tenacity broke up the enemy factions and caused them to flee in panic.
>
> I have never met your husband, but I sensed the warrior spirit in him as he took the fight to the enemy. I sensed his strength of character as he put his life on the line in the defense of others. I sensed his compassion for those who so desperately needed his help. My men and I will never forget the ultimate sacrifice your husband made on November 27, and we will forever be in his debt.

I will forever cherish his letter to us. It speaks volumes of truth about who Troy was, which was evident even to a stranger.

Days later, Troy's squadron, the 309th at Luke AFB, received a letter from the same commander. It is framed and a part of the squadron's memorial to their lost brother.

> My heart is heavy with sadness as I write this, as the thoughts and prayers of our unit are with you and with Trojan's family during this time of grieving. Our entire ground assault force owes Major Gilbert an unpayable debt of gratitude for the actions he took that day. Faced with a crisis situation, we were in dire need of air support to fend off an enemy that had us greatly outnumbered and outgunned. Trojan responded in a calm, collected manner and exuded professionalism and complete control of the situation. We

were in a very vulnerable position on the ground and in great danger of having heavy casualties inflicted upon us. Instead of loitering at high altitudes, Trojan came down on the deck and made it very obvious to the enemy that he was gunning for them. They immediately broke their position and began to flee when he started his strafing runs. During these actions, it was obvious to all of us on the ground that he was singlehandedly breaking apart the enemy forces. Simply put, Troy saved us from certain heavy casualties on 27 November. We are forever indebted to Trojan because of the valorous actions he took. None of us will forget his sacrifice, and we will always be humbled with the knowledge that he gave his life in our defense.

A belief is something you will argue about; a conviction is something you will die for.[2] (Howard Hendricks)

Over the years we have been able to meet many of the men from the unit Troy saved. They told me they still refer to him as "Frosty" because when Troy came on the radio and entered into the chaotic panicked battle scene, he was cool, calm, collected, and in control. They said they immediately knew he was in charge and had come to save the day.

While Troy was deployed to Balad Air Base in Iraq with the 332 Air Expeditionary Wing, he completed twenty-one combat sorties, supporting ground forces routinely under enemy fire. Some were time-sensitive missions: finding and identifying anti-American forces, relaying critical targeting intelligence to the coalition forces, and destroying insurgents using laser-guided weapons. He also volunteered at the Balad Hospital, where he befriended many doctors and saw the other side of war firsthand. He was as loved and respected there as he was at his home base.

Major Troy Lee Gilbert was awarded a posthumous Purple Heart and Distinguished Flying Cross with Valor, the highest Air Force

---

[2]   *"A Lasting Legacy, Howard G. "Prof" Hendricks" Kindred Spirit 37, no 1* Spring/ Summer 2013. 4-7 http://www.dts.edu/download/publications/kindred/DTS-KindredSpirit.Summer.2013.pdf

aviation award. He was the first F-16 fighter pilot lost in Operation Iraqi Freedom. He was the only one whose body was taken by the enemy. More than twenty-six hundred people attended his memorial and funeral services. Once the services were over and friends and family had to return to their routines, I had to face life without Troy, something I had never allowed myself to consider.

Before his deployment, Troy and I had been preparing ourselves for what would have been our twelfth move in thirteen years. This time were headed to Ft. Leavenworth, Kansas, in the summer of 2007. We were already a bit blue knowing how hard it would be to find the quality of friendships and church community that God had placed in our lives in Arizona. As the weeks passed after Troy's crash, I received many e-mails, phone calls, and tributes to Troy. I had a ton of help from family and friends. I saved the hundreds of sympathy cards that arrived daily in the mail, as they are a constant reminder of the compassion Christ displayed through others.

A couple of years after Troy was killed, the kids and I were invited back to a special celebration at our church in Phoenix. I had the privilege of unveiling the new visitors' welcome center plaque; the center had been named after Troy. What a special honor to us and to Troy, as he had earlier poured his heart into creating that very visitors' welcome center. It might be our southern roots or military moving mentality, but Troy and I always felt it extremely important for a church to be friendly. I simply can't imagine that back in the early church days Jesus huddled in the back of the room drinking coffee and only chatting with His disciples. He was about love and openness, so Troy and I believed God's people surely ought to exude a bit of warmth. If we visited a church in a new place and didn't find that warmth, we usually continued looking.

When Troy and I first stepped through the doors of Desert Springs Community Church, we instantly felt that genuine friendliness we sought, and saw evidence of the solid Bible teaching we needed. Wanting to contribute and become involved, we took it upon ourselves to seek out new faces, meet them, greet them, and make them feel comfortable. We served this church in many areas, but the mark I know Troy specifically left behind was that welcome center.

When he told me this was the need the church had and he wanted us to serve in this way, I agreed, but I struggled with the big commitment of setting up and taking down the portable welcome center every Sunday. I wanted to serve, but I didn't want it to inconvenience me too much. Sunday mornings were already hectic with five small children. Regardless, Troy had a vision and a commitment to establishing a real church welcome center ministry. He promised he would help get the kids ready, take them with him, or do whatever needed to be done. Every Sunday he faithfully set up and took down that welcome tent and ministered to newcomers, even in the sweltering Arizona summer heat. I'm very glad he followed through with it, even many times without my support, because I know he touched a lot of people. I just didn't know how many until after he was gone. A woman from church told me Troy had helped carry her child to her car and opened the door for her. It's the little kindnesses people remember long after we're gone.

Desert Springs Community Church has a new building now with a fancy indoor welcome center that Troy never got to see, but there's no doubt his legacy of warmhearted hospitality will forever be its foundation. As you walk in the door, you see a beautiful plaque that reads as follows:

> This Welcome Center is dedicated to the memory of Troy Gilbert, who was killed in action on November 27, 2006, while serving his country with the US Air Force in Iraq. Through his vision and perseverance this Welcome Center was established in 2005, and he was instrumental not only in its inception but also faithfully served here each Sunday morning welcoming visitors until his departure in September 2006. We are grateful for his selfless service and genuine care for others, and we will always remember Troy as a dedicated pilot, a loving husband and father and faithful follower of Jesus Christ.

Dedication of Troy's welcome center at Desert
Springs Community Church 2009

Do not neglect to show hospitality to strangers. (Hebrews
13:2 ESV)

Jesus replied: "Love the Lord your God with all your heart
and with all your soul and with all your mind. This is the
first and greatest commandment. And the second is: Love
your neighbor as yourself." (Matthew 22:37–39 NIV)

Pastor Steve Engram from Desert Springs Church with the
twins, Phoenix AZ, Spring 2007. The Engram family faithfully
carried Ginger and the children through the grief process.

As mentioned earlier, Troy spent a significant amount of time in
Iraq at the base hospital, a makeshift surgical tent, watching the military
doctors administer care to our wounded soldiers. To my surprise, he
told me he watched them work on the enemy's wounded as well. In an
e-mail to me, Troy explained why we would help the enemy: "That is
the type of people, country, Air Force, and Army we are. That's what
makes us different from them."

Sometimes Troy sat with the patients. Sometimes he mopped blood
from the floor or held a patient's hand. I remember him e-mailing me
about a very young Iraqi girl who was wounded and left at the base gates
as a civilian casualty of war. She was treated by our military physicians
and no one had come back to get her, so he asked me if I would consider
adopting her as our sixth child! He didn't see her as a part of the enemy;
he saw her as a potential part of our family. Her family eventually did
return for her. It didn't surprise me that Troy's heart was drawn to
help her.

After Troy died, I received many e-mails from the doctors he worked with. Following are the reflections of one of them:

> Well, after that first visit, it became common to see Troy in the hospital. I never really asked him why he spent so much time at the hospital. I'm still not really sure why, but it was always nice to see him. He was so positive. Everyone liked to be around him. I was working in the ER the night the call came in that one of our pilots went down and the search and rescue teams were out. It really didn't even cross my mind that it could be Troy, but I found out the next day. I've never seen a group of doctors so depressed. He touched so many people, me included. Troy seemed to have a way of making everyone around him comfortable. He always seemed genuinely interested in what that person was saying at that specific moment. His faith was obvious in his conversation. Not pushy. But obvious. He was never negative, which was a true gift around the hospital. Things tend to get cynical here, but he always brought a positive vibe. He was just a good guy. A good man. I only knew him for a few months, but I guess the best way I can say it is that Troy is the man that many of us aspire to be. At Troy's memorial service I learned that he had this effect on everyone. I've never seen anything like it.

Just a few weeks before his crash, Troy showed some of the doctors around the military aircraft on the flight line. They all commented about the specialness of the day when Troy took them on the "field trip" to the flying and operational side of Balad AB. Another doctor wrote the following:

> Despite our very busy schedules, we each spent time in each other's element and learned things that we've never seen before. Troy said that he not only enjoyed going to the hospital to visit with us but it was necessary for him to gain perspective on the war and on life in general. He was an extremely thoughtful and insightful man.

Almost a year after Troy's death, I received this:

> This is probably the fifth time I have tried to write a letter to you regarding your husband and my short but sweet friendship with him in Iraq. ... Another thing that impressed me was the way Troy made everyone feel significant and appreciated. As a Christian, I could tell he was living out the second greatest command of loving your neighbor, but he did it in a remarkable way. He introduced me to the guy who packed their gear, the guy who works on the plane, the guy who calls from the control tower, the guy who ran his office where all the pilots headquartered. In each instance, he relayed their importance, significance and the outstanding job they were doing. It was really amazing and in stark contrast to the way some other high-ranking professionals treated others.

Years later, I still hear from medical personnel who were there in Iraq with Troy, ones who watched him, a fighter pilot, spend his rare off time in the hospital trauma center. I cherish all of the memories that those who knew him over there have shared with me. Those stories are precious gifts to me and the children—a reminder of the wonderful legacy of love and service that Troy left for us to follow.

My grief was immediate and palpable, and felt bottomless for a long while. Troy's sister, Rhonda, explained what losing Troy has meant to her family since 2006. She said, "For me, it was always having someone to rely on. Now that's gone. Watching my parents grieve has been very hard, but Troy left us with valuable lessons: the importance of dedication to God and service to others."

As the e-mails and letters poured in that first week, I continued to wait for the one thing I wanted more than life itself—the Christmas package Troy had previously told me he mailed, more specifically, the video of Troy in the Christmas package. That was one of the first things I thought of after I knew he was gone. A letter and a box from Troy were still headed our way. I had prayed and waited for the postman to deliver it. Talk about begging God for deliverance, not from something but *for* something! God answered. A priceless gift arrived for us four days after Troy died. It was a large package in the mail. There was a beautiful handmade Persian carpet he had purchased for me in Saudi Arabia after haggling with the locals over the price. Another box was full of Christmas presents for the kids: jewelry boxes for the girls, stickers and trinkets for the boys. However, the last gift in the package was the most precious gift I will ever receive. I took it out of the box very gently. It was the videotape Troy had told me about. I would get to see him again, for the last time, on film. I put it in the safe. I didn't watch it for over a year, as I wasn't sure I could handle the heartache of seeing him and hearing him talk to us again. The next year, on what would have been his thirty-sixth birthday, I finally hit play. There he was. It took my breath away. In that moment, he'd never left us. I wept. He was behind the camera for a while at the beginning of the recording. I almost begged him aloud to turn the camera on himself. I hadn't seen him in a year and a half. He gave us a tour of the runways, showing the planes as they took off and landed and taping the busy activity of a base fully operational during war. Later, he prayed with us. He read children's stories to the kids, including one while sitting on top of a building with a gun strapped on his side. I can still picture sweet Troy reading to our children atop that roof in the middle of a war zone.

The children watched the videotape a couple of years after I did. We purchased all of the books Troy had held while reading to his kids through the video camera. They each held their book and followed along, carefully turning a page whenever he did. It was painful but priceless.

The afternoon the package arrived was filled with emotion. Most of all I was very thankful that we got one more moment with Troy. Little did I know that the Lord would give us many moments like that one, an answered prayer, a loving touch in the places that were tender and broken. As I unrolled the Persian rug Troy sent, woven with silken threads of deep red, blue, and ivory, I ran my hands over the plush pile. Smoothing it over the floor of our once-shared bedroom, I lay across it and cried until there were no more tears left to shed. I could almost feel his hands on it too. So began my long and arduous journey of experiencing deep grief while witnessing God's even deeper mercies.

The last Gilbert family photo taken Aug 2006

Chapter 1 *Discussion Guide*

1. Have you or someone you know walked a similar path to the Gilberts because of a sudden drastic life-altering event? Was it crippling emotionally, physically or spiritually? If so explain.

2. Which specific events in your life have had the biggest impact on who you are and what you believe about God? Why?

3. Ginger describes the difference between the muddle and the middle. Describe a time you found yourself "muddling" through and what you learned from that experience. What would you have missed if you had known what the outcome of the situation was going to be before going through the journey?

4. What is the biggest impression Troy's memory has left you with?

5. Ginger describes Troy as a mighty warrior. How would you want someone to describe you after you were gone?

Chapter 2

Andrea

If one person comes to know Christ, it's worth it all.
　　　　　—Andrea Ravella's journal entry of April 3, 2006

This is a psalm Andrea wrote in 2006:

> Praise God, my redeemer.
> You are my Savior.
> My soul is captured by you.
> You alone sustain me.
> Praise God my healer.
> You are my strength.
> I worship only you.
> You renew my being.
> You created heaven and earth;
> There is nothing made that you did not make.
> The earth rejoices at the sound of your name.
> The heavens silently speak of your glory.
> Heaven and earth honor you.
> Abundant blessings come from you.
> Without ceasing I praise you.
> The sound of your name fills me with rejoicing.
> I am your daughter;
> To you I belong.
> You never leave me.
> I will never be abandoned.

You, O Lord, orchestrate my days
And order my nights.
Your provisions cannot be contained.
My fullness overflows.
Praise God, for you are my answer.
When my soul sinks with sorrow, you rescue me.
When I go where I must go alone,
I find you there.
When fear stalks me,
You cover me with peace.
You are worthy of praise.
My blessings outnumber the stars.
You go before me and follow my ways.
My Father, you give good and perfect gifts.
Your eyes never leave me.
I am content in you.

Jim

My desire is to honor Andrea by taking the cold facts found on her death certificate and turning them into the story of who she was and what she meant to me in the hopes that someone else facing difficult times will be encouraged, in the hopes that even in death and "losing" the battle to cancer, I can encourage someone to believe that God loves them.

This is Andrea's story.

On August 23, 2003, our life was typical of an Air Force family, busy and hectic. I was the operations officer of the 90ᵗʰ Fighter Squadron. Our two boys, ages eighteen and eleven, were off to school, and Andrea was scheduled to have her annual mammogram. The squadron had just returned from a deployment the past June, and we were gearing up for another one and a major inspection. I had been deployed for over half of the previous two years, but that was life in an operational Air Force fighter squadron. Andrea and I understood the lifestyle we signed up for, and we loved serving. I say "we" because it takes a joint effort to live the military life. Even though the active duty member is the only one to swear an oath, there is no doubt that you have both "signed up." As a result, your squadron becomes a second family to you. Andrea and I would both ultimately realize how true that really was.

The following four years and four months was a journey of highs and lows. At times we felt like we were lost at sea, unsure of where we were or how it would end; at other times we experienced unexpected peace as we learned to trust that God was in control. When August 2003 arrived, I was ill prepared for the journey that lay ahead of me. However, God does not require us to have every skill necessary to start a journey. In fact, I think the less prepared we are, the greater His opportunity is to use us and show His strength. Trials remove us as the source of strength, so when others say, "I don't know how you make it through the day," we can say, "In Christ alone." And it truly was by His strength and power alone. I did not "tough it out" or "pick myself up by my bootstraps." When the days were hard, I saw how weak and inadequate I really was. I knew that if I was going to "make it," I was going to need someone or something greater than me. Would it be our doctors and their years of education and experience? Would it be modern medicine and the new drug showing such great promise? Ultimately it was none of those. I would learn to fall back upon a foundation that was first formed many years earlier on an unforgettable day when I was just nineteen years old.

It was April 19, 1980. I was a freshman in college. My friend and I were at a stoplight in Wichita Falls, Texas, when I turned to the car next to me and spotted the most beautiful, petite, blue-eyed young woman I had ever seen. It was not just the color of her eyes; it was what I saw in her eyes—something I needed, something intangible and deeper than merely appearance. I can't explain it, but I knew immediately we were meant for each other. The instant our eyes connected, we both knew, I think, that we had met the one person God had created for us. It was truly love at first sight. In those beautiful blue eyes, I saw my future wife. I loved her even before I really knew her. At the time, I had no idea what drew me to her, but I soon learned it was her unshakeable faith in God.

Andrea and Jim's wedding day, April 30 1983

I was raised in an Air Force family. As the son of an Air Force pilot, I was blessed to live out my childhood dream of being a fighter pilot. Born in Abilene, Texas, to an Italian father and Irish mother, I was the youngest of eight kids and felt both Texan and Catholic through and through.

Born in Wichita Falls, Texas, in 1962, Andrea was raised by devout Pentecostal parents. Her father was a pastor, as was her grandmother (very unusual in that day and age) before him. Life was about strict rules. She never wore pants or saw a movie until she was in her mid-teens. As a teenager, the tiny blonde was singing duets in church with her father. She called the church her "lifeline," relying on God for every aspect of her life. Her favorite memories were living next to her grandfather. He was a tall man with a face worn by the hot Texas summers. She told me how she always felt safe in his arms. Once Andrea asked her grandfather if he believed in Christ. She said, "Papaw, you have to choose; it's Christ or the Antichrist." To Andrea, faith was that simple, either a yes or a no. She believed in God, and despite some tough times growing up, she knew that no matter what happened, He was there for her.

It would not be long until her philosophy on life was put to the test. When she was thirteen, her dearly loved grandfather died suddenly of a heart attack. Andrea's foundation was shaken, but she never lost faith in God. Her faith was always like that of a child, pure and trusting. I saw that in her time and time again over the years we spent together. She had reasons to be angry or jaded, even as a young person, but she never was. She made the choice to trust God, not in spite of the hard times but because of the hard times.

June, Andrea's mom, called her daughter "my little miracle baby, a true blessing that was always there for me." June and Andrea liked nothing better than spending time together in the garden while they chatted away the hours. They both got their love of gardening from Andrea's grandfather.

Andrea with her sister Angela and Andrea's great niece
Kaitlyn at her mom's house, Spring 2005

Andrea's sister, Angela, nicknamed her "Jokie," referring to her as "my sweet sister and best friend." No one really knows what "Jokie" means, but it stuck. For the rest of her life, more people knew her as Jokie than as Andrea. Angela and Andrea were as close as two sisters could be. No matter what happened, Andrea would always tell her big sister it was going to be okay.

As crazy as it may seem, Andrea and I began our life together that night at the intersection. She was my first girlfriend. Two months into the relationship, I asked her to marry me. Even though she was still in high school and I had just begun college, I had no doubt this was God's will for my life. We were engaged for three years and married on April 30, 1983, the week after I graduated from college.

We started our life together in San Antonio, Texas, where our first son, Nic, was born. He was a fun-loving boy, with blond hair and blue eyes like his mother. I was a proud father and was learning as I went along. At the time, I was working as a salesman for a hardware company. The money was good, but the work left me unfulfilled. When Nic was one month old, I told Andrea I wanted to follow my dream of becoming an Air Force fighter pilot.

Jim, Nic, and Anthony watching an airshow from Jim's F-15E

Even though it meant giving up both our jobs just three months after we had our first child, Andrea did what she always had done: she supported me. This case was no different. I was soon enrolled in Officer Training School. Andrea and my father pinned my pilot wings on my chest after sixteen months of grueling work. Then, Andrea and I set off for what would become a typical series of assignments, both domestic and international. God blessed my career. After serving as an instructor pilot for four years, I was selected to fly the F-15E, the newest fighter in the United States Air Force at the time. The Air Force afforded me amazing opportunities, including being a National Defense Fellow in Washington, DC, commanding a squadron, and serving as the first F-35 operations group commander at Eglin AFB, Florida.

Andrea pins on Jim's pilot wings, April 1986

Andrea had always dreamed of raising a little girl, but we were not able to have any more children after Nic. We went through years of infertility, and were never able to have another biological child. But God had another plan for us. In 1992 we adopted our second son, Anthony. He was two years old and a gift from God. I loved being a dad to two boys. Dads of boys get the chance to relive their childhoods. I taught my sons to do all the things I enjoyed: fishing, skiing, and building things. Andrea loved our boys with all that was in her. She also cherished spending time with young girls and passing along her talents and wisdom. I have many good memories of watching Andrea with her niece in the garden and with our best friends' daughters in the kitchen teaching them how to cook. There would always be a big mess, but Andrea would tell me to relax, saying it's how they learn.

Growing up in the Catholic Church, I learned about God. But Andrea taught me to know God and have a relationship with Him. Faith and church were important to our life and relationship. Like a lot of Christians, I *perceived* my faith as my center; however, I also allowed myself to become distracted by the trappings of modern life. Occupied by a busy life and unaware of what lay ahead is how I remember the day before my life changed— the day before Andrea told me she found a lump in her breast.

If you have suffered a tragedy, it's common to think about the moment before everything changed. Like the Israelites who wanted to go back to Egypt when faced with life in the wilderness, we often want to return to the familiar when we fear the future. But as God proved Himself to be their Provider, assuring them of His presence by appearing as a pillar of smoke in the day and a fire at night, He will do the same for us. His faithfulness was something Andrea and I needed to remember in 2003 when cancer became part of our life together.

We were shaken to our core, but we would learn what it meant to lean upon God, strip away our own desires, and find rest under the shadow of His wings. Learning to trust is not an easy or instantaneous process. It was a journey we had to walk—and often crawl—together. But we were never alone, never abandoned. I remember feeling like I was hanging on by my fingertips to the edge of a cliff, unable to hold on one moment more. Like an actor in a movie, my fingers were slowly slipping away from my source of safety and there was nothing I could do about it. Too weak to hold on any longer, I was going to fall. It felt like my fate was sealed. I had to face the limits of my own abilities. But as I lost my grip and my fingers slipped from the edge, I did not fall. I wasn't harmed. I broke down and cried when I realized I was never the one truly holding on, but that it was God who had been holding on to me.

In retrospect, I thought back to the letters Andrea had written to me while I was deployed, before she was diagnosed. She told me she was very tired. She would even fall asleep in the car while watching the boys' sporting events. She said she was unable to find the strength to get things done. This was not her usual self, but deployed life was anything but normal, so we attributed it to her being a single mom running the household alone.

After I returned from my deployment in the late summer, Andrea felt a small "pea-like" bump in her left breast. We thought little of it because her last mammogram had been only six months prior and had shown no signs of trouble. Cancer never even crossed my mind. Andrea was a healthy forty-one-year-old who was rarely sick, never smoked, and had no history of cancer in her family.

I remember when Andrea contacted me after her doctor's appointment. I expected the usual "everything's fine," after which I would get back to my busy day, but that's not what happened. Instead, she told me they confirmed the lump, but only after she insisted the doctor perform an ultrasound when the mammogram failed to show anything.

Andrea knew she had felt something, and her intuition was correct. The doctor told her not to worry, as it was small, she was young, and 95 percent of lumps turned out to be nothing. It was our first introduction to the world of chance and statistics—life and death reduced to a percentage. The numbers would prove worthless; odds mean nothing if you are the other 5 percent. It was another lesson I would learn later.

Andrea just before she started chemotherapy, September 2003

It was a few weeks before we got the official word that it was cancer. Those were painful and difficult days of waiting. It was a mental battle every day to fight back the unknown. In many ways, I think the waiting was harder than fighting the actual cancer. At least once we knew the enemy; we could focus our energy on the fight. Waiting created a void that my mind was all too happy to fill with every worst-case scenario. The Internet only fueled this as I became "educated" from unknown sources that knew nothing of our specific case.

I will never forget hearing the doctor tell us that Andrea had invasive ductal carcinoma. The medical lingo made it sound not very bad, maybe because he didn't say the word *cancer.* Everyone knows that the word has too negative a connotation. I think it really began to sink in the day Andrea and I went to the oncologist. That's when it all gets serious - when you are handed off to a specialist because your first doctor is no longer qualified to treat you. You must, instead, see someone trained to treat your "condition."

I called our first appointment with the oncologist "formalities and fear." I had already come to hate waiting in those little rooms with Andrea lying on the table in her gown with the instructions, "Open in the front, please." You sit there and try to fight back the tears and fears. Unable to comprehend it all, my mind blocked out the reality of what was happening. I was in denial, trying not to think that my wife was seriously ill. She looked the same. She felt the same. Maybe this was all a mistake and the oncologist would burst in and tell us they had mixed up Andrea's test with that of some other poor soul and that we could go home, back to our life as it was the day before. Instead of that, the doctor came in and started telling us treatment options. This was really happening. And it was happening to us.

Jim and Andrea after Andrea completed her first
round of chemotherapy, Jan 2004

Cancer is hand-to-hand combat. As cancer tries to overwhelm you, you try to keep your distance from it. Like a fighter trying to stiff-arm his opponent so he can catch his breath, you try to give yourself some distance from your adversary so you can figure out what's going on. As in any battle, you need to survive the initial blow from your opponent. You are a new recruit, inexperienced in the ways of the war. Meanwhile, cancer is a seasoned veteran. It strikes you with blow after blow as you fall to your knees trying to block the attack. You can't even think of going on the offensive. Instead, it soon becomes a matter of survival. Soon you are in the fetal position on the mat praying for the bell to ring and end this round of the fight. You desperately need to get to your corner. Success means to live to the next day, the next hour, or maybe the next few minutes. Victory is no longer the goal. All you are focused on is just survival at some point.

I remember looking into the doctor's eyes and searching for some hope, some indication of impending good news, but this was "just another case of breast cancer." I was certain it was her fiftieth patient in another hectic day. Her words were without feeling or emotion, never acknowledging what we were experiencing. Andrea's diagnosis of invasive ductal carcinoma was completely foreign to us, but this was certainly not the doctor's first experience with it. And I'm sure it wasn't her last.

We wanted to be told it was okay, to hear the optimistic confidence of a trained professional. We were hoping the cavalry would arrive, just like in the movies. We wanted to meet a strong leader, some amazing cutting-edge oncologist who would lead us to victory. But in reality, I left thinking it was still just Andrea and me who would battle this alone. We didn't know much, but we knew our life would never be the same. There is life before cancer and life with cancer, but between the two is a very definite line that you can't cross back over.

I found an interesting contrast in the exam room, between the methodical detached efficiency of the doctor and the mayhem and panic of the patient. We were nauseous from our nerves and the fear of what was happening to us. Our world had been turned upside down, and in an instant we were thrown into an environment where we didn't even speak the language. In the end, the doctor offered options and told us, "You have to decide how you want to be treated." I remember thinking, *Aren't you the doctor here? You're wearing the white robe. You have the nice diploma on the wall and the stethoscope around your neck. Aren't you the one who is supposed to tell us what to do?*

It seemed crazy. Not only were we dealing with the diagnosis of cancer, but also we had to select the treatment plan. Suddenly, doctors were too timid to tell us what to do when life and death were on the line. I wondered if the doctor did not want to be held accountable in the event things "didn't work out."

Andrea was told to get dressed. As we left, we were handed a pretty pink box. When we got home and opened it, we found a video about dealing with breast cancer, a nice notebook, a pen to record thoughts, a pink candle, and a pink magnetic ribbon. We looked at one another and realized we were now officially "breast cancer people." Pink would be our favorite color; *hope* and *courage*, our favorite words. I know the doctor's office was trying to do something nice, but at that moment the gift seemed very out of place. A mere thirty minutes earlier, our life had been "normal." Now our minds were reeling from the life-changing diagnosis. Somehow the box felt like an inadequate parting gift, like a consolation prize for playing the game of life and not being the winner.

As with all journeys, it seems you are never the same at the end as you were when you began. This journey was no exception. I suppose the true tragedy would be to face a trial and come out unchanged, quickly returning to your old ways. I remember the day Andrea and I went in for our pre-chemo briefing. We were handed a VHS tape and shown into a private viewing room with two chairs, a TV, and a VCR player. I concluded that cancer must be too difficult a subject for anyone to sit down in person and talk to us about it. The viewing room was adjacent to the chemo room, so as we walked in we had our first glance of what lay ahead.

It was a large room with about twenty La-Z-Boy recliners. The patients sitting silently in the chairs all seemed to have the same blank stare, some watching TV, but mostly all sitting alone. At that moment I swore then that Andrea would never be alone in that treatment room. We went into our viewing room as if it was a safe haven from what lay beyond those doors; as if we would somehow escape what was ahead. For the moment we felt safe, like children hiding in the closet to avoid a parent's discipline.

We hit "Play" and began watching beautiful scenes of the countryside and smiling people while a narrator described in a calm, soothing voice the common side effects of chemotherapy. All the while, beautiful music played in the background. The side effects seemed endless as the soft voice explained, "Some people experience fatigue, vomiting, diarrhea, and constipation." One couple rode horses while laughing together in the background. The film was the best possible spin you could put on chemo, which fit nicely with our naivety about the reality of the journey we were about to embark on. Then we noticed a disclaimer that was a pretty good indication that we were in for a little more than what the video conveyed. The disclaimer talked about different chemo drugs and expounded on the various side effects. The final side effect always seemed to be "and/or death." Yes, I guess that would be the ultimate side effect.

We knew Andrea would be sick, maybe tired at times. We had no idea the extent of pain she was about to endure. As we were leaving our private theater, a chemo nurse stopped us and said, "Honey, did they tell you that you will lose your hair?" We said yes, but mentioned that the video said that only *some* people lost their hair. We were hoping Andrea would not be one of them, but that was not to be. The "some" people who lose their hair turned out to be 99.99 percent.

The nurse went on to say, "No, honey, you will lose your hair, but not just the hair on your head. You will lose *all* of your hair." We walked away wondering what she meant by that. We quickly learned this was no vacation club and there wasn't going to be any pretty music in the background of our life for the next six months. It was going to be bad beyond anything we could imagine.

Andrea's first chemotherapy treatment was a little scary, to say the least. We walked into the chemo room feeling totally out of place. I wanted to shout to everyone, "We don't belong here!" But chemo meant we were fighting back, and fighting back meant we had a chance. It's amazing how much hope you can build from such a sliver of a chance. It didn't matter that the odds against Andrea beating cancer were one in a million; with that as our only hope, it suddenly seemed possible.

Once Andrea found her chair, the IV stand was brought to her side. I tried my best to remain strong for Andrea, but I'm sure she could see the fear in my eyes. We remained upbeat even as we looked at the others in the room. They all seemed close to death, very weak, with empty stares and hopeless eyes. I couldn't help but think, *Is that what we are going to look like?* Were they looking at us remembering their first day, when they had hope and strength too, before the reality of chemo hit them and the softness of that video was erased from their minds? The nurses hooked Andrea up through her newly installed chemo port, a small device surgically implanted under her skin where the IV needle was inserted. The port had a long tube that ran directly into Andrea's heart, so the drugs were quickly pumped throughout her body. Watching, I couldn't help but think she seemed like someone on death row.

The nurse then brought Andrea's first chemo treatment, AC as it was called—the "red devil." I referred to it as liquid death, deceptively cloaked in a pretty red Kool-Aid color. When the nurses hooked it up, Andrea and I watched it slowly flow from the IV tube, inching ever closer to her body. She was scared and rightly so. She later told me she wanted to rip the IV out and run, knowing what it would do to her, but she knew this was also her "cure." That little pea-sized lump was about to get it, but sadly so was the rest of Andrea's body. I hope the world soon develops a better way to treat cancer. I'm sure one day we will all look back at some of the drugs Andrea took in the same way we now look back at the practice of using leeches in the Middle Ages.

As it turned out, the first treatment was not that bad. We returned in three weeks for Andrea's second treatment, which sadly hit her with a vengeance. Within five hours, she was vomiting, which continued for the next three days. She didn't have the strength to move, with the exception of getting out of bed, crawling onto the sofa, and trying to make it until 8:00 p.m., when she would crawl back into bed. Once her nausea passed, she would walk into the kitchen to tell me she was hungry. Those were hard times for us both, obviously more so for Andrea, but as a husband it was hard to watch my wife be that ill. I took on the role of nurse and caregiver. I kept track of all her medicines and when she had to take them and wrote notes about the side effects for the next doctor's appointment. It was busywork, but at least I felt I was doing something for her. It became my labor of love to let Andrea know I was with her in this fight. I'm thankful for the support of my great bosses and my squadron mates who picked up the slack at work and allowed me to attend every appointment with Andrea unless I was deployed.

Between Thursdays at 6:00 p.m. and Sundays at 10:00 p.m., Andrea didn't talk and could barely keep down food, not even dry crackers. Anthony would read her the Bible because she didn't have the strength to lift her head. It was the most horrific three months we had ever spent.

Her last AC treatment was on December 31, 2003, not how we wanted to spend New Year's Eve.

Andrea with Anthony after his club soccer
game, Goldsboro NC, Spring 2006

Andrea went into her next round of chemotherapy marked with extreme fatigue and body aches. She was wiped out. One day she was sitting on the floor in the kitchen next to the heater and didn't have the strength to get up and walk across the room. Unable to move those ten feet to the chair, she said it might as well have been a thousand miles.

Soon, Andrea did lose her hair. It was hard to see it fall out in clumps. One of the things that surprised her most was how much her head hurt just before her hair would fall out, as if her head had been burned. To make it easier, she had her hair cut short before chemo started and donated it to Locks of Love, a company that makes wigs for children with cancer. As her hair thinned, I shaved her head. I soon learned that Andrea had a beauty and elegance that seemed to shine no matter what her outward condition was.

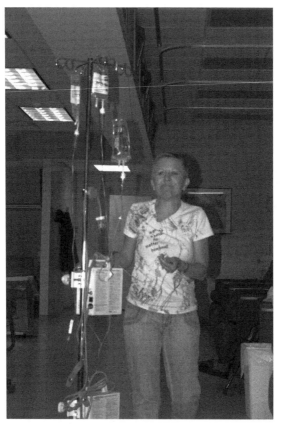

Andrea at chemo treatment, Spring 2006

By now, we realized we were in for a much tougher fight than we could handle alone. We would need to depend on our faith. God used the help and prayers of friends to make this fight a little easier. A bright spot for us in all this turmoil was meeting a fellow Air Force fighter pilot family, Lori Jo and Mike Duvall and their three children. We were all stationed together in Alaska and later in North Carolina. We forged a bond that would long outlast the cancer.

Andrea and Jim with Lori Jo and Mike Duvall,
Elmendorf AFB Alaska 1994

I learned the importance of having a support system around you
when you find life overwhelming. It could be twenty people or it could
be one close friend. Those people become the hands and feet of God.
When you silently cry out for help and someone suddenly shows up,
you realize you are not alone. They don't have to have the perfect words
or do very much at all. Just showing up is often enough. What they
do or say is not what's important. To the one hurting, it's important to
know you are not forgotten and that someone was willing to leave their
"normal" life and come into the pit with you. Mike and Lori Jo were
those friends for Andrea and me. I remember how they included us in
their family activities, whether that was going to the beach, watching
American Idol, or eating dinner together. Most importantly, they prayed
with us and for us. I remember the strength I received when Lori Jo's
father, who has since gone to be with the Lord after his own battle

with cancer, would pray or anoint Andrea with oil. Like a tag team partner in wrestling when Andrea and I were drained, Mike and Lori Jo would jump into the ring with us. It was the best therapy we could have hoped for.

Andrea's first two years of battling cancer were intense. We were often on our knees seeking answers to our prayers. Yet God seemed to ignore our prayers. Cancer continued to torment Andrea. By June of 2005, medicine and doctors lost the ability to heal her. We were told her cancer had spread to her bones, liver, and lungs. We still believed God could heal her, but without His touch she would die. We knew healing was never beyond Him and never out of His control. But in November of 2007, my worst fear began to come to fruition as I realized time was not on our side.

Nic heading back to college after Thanksgiving break, Nov 2006

Anthony and Andrea after Randolph AFB High
School Homecoming Game, Nov 2007

It was on November 25, 2007, just after Thanksgiving. Nic was a senior at American University in Washington, DC, and had returned to college that weekend. Anthony was a sophomore in high school. We had just finished an incredibly busy month. My mom passed away the month prior, only days before she was supposed to come to my brother's wedding in Austin, followed by my promotion ceremony to colonel. It was supposed to be a time of celebration for my family. Instead, Andrea and my sister, Maureen, pinned on my colonel's rank in the back of the church at my mother's funeral.

Jim's sister Maureen and Andrea pin on Jim's colonel rank,
with his brother Neil watching, October 2007

All of this exhausted Andrea, I could tell. She began requiring oxygen, which was never a good sign. At the time she seemed to be stable, but that November night she was feeling a little more short of breath than usual. I found her oxygen and gave it to her, and then we went to sleep. It soon turned into a restless night with Andrea unable to catch her breath. As she began to gasp for air, I increased the oxygen from her normal level to the maximum the machine would allow. But she was still having trouble breathing. I prayed for her and pleaded with God, knowing we were approaching our last hope. I just wanted her to be better and to go back to sleep. I just wanted this to go away, but it wasn't going away.

At one point Andrea asked me to call 9-1-1, but I couldn't. I was scared. I didn't want what was happening to happen. After trying to talk her out of going to the hospital, I knew deep down she had to have more help than I could give her. I finally said, "Just let me take you. No ambulance." I helped her get dressed and then left the room, trying to gather my strength and thoughts. Andrea sat waiting on the bed as I paced in the living room trying to get ahold of myself. Finally, I walked back in and helped her to the car. My mind was racing. I hoped

I wouldn't say what was I fearing, which was, *I don't think you will come back home once we leave here tonight.*

When we arrived at the ER, I put Andrea in a wheelchair. As we stood at the entrance, I turned to her and asked, "Are you sure you need to go in?" Inside I was pleading, *Please don't let this happen.* Andrea replied with, "I have to go in." And for as long as I live I will never forget what she said next. She looked right at me and said, "Jim, you have to be strong now." Those were her last audible words to me. I have thought about those words many times. They were the words of a godly woman and the encouraging words of love of an unselfish wife. She knew I was scared, yet she sat patiently on the bed as I tried to come to terms with what her request to go to the hospital actually meant. Andrea did not run and was not afraid. She was the one facing the ultimate challenge, yet she was telling me to be strong. I know in my heart she was not asking me to be strong enough to walk her into the ER, or even for the brutal weeks that lay ahead. I believe she was asking me to be strong for the years that lay beyond her life on earth with me. She was telling me to be a faithful servant of God, a steadfast father, and ultimately a strong person for a new life without her in it. I think she knew the reality of her condition more than I did. That was Andrea - always encouraging, always patient, always full of faith.

The decision was made to move Andrea from the ER to the ICU when her oxygen level dropped from 100 to 60. She began to struggle to breathe and was trying to get the mask off her face. I could see the panic in her eyes. I tried to calm her, to no avail.

Her oxygen continued to drop, first to 50 and then to 40; her heart rate dropped to 52. I knew enough to know this was serious. In a flash, there were doctors and nurses swarming to her bed, everyone barking commands. Andrea's feet were turning a little blue. For the first time ever, I thought, *Andrea is dying.*

I stayed at the foot of her bed and held her feet as I prayed. I was very scared. Once Andrea was sedated, the doctor began to insert the tube for the breathing machine. I looked up. A man asked me, "Are you her husband?"

"Yes," I answered.

He said, "Hi. I'm the on-call chaplain." I held onto the bed, fearing I was going to pass out. Chaplains usually only show up when the outcome is expected to be dire.

Once Andrea was stabilized, friends began to stop by and visit. I enjoyed having people with me in the ICU. I knew Andrea could hear the voices because she would try to open her eyes. At the same time, I also really enjoyed the time alone with her. Right before I left each night, we would pray together. I would read her favorite scriptures aloud, speaking them over the rhythmic sounds of the ventilator. Despite the fact that Andrea was not conscious most of the time, it was important that we kept our habit of ending our day in the Word.

Although Andrea and I had spoken of her funeral only a few times, I think in some way I was preparing myself for the potential of losing her. Andrea told me she did not want to plan her funeral until the cancer came back, yet even when it did come back, I don't think we were ready to have that talk. It would take time for us to discuss her wishes. Although I don't think we ever finished the conversation, I did know most of her desires. Naturally, I would find myself asking what I would do for her service, how would I plan it, and where should it be. I hated when I had those thoughts, but I couldn't stop them. They are part of the cancer package when the doctor says you have incurable stage IV cancer. There are many things in that package: fear, worry, dread, darkness, gloom, and a heaviness on your shoulders you can't seem to shake. You bring your own package to the party too. You bring love. You bring faith—maybe not enough, but you bring what you have, and you pray for more. You also bring family and friends, those who stand beside you and help carry the weight you bear. Those who call even when they don't know what to say. Those who write letters struggling to find the right words. Those who pray with you and are willing to sit in silence because you are unable to express what you feel. You bring a loving God who gave us the Word filled with reminders of His character and promises. All of it sustained me and Andrea on the darkest of nights.

Andrea and I talked many times about the reality of what she faced. She was honest with herself and also told me what her prayers were for our children's future and for my life. She was also a fighter, so she fought—because she believed God could heal her. She fought because she had much to live for, grandkids to see, sons to watch grow into men, and family and friends whom she loved.

Andrea's twenty-one days in the ICU were filled with daily, if not hourly, ups and downs. Two events best illustrate our days in the ICU. The first occurred after Andrea's first week in the ICU. She had been pretty much the same, with glimpses of her getting better but never getting over the hump. Her oxygen levels became a critical data point to determine her breathing effectiveness. The doctors decided to put a line in her artery that would provide a constant measure of her oxygen level.

After several failed attempts, this strategy was abandoned. The next day the doctor, Dr. "Doom and Gloom," as I called him, asked me to step into the hallway. He told me Andrea was about to die and said that I needed to call the family. He had seen some bruising on her hip and back and said she had internal bleeding. I remember walking back into the room with the boys. We were crying. Andrea looked at us with an expression of "What's going on?" We told her that nothing was going on, because we didn't know what else to say.

About an hour later, Dr. Doom and Gloom called me back outside the room and said, "Oops, sorry, everything is fine. The bruising was from the failed attempts at the artery line." Really? I have to be honest, I lost it. But when I walked back into Andrea's room, she was smiling at me.

That was December 7, 2007.

The second event happened a couple of weeks later, still in the ICU. The doctors said that since two weeks was about the limit to leave someone with a vent tube, we needed to consider having a tracheotomy performed. This would allow Andrea's vent tube to be removed from her mouth and connected though the opening in her neck. She would still rely on the vent to breath for her. But having the vent connected like this would be more comfortable for Andrea and allow her to "mouth" words. I gathered the team of doctors involved in Andrea's care and asked if this was worth the risk, given that surgery for Andrea was very dangerous on account of her weak condition. They all felt this procedure would give her the best chance to get off the vent and back into chemo.

I wanted to know if Andrea's oncologist felt she had a chance to get back on chemo. If not, there was no need to have Andrea suffer through surgery. The doctor's answer was yes, she still had a chance to get off the vent, and yes, if she could get back on chemo she had a chance of getting better.

We all walked into Andrea's room. In front of the doctors I asked her if she wanted to have the procedure done. She nodded yes. I asked her three different times to be sure. Andrea wanted the surgery. The next day, she was scheduled for the operation. An hour beforehand, the doctor came in and told me he would not do the surgery because she would die on the table.

I explained that I knew her chances were about one in a million but that without this, her chances were zero. I asked that he give her that one-in-a-million chance. After my sister and I pleaded with the doctor for another hour, he finally agreed. Andrea came though the surgery with flying colors. The next day she was awake, alert, and without the tube in her mouth. She was even able to mouth words to us. It was such a blessing to be able to kiss her on the lips.

That was December 12, 2007.

I'm sure we all have a day that marks an event in our life. No longer just a day on the calendar, it is a day we can't forget, whether it be a really good one or really bad one. December 17, 2007 is my day. The hardest day of my life - the day I said good-bye to Andrea. As I drove to the hospital that morning, I was tired. Tired of seeing my best friend suffer with this never-ending battle. There is a time when the greatest expression of love is to let someone go. I know that may seem impossible to some reading this. It would have seemed that way to me too any time before that December day. All I can tell you is, it is hard to say what you would do until you are faced with this situation. All we can do is our best. There is no right or wrong answer.

Over the previous three days, Andrea couldn't keep any food down, not even with a feeding tube. So we switched to feeding her through an IV, a risky procedure according to her doctor and one I had to plead with him to do before he agreed. The doctors and nurses knew far more than I did about medicine, but I knew Andrea. Sometimes I had to fight for her; to be her advocate with well-intentioned doctors who were making decisions based on odds. I had to insist we make decisions based on Andrea. She was not just another patient to me. She was my wife. If you find yourself in this role, I encourage you to speak up for your loved one. They need you to be their voice.

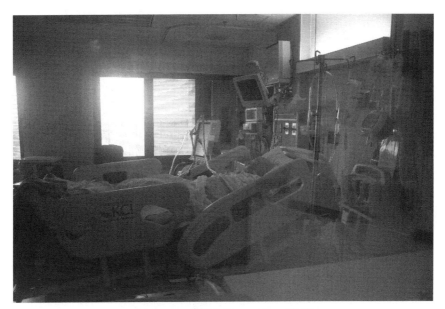

Andrea in ICU, December 2007

The only time Andrea told me she was hurting during her twenty-one days in ICU was when she mouthed, "My stomach hurts. I'm so hungry." I would dip a sponge in Coke and put it in her mouth with a piece of ice. One day, I brought in a chocolate bar, broke off a small piece, and put it against her cheek. She smiled at me. Then the nurse caught me and posted this sign above her bed: "Do not give this patient any ice or anything to eat!"

Sometimes I thought the hospital staff lost sight of what was happening in the ICU. And no, the sign did not stop me. To this day, it brings tears to my eyes to think of that moment. As a husband, I wanted to take care of my wife, protect her, comfort her. I was sick of being so helpless, unable to change the course of events. I would give her a smidgen of chocolate if I wanted to.

The day came to try the feeding tube again, at the rate of a Coke cap full every hour to see if Andrea's body could process the food. I was by her bed when it was time for the nurse to suction her stomach and measure the success of the feeding tube. I'll never forget when she drew back the syringe and found that the tube had filled with a bloody liquid.

I remember saying, "That's not good." The nurse agreed and left us alone. I tried to explain the gravity of the situation to Andrea. "Andrea, you are not able to eat, and that is our first priority. You need to eat to have strength to get off the vent, because until you do they can't start your chemo."

It sounded impossible as I listened to my own words. I hadn't thought of the whole process until then, as I had always taken it one step at a time. It seemed manageable and possible, but when I said it all together, it was overwhelming. I was losing my wife. Andrea's response was a smile. I said, "Are you okay? If you are too tired, I understand."

There comes a point when your love for someone is no longer tied to what you get from the relationship but is tied to what is best for them. I could not allow Andrea to suffer for me. She had done too much of that for four years. She just nodded, as if to say, "I'm okay."

As I started to leave that night, Andrea and I had Communion together. Of course she couldn't eat or drink anything, but it had become our nightly routine. When I finished, she was staring at the ceiling, so I asked her if she was okay. She looked at me and nodded, and then went back to staring at the ceiling. I kissed her good night and walked out of the room. As I was leaving, I looked back through the window and saw she was still staring. So I went back in and asked her again if she was okay. She nodded yes. I told her she was scaring me. She mouthed, "I love you."

That was December 16.

As I drove to the hospital the next day, I prayed to God that I wouldn't have to decide if Andrea would stay on the ventilator. I had always feared that decision, never wanting to give up when Andrea wanted to fight. I had fought for her every inch of the way. As a caregiver, I found myself in the role of Andrea's advocate. I took notes at every doctor's visit in case Andrea missed something. I kept the calendar of all her appointments and medicines, and the records of her blood work. In the end, I could read the ventilator readings as well as the nurses could.

I'm thankful for people who choose to work in the medical field. It is something I could never do. I'm grateful for those who answer the call to serve the sick and dying. I made very good friends with many of the nurses. Andrea's doctor in North Carolina also remains a close friend. But I also saw the other side of medicine, namely, the doctors who were so busy that they never took the time to know Andrea. She was just a case. I always felt they were the unlucky ones. She was so worth knowing.

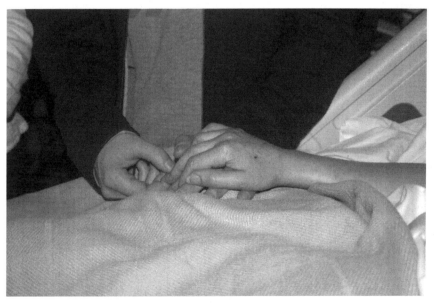

A mother's touch. Andrea and Nic during Andrea's
final days, ICU, December 2007

When I walked into the ICU at 9:00 a.m., there were several nurses and doctors around Andrea. I knew then that something was wrong. They told me her lung capacity had dropped by 75 percent during the night and they didn't know why. They had tried to talk to her, but she was unresponsive.

That was December 17.

I walked up to her bed and said, "Jokie." She opened her eyes just for a second and then closed them. I asked her caretakers to wait while I called her oncologist in North Carolina. He had treated Andrea's metastatic cancer for two years. I trusted him, but more importantly, Andrea trusted him.

It was 10:15 a.m.

I explained the situation, after which he said it was time. I knew what that meant. I called Andrea's current oncologist in San Antonio and asked him to come over and confirm my thoughts. In the meantime, I called our sons and told them they needed to come to the hospital. Then, I called family and friends and asked for prayer. The boys arrived and were with Andrea while I was outside her room on the phone. I saw her oncologist arrive. At the same time, Nic came out of Andrea's room with fear on his face and said, "Mom is spitting up blood." That was it. Andrea helped me make my decision. Her fight needed to end. I didn't need a doctor to tell me what to do. I apologized to her oncologist for making the forty-five-minute drive to the ICU.

It was 11:30 a.m.

I walked into Andrea's room and wiped her mouth with a tissue, one that I keep to this day. I told the doctor he could remove the ventilator tube. He explained the process. The vent would not be turned off. Instead of forcing air into her lungs, it would blow across her trachea opening so she could still breathe. She would have to pull the air into her lungs herself.

I don't remember it happening, but soon all the IVs were removed from Andrea and the machines that had once displayed everything about her condition were turned off. The room was stark and quiet, the only IV a morphine bottle. The only people in the room were our two sons, a nurse to release the morphine if she sensed Andrea was in pain, and me.

It was 12:25 p.m.

The boys and I prayed with Andrea, telling her we would be okay and that we would take care of each other. We said that we loved her and were proud of her, proud to have her as my wife and their mom. Then I sang to her a song we sang in our church, but I replaced the word *life* with *wife* and the word *it* with *her*. It went like this:

> Here's my wife. I lay her down. I surrender her all to You.
> Here's my wife. I lay her, I lay her down.
> I surrender her all to You; I surrender her all to You.
> I let go and give her to You.

Andrea took her final breath as I uttered the last words of that song. It was 1:07 p.m.

Her body now looked different to me because she was no longer there. Only a broken shell remained. She was free from the pain and the suffering of cancer. I kissed her cool lips, and then the boys and I left—to what, I had no idea. Everything about me, my hopes and my dreams, were mine and Andrea's together. I no longer knew who I was. When you lose your soul mate, your identity seems to disappear along with them.

Jim, Nic, Anthony with Andrea's Mom, June at Andrea's
Funeral, Randolph AFB, TX, Dec 21, 2007

Among the shows on the Discovery Channel is *Planet Earth*. As
I watched the scenes of the Arctic wolves and their search for food
and attempts at survival, I noticed how they stalked the caribou herd,
looking for the weakest and easiest prey. The chase was on as the herd
darted, panic struck, and a threat was sensed. The wolves pursued until
the slower or weaker caribou were separated from the herd. It was now
down to one caribou and one wolf. The caribou began to run for its very
life, darting and changing direction in an effort to shake the relentless
pursuer. As I watched, I could feel the exhaustion of the caribou, yet
to rest was certain death. There was only one option: run and keep

running. Before long, the caribou had no strength left and collapsed, accepting the fate that awaited him. The desire to live was lost in the inability to go on. That, to me, is what it's like to fight cancer.

Once told you have cancer, you soon learn it can be a relentless pursuer, forever on your mind, always making you wonder if it's about to strike back. You hope you don't reach the point where you are so tired that you can only drop and accept the fate that awaits you. So you keep fighting until the point when the fight is so exhausting that you can't go on. That's what makes even the smallest of victories so sweet. These little victories are resting points when you can take a break from the chase. You have to find these moments or else you will lack the strength to fight. It may be a day where you feel "normal" or a day without pain, a day when you don't think or talk about cancer. As Andrea once said, "Remind me how good I feel today next week after chemo." You have to remember that the exhaustion, fatigue, and sickness will pass. That there is life after all this. Otherwise, you lose all hope and soon stop and accept what appears inevitable.

I also thought about how cancer comes to us spreading fear as those around us sense the sudden closeness of cancer. We all hear of cancer, but when you learn of a friend or family member with the disease, it suddenly seems too close for comfort and a much greater threat in your own life.

I felt as if cancer had singled out Andrea for the chase. She had been fighting it with all she had, and with the strength and the faith granted her by God. She had been running and giving all she had. There were times when the cancer drew very close, nearly taking her. But by the grace of God she escaped the grasp of death.

I couldn't help wondering why we were chosen from the herd. I knew that God had used this burden He placed upon us to change Andrea and me, as well as many others around us. Unlike the caribou herd that scatters when the wolves begin the chase, our friends and family had come to our defense. They were true friends who never left us alone to fend off the pursuer. Friends who wrote, called, sent flowers, cards, meals, or gifts of encouragement, or simply sat with Andrea during her treatment. Our friends never scattered from the fear of cancer, but looked it in the eye with Andrea. They shared in the suffering, but they also shared equally in the joy. When we saw the exhaustion on her face, we were all there encouraging her to keep running, to keep fighting, calling out, "Run, Andrea, run!"

One night Andrea and I were reading our Bible and came across comforting verses in 2 Corinthians 1:3–11. I still love these verses and want to share them because they express the way we felt about those who stood beside us during our darkest hours. They also gave us perspective about the suffering we endured.

Andrea's gravesite Fort Sam Houston National Cemetery

No matter where you are in life, whether you find yourself on your own difficult path or providing a shoulder for someone else to cry on, these words offer you purpose and hope in knowing that we all share in Christ's suffering. It teaches us to rely not on ourselves but on our loving God.

> Praise be to the God and Father of our Lord Jesus Christ, the Father of compassion and the God of all comfort, who comforts us in all our troubles, so that we can comfort those in any trouble with the comfort we ourselves receive from God. For just as we share abundantly in the sufferings of Christ, so also our comfort abounds through Christ. If we are distressed, it is for your comfort and salvation; if we are comforted, it is for your comfort, which produces in you patient endurance of the same sufferings we suffer. And our hope for you is firm, because we know that just as you share in our sufferings, so also you share in our comfort.
>
> We do not want you to be uninformed, brothers and sisters, about the troubles we experienced in the province of Asia. We were under great pressure, far beyond our ability to endure, so that we despaired of life itself. Indeed, we felt we had received the sentence of death. But this happened that we might not rely on ourselves but on God, who raises the dead. He has delivered us from such a deadly peril, and he will deliver us again. On him we have set our hope that he will continue to deliver us, as you help us by your prayers. Then many will give thanks on our behalf for the gracious favor granted us in answer to the prayers of many. (2 Corinthians 3–11 NIV)

Last Ravella family photo taken, Nov 2007

Chapter 2 *Discussion Guide*

1. Have you or someone you love been touched by cancer? How did you or they face the initial diagnosis?

2. Jim makes the parallel between wolves chasing their prey to battling cancer. Have you ever felt defeated or exhausted from a life that you wanted to give up? If so how did you cope with those feelings?

3. Jim described Andrea's ability to balance fighting to survive while trusting God's sovereignty. Have you had to balance the "good fight" in a situation with not knowing the outcome?

4. Jim describes Andrea, above all else, as a woman of faith. It was the one statement he wanted on her headstone. What is the one phrase you might like on yours?

5. What is the biggest impression Andrea's story left with you?

Chapter 3

Beauty from Ashes

Circumstances do not define God.

I will lead the blind by ways they have not known, along unfamiliar paths I will guide them; I will turn the darkness into light before them and make the rough places smooth. These are the things will I do; I will not forsake them.

—Isaiah 42:16 (NIV)

Those who sow in tears shall reap in joy.

—Psalm 126:5 (NKJV)

Jim

After the deaths of Troy and Andrea, Ginger and I each found the one person we could talk to about anything: we found each other.

But the story starts before Andrea's death. Andrea "knew" Ginger, and Ginger "knew" Andrea, long before the day Ginger and I actually met. Back in January of 2007, Andrea had gone into the hospital. She was fighting yet another side effect of her compromised immune system, pneumonia this time, and her doctor suggested she be put on a ventilator. Andrea agreed and was taken to the ICU, her first time there. Once in her room in the ICU, she and I prayed and talked until I was asked to leave for a while so the staff could intubate her.

When I returned to Andrea's room, she suddenly looked very sick to me. She was motionless, the tube in her mouth and the rhythm of the breathing machine the only sounds. I left and went home, scared but trusting the Lord. I wrote an e-mail update to our friends explaining what had happened and asking for prayers. It also expressed my faith that God was still in control no matter what was happening or how frightened I was.

Ginger

That same January, I was really questioning God's goodness to me and His plans for me. I was struggling to find anything to be thankful for, when I received this forwarded e-mail from a friend. It spoke loudly yet gently to me in my distress. It was written by a total stranger who was struggling but finding victory in his own trials:

> I won't, by the strength of God, give up on all I believe, nor get mad because I don't understand why. God is still God no matter how these events transpire. Circumstances do not define my faith or my God. God is unchanging. He is the same yesterday, today, and tomorrow. Being a Christian does not mean we are given a guarantee of a trial-free life or pain-free life. In contrast, it means we will face trials and pain.
>
> Our guarantee is He will never leave us nor forsake us. We do not face trials alone. And through our faith we glorify our Creator and our Savior who gave us another guarantee: that we will live for eternity with Him. So as we get ever closer to the edge of this furnace and as we begin to feel the heat from the fire, we know the flames do not control our destiny. And we rest under the shadow of the Almighty.
>
> —Jim

That stranger was a man named Jim Ravella. It would be those last paragraphs, the conclusion of the e-mail he wrote to his friends when Andrea went into the ICU, that resonated in my soul and reminded me of real truth when I had been believing lies.

> Though the fig tree does not bud and there are no grapes on the vines, though the olive crop fails and the fields produce

no food, though there are no sheep in the pen and no cattle in the stalls, yet I will rejoice in the Lord. I will be joyful in God my Savior. (Habakkuk 3:17–18 NIV)

From the rising of the sun to the place where it sets, the name of the Lord is to be praised. (Psalm 113:3 NIV)

I literally received dozens and dozens of e-mails every day. I was completely overwhelmed, depressed, and suffering from the fog of grief and severe insomnia. The thought of reading and responding to hundreds of e-mails seemed a bridge too long to cross, so sometimes I just scanned the messages aimlessly. Why I stopped on this particular forwarded e-mail, I can only see in hindsight. I not only read the e-mail but also actually reached out to the couple from whom it originated whose words spoke exactly what I needed to hear at that time. My dear friend Jennifer forwarded it to me from her friend, a woman named Terri Otto, who happened to be a dear friend of Andrea's. Terri was a godly woman and a mother who often prayed for Andrea. Ultimately, Jim and I believe God used her to introduce us. I met Terri right after Jim and I married. The following year she was tragically killed after being hit by a truck while jogging. I couldn't believe the timing of it all. She left behind her own grieving family. She will forever have a special place in our hearts.

Below is my e-mail to Terri and then Terri's e-mail to Jim:

Date: January 6, 2007
Time: 11:30:37 a.m. CST
From: Ginger Gilbert
To: Terri Otto
Subject: Friend of Jenn Gordon's

Terri,

My name is Ginger Gilbert. I am a good friend of Jenn Gordon's. She forwarded me an e-mail from Jim about his wife and their faith, and it touched me. I don't know them or you at all. My husband was Troy, and he was the F-16 pilot who was killed in Iraq on November 27. I am a believer. I love the Lord, but I am struggling. I am left with five small children, and the reality is starting to sink in. I really needed the spiritual encouragement he enclosed in his e-mail and wanted to e-mail him and his wife if possible. Totally different situations, but still pain is pain. If you think it would be okay, could you send me his e-mail address? Thanks so much.

Ginger

Date: January 6, 2007
From: Terri Otto
To: Jim and Andrea Ravella
Subject: Friend of Jenn Gordon's

Jim,

I just received this e-mail. A friend of mine is very good friends with the family, and she forwarded Ginger your e-mail about Andrea. Ginger would like to e-mail you. I hope you don't mind, but I gave her the go-ahead. I am sure that you heard about her husband dying in Iraq. Anyway, she is struggling, and I know that she was encouraged by your and Andrea's faith. You will be hearing from her soon, I am sure.

P.S. Love you guys and am sooooooo happy to hear of Andrea's recovery and good humor! Like you say, "small but mighty!"

Terri

Thus began the relationship between Jim, Andrea, and me that would one day lead to my meeting Jim. Sadly, I never had the chance to meet Andrea in person. Yet, as I learned about their faith in the face of sickness and death, I saw two people who did not turn their back on God, even when all the circumstances could have tempted them otherwise. I could see they were confidently betting all they had on God. They trusted Him no matter what His decision was. That was real inspiration to me. Because if Andrea really *was* dying and was joyful and hopeful, then couldn't I possibly be joyful and hopeful when it only *felt* like I was dying?

Jim

Soon, Andrea and I were exchanging e-mails with Ginger. We tried to offer our help and words of encouragement as Ginger was dealing with the loss of her husband, Troy. Her e-mails were difficult to read at times. Although Andrea and I had been facing the possibility of death for over three years at this point, the fact of death in Ginger's life was not a possibility but a sad reality.

Unlike Andrea and me, Ginger was not given a gradual adjustment to a potential loss. Her devastating and final news was a sudden shock, the dreaded knock at the door. Her life went from normal to abnormal in a matter of seconds, and her struggle with God and faith reflected that swift switch. Andrea and I felt inadequate to offer advice, but we did the best we could.

Usually, Andrea would be lying on the sofa sick from the effects of her chemo as I would sit at the computer to read Ginger's e-mails aloud. Andrea would dictate what to write in response. The eleven months of back-and-forth correspondence became a special bond between us as families.

After Andrea passed, I was looking through Andrea's prayer journal, where I found Ginger's name on her prayer list. I wondered what exactly her prayer words for Ginger might have been. Our marriages had been similar, both loving and stable, with devout Christian spouses who served the Lord. It was only after Andrea passed that Ginger and I talked on the phone. On our first call, she offered her condolences, and I told her I was sorry if I had ever said anything stupid when trying to give her advice for dealing with the loss of Troy. Following four years of battling cancer through Andrea, I thought I understood death, but when Andrea passed I realized how little I knew. I was an expert at dealing with the possibility of death, but I had no idea what it actually meant to deal with the death of one's spouse. Ginger became a source of comfort and support. Her words met me in my grief and spoke to my heart. She knew the pain I was going through. She had become the veteran now. Her year of experience with loss and grief permeated her words and spoke to me in my need.

Ginger and I never meant to meet so soon after Andrea had passed away and certainly never meant to rush into a relationship. What we had in common was shared pain. Some people thought we had lost our minds. Yes, we moved far faster than "normal," but it started with the experience of our individual suffering, founded upon our faith, a faith we had shared with each other over the previous eleven months. Andrea and I had both gotten to know Ginger through the depths of her pain.

We discovered that God's direction for our lives doesn't always fit either our or others' acceptable time lines. There was never an acceptable time to get a terminal illness or never to return home to your newborn babies. We also learned there is no right way to grieve, to meet your future spouse, to remarry, to parent children you did not birth, or to start over in a new life when you weren't ready to surrender your old one. Walking a mile in someone's shoes does a great deal in helping you learn true empathy. Ginger and I also knew through personal experience that lives can be turned upside down in an instant: one knock on the door, one doctor's report, one phone call, one bad decision—one move on the freeway of life could change its entire course.

Once we met, we had no doubt we were meant to be together. We also knew the implication of what that meant in our lives, the pain and loss we both had to experience first. While we leaned on each other, God saw our needs and heard our prayers. In Him, we were reassured He was with us. We learned how to smile again, no longer alone in our grief.

The day after Andrea's funeral was the day Ginger and I talked on the phone for the first time. We decided to meet in person while she and the children were back in Texas visiting family. Though we did not plan it this way, the day we met was Christmas Day 2007. We were both in Dallas at the same time visiting loved ones. The Four Seasons Hotel parking lot was our meeting place. For me, I remember feeling like I was about to meet someone I already knew even though she was a stranger. I had seen her pictures on the news, but I was still a little anxious. We ended up talking in the parking lot for about twenty minutes. I already knew the most important thing about Ginger—that she knew God and had experienced love and loss just like me.

Ginger

It was a while after the Ravellas and I began corresponding before I even knew Jim and Andrea were a military couple like Troy and I were. In the beginning, the only thing I knew the three of us had in common was the challenge of reconciling suffering with faith, which was certainly all I needed. We seldom talked about anything personal in our e-mails. We discussed theology, prayer, God's supreme sovereignty, life, death, and other "light" topics. Suffice to say that the weather or idle chitchat was never brought up! Honestly, I actually remember thinking, *I will never see these sweet people, so I can definitely share my real and raw feelings and never have to worry about running into them anywhere.* That thought must have made God smile.

When Jim and I met a year later, after Andrea's death, there weren't any preconceived notions or expectations. He was a little older than I thought he would be. Colonels were still the "old guys" to me at that time. I had one-year-olds in diapers, whereas his oldest was about to graduate from college. As we continued to learn more about each other, I was confident of what kind of husband he had been—the same kind of man that Troy had been: adoring, loving, thoughtful, *devoted*. Jim's passion for the Lord and his dedication as a husband was the same as Troy's. We were able to skip past all the small talk and get right to the deep stuff. I remember how sad his eyes looked the first time we met, because it was the familiar sight I saw when I looked in my own mirror. I recognized it well—grief.

Because it was a holiday and no restaurants were open, we went to Jim's sister's house for dinner. I had just met Jim minutes before, and now I was following him to his extended family's formal Christmas meal. Since so much madness had ensued over the previous year, I don't think I was much fazed by the potential awkwardness of the situation. I can't say the same for his family. Still, they were very welcoming. His sister, Maureen, had set a beautiful table with fine china and silver. I smiled, thinking of the kids and our sit-down dinners, which were more along the lines of sippy cups and paper plates. Later, we all moved to the living room, where we had wine and talked politics. At my house, we might have had wine, but we talked potty training, which was more immediately relevant than politics. At one point during the political discussion, I leaned over to Jim and said, "This is nothing like my life." He laughed. I stayed for the family's Christmas gift unwrapping. I can't even believe I did that. I guess I just didn't know how to eat and run.

I thanked everyone for a nice evening. After agreeing to Jim's invitation to meet him at Starbucks the next morning, I left. I didn't know it at the time, but he doesn't even drink coffee. Thinking of that now makes me smile.

Jim

Before Ginger and I met again the next morning, I remember waiting for her while I had the oil changed in my car. As I sat in the Jiffy Lube waiting room, I began to write a note to Ginger to explain things about myself—my strengths, my weaknesses, my likes, and my dislikes. I'm not sure why I told all of that to someone I had just met, but I did. I kept that page of notes. It's in my Bible today. Sometimes I take it out just to remember that day in December.

Throughout the next days and months to follow, I was very conflicted. I found strength in Ginger's words and presence, yet she was the beginning of a life without Andrea. Ours was the first relationship that Andrea and I would not share. All of my other friends knew Andrea personally and had been a part of our life. This person was unique to my life alone. That in itself was a reminder that life goes on. My friendship with Ginger was a step I had to take in order to begin to heal, yet it was a step that reminded me that it would create a certain distance between Andrea and me. Survivor's guilt was very real for me. The thought of going on and being happy without Andrea would often bring me to tears.

I hated the thought that Andrea would fade with each passing year, with only the brightest of memories remaining. I wanted to hold on to all of those memories as if I had just lived through them, but my moments with just Andrea in my life ended that Monday morning. I was sitting in a coffee shop with another woman, yet I missed my late wife deeply. When I was in our hometown just days prior, I went to the place where I had met Andrea's eyes for the first time. I went to the light pole on the college campus where I had written our names in wet concrete twenty-five years prior. Now I was in Dallas to visit my sister, Maureen, who had been by my side many of the days in the ICU and whose faith was always a source of strength for me. Strangely, I realized, I wasn't married anymore and was sitting across from a woman in Starbucks telling her my life story. Sadly, the world does not stop so we can deal with our pain. There are no timeouts in life. Oil needs to be changed, kids need to go back to school, life pulses on. You have to keep moving. The bold landmark death leaves begins to fade as time pushes us through the crowd. Though I had wondered what it would be like if Andrea had survived the cancer, I had to face that the life I had had with her was now in the past.

Ginger

During our e-mail correspondence over the previous year, Jim made it very clear that he was a married man and loved Andrea very much. He would sign his e-mails, "Jim and Andrea." I remember thinking how lucky they were that at least they got to go through their trials together. I often thought it ironic that the only person I truly needed to help me through the loss of Troy was Troy himself. That still seems a cruel twist of fate.

Regardless, I hoped and prayed I would remarry someone someday and that the children would have a father again, a man whom the Lord would have to choose for us. Still, I couldn't imagine that any man could love us like Troy did. In fact, during those first months after he was gone, I was constantly seeking immediate rescue from my pain. My first thought was that surely it would come through a relationship with someone I knew, someone who really loved my children and me. Looking back, I see that I wanted an escape instead of having to go through the whole process of grieving. I didn't *want* to go through the muddle and misery.

The difference between the "muddle" and the "middle" is very slight, and it doesn't consists merely of the difference between a *u* and an *i*. Whenever you hear the phrase "muddling through," it definitely doesn't make you think of achieving a quick, trailblazing, easy passage. It evokes a much more dark, confusing, and slow process. However, it's in the middle and the muddle of a trial that we must draw close to Christ. He does His best work in us when we realize how much we need Him, especially when we are amid circumstances beyond our control. How many songs and poems have been written about that dash between the year of a person's birth and the year of that person's death on a headstone? I certainly always desired for my "dash" to count and to be about things of eternal value. I just didn't want to suffer for it. I am not saying God necessarily wanted me to suffer, but I know He allowed me to suffer so that I would put the full weight of my trust in Him for His power to be more fully known. I was reluctantly willing to sign up for glorifying Him in some way through my grief, but I most certainly wanted the Lord to give me a date, time, and place for when my heart would mend and my life would be whole again. In retrospect, however, I realize that if He had revealed His plan to me, I would have only lived for *that* day and would have missed massive spiritual growth and the intimacy of solely trusting Christ with my future and the future of my children while I waited.

On the other hand, Jim's grief didn't start on December 17, 2007. It was four years in the making, beginning on the day Andrea was first diagnosed. Now, it had simply moved to its final stages. With no checklist to complete our grieving timetables, we cried together, painfully said good-bye to our spouses, cleaned out their closets, sorted their belongings through our sorrow, and tried our best to settle into a new routine. Even as we chose to move forward, I still missed Troy, and Jim still missed Andrea, every single day. However, within weeks of our meeting, it was time to approach our friends and family with the news of our relationship. Here's what Jim wrote:

> I want to tell you all how fortunate I am that God has blessed me with another wonderful woman in my life. Her name is Ginger Gilbert. She is the woman Andrea and I had been e-mailing for a year after Ginger lost her husband, Troy, in an F-16 crash in Iraq in 2006.
>
> Ginger was dealing with a depth of pain I could not understand at the time while Andrea and I were in the throes of our second battle with cancer. All of us were trying to understand our life that had suddenly changed, all of us seeking God for strength. [Ginger and I] have been friends for a year, and then quite unexpectedly, the Lord turned our friendship into an amazing relationship.
>
> Troy was a loving father and dedicated husband but most of all a man who loved and served God. He and Ginger had a marriage very similar to Andrea's and mine. I'm thankful Ginger has loved so deeply, yet I grieve with her, as I understand the pain that comes from losing such a love.
>
> She is a godly woman, so tenderhearted, full of so much love for me. I cannot put into words the depth of our feelings. Had I asked God for her, I could not have imagined such a loving woman who understands me in ways I did not even know to ask, who wipes my tears with her words, and who gives me hope in a life ahead.
>
> My prayers for her would have fallen far short of the perfection God has blessed me with. She has helped me walk the difficult steps of adjusting to being a widower. She has listened to me cry and given me reason to smile.

We share a special bond built upon a shared grief I hope none of you ever experience. Most importantly we share a faith in Christ that guides both of us into this relationship, a relationship that is orchestrated by God. We love each other deeply and we have begun making plans for our future. Please pray for us as we continue this relationship.

I know this seems way too sudden to all of you. But I also know that when God moves and does miracles, He chooses to do so in His own timing. Though it may seem awfully quick, Ginger and I have suffered for a long time and gratefully accept His blessing of our relationship with total peace and confidence.

Jim

Andrea talked to me and the boys several times about the possibility of my remarrying and told me it was what she wanted. She told me it was not good for me to be alone, and said that the boys would need another mother. It was one of the most unselfish acts I have ever witnessed, one that I have often wondered if I could have done. But that was Andrea. At the time, it was very hard for me to have that conversation or even think about what she was saying. However, shortly after I met Ginger in Dallas, I knew I felt drawn to her. It scared me in some ways. Was I thinking clearly? Could I even have such thoughts right now? Then one day shortly after I met Ginger in Dallas, I was at home reading through Andrea's journals and came across a heart-wrenching entry. It was written in 1998, five and half years before she would even find that tiny lump in her breast. These are the words Andrea wrote:

> About eight months ago I dreamed I had a lump about the size of a golf ball in my stomach. I could feel it in the area just under my ribs, right in the middle. Anyway, I was told I had cancer and I was dying. I was telling Nic not to be sad and be strong. I told Jim to remarry. He said he would never be able to replace me and that he would be afraid to remarry because he was afraid it wouldn't be like our relationship.

He asked me how he could ever know if he found the right one. I said, "You will know, just like you knew with me. If there's any doubt, she is not the one." That was the end. Talk about a depressing dream!

As I sat and cried over Andrea's words, I felt a love that I never deserved in her. I closed the book and knew God had called me to Ginger. Andrea confirmed it. As crazy as it seemed, this was the right thing to do.

I remembered a question Andrea asked me back in March of 2007. We had just received an e-mail from Ginger; Andrea was telling me what to type in reply. As we got up and walked back to our bedroom, Andrea asked me, "Jim, are you going to marry her when I die?" I said, "What? Don't even talk like that. You are going to be fine!" We never talked about it again. We just went back to fighting cancer. We still corresponded with Ginger over the next three months, and then we moved to Texas and lost touch with her until November, when Andrea was back in ICU and Ginger was at the one-year anniversary of Troy's crash.

Ginger's and my consideration to marry, rather than date indefinitely, was strongly based on the needs of our children. I knew that Boston, Greyson, Bella, Aspen, and Annalise needed a dad again. Anthony was in his struggling teenage years and needed more love and structure than I could give him alone. We all needed to be a part of a family. God had provided us that gift once again.

> The Lord gave and the Lord has taken away; may the name
> of the Lord be praised. (Job 1:21 NIV)

Looking back, I know that my and Ginger's decision to remarry so soon caused pain for my boys. While I tried my best, I did not find it easy to make perfect decisions. I asked my boys to trust me, remember who I was as their dad, and remember the years we had together. I made sure they knew I still loved them just the same as before. While my decision to marry Ginger so soon did not give my boys and me the time to grieve Andrea's death together, I knew that God had given us the opportunity for the nine of us to come together and support each other in dealing with all of our losses. Sometimes I have wished I could take away the pain for my sons or I had communicated this better to give back their initial grieving time. My hope is that all seven of our children, each of whom lost a parent far too soon, know how much we have always considered their feelings and love them.

As Ginger and I pressed on, God showed His love to both of us over and over again through friends like Lori Jo Duvall, who acted as the hands and feet of Jesus on our journey. She shares some of her perspective here:

> Andrea passed away the week before Christmas. She was gone, and all we had left were memories and our love for each other's families. Jim was filled with grief. It was my duty to my dearest friend to help the man she loved through this process. The Holy Spirit gave me words for Jim, but at times there was just silence. We often spoke on the phone as he worked through his grief. I was lying on my bed during one of these long phone conversations when Jim said, "Can I ask you something?" I thought that he knew that he could share anything with Michael and me. He said that he had begun talking with a widow. They were sharing their unique feelings of grief. He wanted to know if I was shocked or thought he was terrible for moving so quickly. The Lord had prepared me in advance for this. I said I was not shocked. Andrea had spoken with me about this very subject. She said, "If I die, Jim will not be single very long. He needs a helper." My mind went immediately to that conversation. Andrea knew this would happen; she wanted Jim to move on in a new relationship. I supported her wishes and encouraged Jim, saying that pursuing this relationship was okay. My words confirmed that he had been faithful to Andrea during her entire life. He was a wonderful spouse, but their wedding vows ended with "until death do us part." The marriage covenant that he had made before God was fulfilled. I gave the example of David. When his child with Bathsheba was

ill, he would not eat and would not change his clothes. The grief spurred him to continue to ask the Lord to spare the life of the child. When the Lord finally gave the answer and the child died, David got up and changed clothes and ate food. Others around him questioned his behavior. He said that once the child died, he could no longer ask the Lord for the life of the child. He moved forward in life. It was time for Jim to start looking toward the future too. Four years of his life had been consumed with cancer. He was faithful in every way to his beloved wife Andrea.

After I gave Jim my blessing, I was shocked to hear that many people did not feel the same way about the situation. They felt that Jim was moving too quickly. Others asked what I thought about this situation. I admit it was a whirlwind romance. Maybe I could have had more reservations, but the peace of God allowed me to say words that would normally seem foreign to me. Friends would reject Jim because of his pursuit of Ginger. I still shake my head at this reaction. Hadn't he suffered enough? Were these friends the ones praying in the middle of the night as his wife was suffering in pain? No. Again, they had no right to pass judgment on this sweet man. He had been loyal until the end.

Michael and I planned our move to New Mexico around Jim and Ginger's wedding. I would attend Jim's marriage to Ginger and show my support for the union of two people hurt by the ugliness of living in a fallen world. In my mind I planned it as a getaway for Michael and me. It had been a stressful time for us. My father had died of renal cancer in May while visiting us in Hawaii. We shipped a body over an ocean and planned a funeral thousands of miles away. We moved from Hawaii, and we sent our son to the Air Force Academy. All of this occurred within a four-week period. I was tired and worn out. It would be cathartic to see Jim, Nic, and Anthony. I would meet Ginger and try to begin a friendship with her because I loved Jim.

I visited Andrea's grave that weekend. It seemed strange to see the place where her frail body had been placed. Michael, Jim, and I cried for our loss. I thought that was all of the cleansing I needed for that day. Jim was clearly taken by Ginger, a beautiful tall brunette. I was happy that she didn't look anything like Andrea. They were complete opposites. I was thankful that I didn't see a replacement wife in her beautiful face.

We arrived at the Officers' Club for the wedding. I was going to sit in the back so that I could slip out if it became too painful. Thoughtful as always, Jim had seated us at the front at one of the head tables. This was going to be okay. I could control myself during the ceremony. At least I thought that I could. As they said their vows, the tears began to flow—and then they began to pour. Finally I reached that point where the sobs were shaking my shoulders and I muffled the ugly sounds that wanted to come out of my mouth.

It is true that I will never forget Andrea. Who could forget the impression that she made on many of us? But life proceeds in this world. We can't wish and hope that death didn't happen. We must move on. Our perspective needs to be encouraging to the ones left by the dead. God loved Jim and Ginger very much. He was providing for their future in a new way. God had formed this new family out of two broken people. God was giving an earthly father to the fatherless. My tears were grieving for my lost friend, but also for the beautiful hope that only our Savior could join these two together.

We know that God prepared us to be where we are today. The same God who led me to Andrea and who led Troy to Ginger, all while we were still teenagers, is the same God who led Ginger and me together in 2007. I knew that God's plan was not just for Ginger and me, but for all of us.

When I hold the girls or put my arm around Greyson or Boston, I feel a sense of peace. When Ginger talks to Nic or Anthony and expresses her deep care for them and a desire to be in their lives, she knows she wouldn't ever try to replace Andrea. Despite the fact that none of us chose this path, we are confident we are exactly where God placed us. We await the revelation of His remaining magnificent plan, or "Glorious Unfolding," as referred to in the Steven Curtis Chapman song.

Ginger

Jim and I had a wonderful engagement party. It was a night to thank God for His numerous provisions, celebrated with many of those who made up my loving network of friends in Phoenix from both before and after Troy died. I call them my "family in the desert," which they were, literally and figuratively. My words will never do justice to the love and gratitude I feel for them.

Jim and I feel a debt of gratitude to all who cared for my children and me when I went into a seemingly bottomless fall from my safety net in November of 2006. These friends bore the brunt of my pain and suffering. They are the ones who loved on the kids when I was lost in grief. They are the ones who took care of the house, paid the bills, and ensured that even the mundane tasks of life were handled. They helped me move to a new home, where they hung pictures, organized closets, unclogged toilets, and threw a first birthday party for my twins. These and countless other acts of love and kindness are the essence of selflessness.

One of the "side effects" of losing a spouse at such a young age is that everything in life becomes more uncertain. My children and I came to realize that anything is possible and that life promises no guarantees. We try not to live in fear, but at times the struggle is real!

> For God has not given us a spirit of fear, but of power and of love and of a sound mind. (2 Timothy 1:7 NKJV)

The simple thought of me going for a routine mammogram strikes fear in Jim. The idea of Jim flying solo again does the same for me.

Living together forever is no longer a given. The thought of dying young is no longer an improbability. I haven't told many people this, but sometimes I take pictures of Jim or the kids all by themselves because I remember going through photos after Troy died and wishing for more of just him—without hordes of kids or friends or even me in the photographs with him. Maybe that's morbid. In some ways, the untimely death of a young loved one steals from us the simplicity of carefree living. But in another way, it helps you purpose more moments than you ever did before. As Jim and I set out on a new life together, one filled with uncertainty, we remembered that there isn't always an answer to life's uncertainties. But peace can be found through prayer, as God orchestrates our healing.

I recall a conversation Troy and I had when he volunteered to go to war in Iraq. I told him we would never forgive ourselves for signing up if something happened to him. He assured me he would be fine, saying that if he wasn't, we had to know it was God's will. Troy always had this confidence about him; it was one of the things that attracted me to him. He was Superman to me. But when he spoke those words to me that day, I knew his confidence was in who he was in Christ, *not* in himself.

> But seek first his kingdom and his righteousness, and all these things will be given to you as well. Therefore do not worry about tomorrow, for tomorrow will worry about itself. Each day has enough trouble of its own. (Matthew 6:33–34 NIV)

These verses remind me how great God is and why He is worthy to be the center of my life. To this day, there are moments when I still struggle with anxiety, fear, and worry—more than I used to. Yet there are many more moments when I remember I wasn't left in the painful lonely places to fend for myself. These and many other scriptures remind me that God's great nurturing love for me gives me the freedom to live without worry.

> Are not two sparrows sold for a penny? Yet not one of them will fall to the ground outside your Father's care. And even

the very hairs of your head are all numbered. So don't be afraid; you are worth more than many sparrows. (Matthew 10:29–31 NIV)

Jim

We set our wedding date for July 5, 2008, which was seven months after we first met. Ginger and the kids were coming to San Antonio in May to begin moving into our new home. Anthony and I would remain in Randolph AFB housing until after the wedding. But two weeks before Ginger packed, we decided it would be best if we started our new life together as a family from the moment Ginger and the kids arrived in San Antonio. So we joined our lives in holy matrimony on Monday, May 5, 2008, in Phoenix, Arizona, before a very small group of family and friends. We kept our July 5 wedding, as we still wanted the celebration with our larger group of loved ones. Plus, everything was already ordered and paid for! Ginger always teases me by saying that if I miss one anniversary, I still have a shot that year.

Ginger and Jim's Wedding Day, July 5, 2008

We trusted God as He led us into this phase of our lives, knowing that our meeting was part of His plan. We also believed this was a continuation of the thread of our growth and maturity in our faith. It was an amazing gift to be loved twice in a lifetime by another individual. As we continued working our way through the grief of losing Andrea and Troy, we did so with much thankfulness and a hard-earned but necessary eternal view of life and marriage. We also realized that much like a parent loving subsequent children following a firstborn, a bereaved spouse has the miraculous ability to love a second spouse completely while still loving the first one just as much.

Following the ceremony, we had a restful honeymoon in Maui. We sat on the porch overlooking that beautiful Hawaiian island and talked not only about our lives together, but also about Troy and Andrea and all that they had meant to us. As strange as it sounds, it was almost as though they were with us.

These thoughts included our seven children, all of whom have endured pain and learned the harshness of life at far too young an age. Our home was forged in the pain of loss, but it was *our* home.

> Then choose for yourselves this day whom you will serve.
> But as for me and my household, we will serve the Lord.
> (Joshua 24:15 NIV)

Ginger

I prayed that the Lord would continually show us how to fully embrace His newly revealed plan for our time left on earth and that He would help us trust Him through any rough patches ahead. We knew so many had prayed for a miracle for us. And behold, this was it. So we rejoiced in this new, unique blessing of a second marriage and new children entering our lives.

> Among the gods there is none like You, Lord; no deeds can
> compare with Yours. (Psalm 86:8 NIV)

> See I am doing a new thing! Now it springs up, do you
> perceive it? I am making a way in the desert and streams in
> the wasteland. (Isaiah 43:19 NIV)

We knew that many looked at Jim and Andrea's defeated battle with cancer as an instance of God being neglectful. I'm sure many others saw the tragic death of Troy as an instance of God turning His back on us to be left alone, wandering in the desert. I know they questioned God's love and sovereignty. We certainly did at times.

Jim and I would be lying if we said did not feel some level of abandonment at points. Why were we the ones left to pick up the pieces? Death made breaking news right in the middle of our happy lives. We faced this question: would we wallow in the ashes or allow beauty to rise? I think that as Christians, we often want the benefits of a reconciled relationship with God without any of the responsibility resting in our laps. I began to see the miraculous way our wounds were healing and our new marriage forming as an entirely outrageous opportunity to tell others what a great and mighty God we serve. I saw my past experiences, and Jim's too, as crushing but not defeating. The mountains to climb turned into stepping-stones leading us to this place together as a new couple with a new ministry to the hurting. Each milestone we passed served as a benchmark reminder of how to live on this earth with a heavenly perspective. As we realized, eternity can begin in the blink of an eye.

In a world teeming with self-love, Troy and Andrea radiated selflessness. They never seemed to doubt God's loving care, not even in the face of death itself. Jim calls our meeting the "miracle of the moment" because it happened so quickly and had the Lord's handprints all over it. We now understand that a loving God can permit unspeakable tragedy to suddenly enter our lives, but that He can equally bring sudden, unspeakable joy. Ironically, joy and sorrow can coexist.

We've felt Christ weep with us. We know His compassionate hand has been upon us. In short, we know better than before that He is real. He will move and work in us despite our setbacks and our heartbreaks. His Word, the Bible, is daily food of which we must partake. He gives us the strength to follow Him in the darkness. There were many days when I followed but admittedly went kicking and screaming along the way. I hope I have become more in tune and have submitted to "hearing" the Lord speak to my heart. Some days I would say I have. Some days I see I still put my hope in the securities of this world or am just too plain busy to hear His whisper. However, I remember that it takes less rebellion and struggle on my part in order to surrender my own agenda to His. I truly want to see situations, good and bad, through Christ's eyes.

> And we know that God causes all things to work together for good to those who love God, to them who are called according to His purpose. (Romans 8:28 NASB)

Our goal as we wade through the deep waters of affliction or adversity should be to emerge better and not bitter, which I know is much easier said than done. Just as a parent lovingly seeks to nurture and develop her child in wisdom and stature, our Father loves us and wants to grow us to depend on Him. The rub comes when we seek our desires above His. If you have lived very long at all, you probably already know that His plan for your life can look drastically different from yours. Putting God's will first is always going to be our challenge, but Jesus modeled it perfectly for us.

> Father, If you are willing, take this cup from me; yet not my will, but yours be done. (Luke 22:42 NIV)

Jesus didn't say, "Father, please leave the cup. I want the cup." He asked Him to take it, but then He ultimately said His will had to take a backseat to His Father's. When you think about Christ being all human and all God, you know that the human part was frightened. But Jesus never panicked, because He ultimately knew that the will of His Father was always best.

Jim and I leaned on Andrea and Troy at times much more than we did the Lord. We know these were our past weaknesses, finding our identity and security in our relationship with former spouses. We knew that we must not first look to one another for all the answers or for our fulfillment. Even the best spouse makes a poor substitute for God.

> Love the Lord your God with all your heart and with all your soul and with all your strength. (Deuteronomy 6:5 NIV)

The first year of our marriage was *hard*. Our family, our feelings, and everything else was just so complex. With forty combined years of marriage experience, we both had already become set in our ways of doing things, and we each kind of liked our own ways. When tensions rose, we had to make ourselves stop, laugh, and say, "Oh, isn't this the way everyone does it?" Starting over required we put all of our energies into making this transition work. There was not a blueprint in the attic for this. We stumbled some but most certainly surrendered more. Yet our goals back then are still our goals now: to grow in grace, flow with love, spread hope, and accept the blessed gift God has provided—a new us.

Jim

Establishing traditions, especially holiday traditions, is part of the union of marriage and family. Nothing highlights the blended family like the Christmas holiday does. As you get the tree out to decorate, you realize you each have traditions and expectations that are inevitably not the same. Some like real trees, whereas some like artificial ones; some open presents on Christmas Eve, whereas others open the gifts on Christmas morning. And don't get me started about Santa!

Of course Ginger and I had this same experience our first Christmas, so we compromised. We opened one gift on Christmas Eve and the rest on Christmas morning, including gifts from Santa. We also had two Christmas trees, because when you are married to an interior designer (which is Ginger's occupation), one is not enough. The first tree was artificial. This perfectly shaped tree had perfectly spaced lights with perfectly coordinated ornaments placed by Ginger's skillful hands. It could have been in a magazine.

Just past the entryway in the family room, opposite the fireplace where nine stockings hung, you would find the other tree, the Ravella–Gilbert family tree—the real tree. It was a little too fat at the top and didn't come to a point as a good Christmas tree should. The branches were irregular, interrupting the tapered shape that a Christmas tree is known for. There were gaps where branches should have been, and dry needles began to sprinkle the floor. There were places where the lights were a little too sparse, but those were offset by the spots that had excessive lights. All in all, it had many flaws. There were no color-coordinated ornaments, nor was there a theme for this Christmas tree. Instead, it was covered with homemade ornaments, each proudly made by a child's tiny hands. There were store-bought ornaments with a story behind each. There were ornaments that had been gifts—some from grandparents, some from good friends, some from squadrons—marking periods of our lives.

The ornaments spanned the years 1983 to 2008—twenty-five years—two families, eleven lives, and countless memories. Many of our ornaments are missing pieces and have chips and colors worn thin from age, yet each is beautiful in its imperfection for the memories that each one holds. As I was sitting in the family room, the kids were fast asleep in their rooms and the tree sparkled before me. Silent yet seeming to want to speak to me, the tree stood erect, almost as if it felt honored to have given its life to hold such special decorations on its branches.

Hours before, all the children dug through boxes of ornaments, excited to renew a tradition and recount the stories of each ornament they selected. In that moment, I witnessed two families becoming one. Ginger and I exchanged glances, both realizing the significance of this moment. We both felt the sadness and the joy that were intertwining before us. We snuck off to hold each other as an attempt to help with the pain. Sometimes it's just going to hurt and nothing can spare you from that. Love is the only thing that makes it bearable.

We hung clay ornaments shaped like a mom, a dad, little cowboys, and dancing ballerinas. We hung pink ribbons, and angels with "Hope" written on their wings. We hung an F-16 and an F-15 ornament. We hung a red bulb with "Andrea 2007" written on it. It was one of Andrea's last ornaments, a Christmas gift from her friends—a gift she never got to open. It hung on the center of the tree, the shiny red bulb reflecting the white lights on the tree. There was a Middle Eastern wooden bell with a camel on it. Troy had mailed it to Ginger from Iraq. She received it just days after he had been killed.

If you took the time to look closely, you would see Troy and Ginger's first Christmas ornament—two hearts intertwined. You would see Willow Tree angels for hope and healing, snowman ornaments from Alaska, lighthouses from North Carolina, lots of princesses, Popsicle reindeer, and paper angels poorly colored to perfection. You would see a football, a soccer ball, a basketball, a hockey player. You would see bells from Italy, wooden shoes from Holland, a British flag. There is a Texas A&M and a Texas Tech ornament. It is a hodgepodge of ornaments representing two different families' full lives. It was beautiful to me.

Adding to the imperfection and to the tree's beauty, the bottom branches were overweighed with ornaments, because that was as high as three little girls could reach. There were branches with two ornaments in the same spot. And yes, there were places with no ornaments at all.

This tree represented us, an imperfect family brought together in the worst of circumstances. At times Ginger and I do not understand why we were brought together. At other times, and sometimes in the same moment, we see the blessing of our meeting. Though it is totally unfamiliar to us, we have tried to make our way on this road where hope was found, knowing we surely are making many mistakes along the way. We try not to hide our imperfections or to give the impression that bringing two families together is a cakewalk. It's certainly been anything but.

Sometimes as believers, our lives are much like our two Christmas trees. When you first enter or meet someone, you are presented the "perfect-looking" version—the one that looks whole and flawlessly put together. But upon closer inspection, you find it's not real. It's got wires and plastic and such. When you look past the artificial tree, you will see the real tree. It will have imperfections. Yet our victories and tragedies have formed who we are. It's in our weaknesses where you can see the true beauty of Christ. He takes our struggles to demonstrate His strength. The only "realness" we have to offer people is who we are in Christ. He is genuine love and grace. Faith and hope are found in Him alone. Our prayer is that everyone sees Jesus though our lives and knows that our triumphs are not because of us but because of Him in us.

One weekend Ginger was away at a women's church retreat. It was a much-needed trip for her because, having been a leader in the women's ministry in Phoenix, she had lost that connection with two recent moves. For me, it was a chance to spend a weekend alone with the kids.

While Ginger was away, I decided to challenge myself by getting five kids fed, ready, and to church on time. It turned out to be surprisingly simple, because the kids were already very responsible when it came to doing tasks themselves. I had nothing to do with it.

As we sat in church and sang worship songs, I looked at Boston, Greyson, and Bella beside me and felt the joy of being a father, but also the pain of loss, knowing Troy would have loved this moment. Have you ever felt like you were living someone else's life? There is a guilt that underlies the joy. I knew I suffered from survivor's guilt when thinking about Andrea. Now I felt it again, but this time for Troy. I felt guilt for living when Andrea had died, guilt for moments like this on a beautiful Sunday morning with Troy's kids.

As I sang with the kids, I felt Bella lean into me. I knew she needed the comfort of her dad's arm around her. In times like that, I can't help but think of Troy. There are a few times in my life when I know exactly where Troy would be and in some ways know what he would have been feeling. Telling Ginger goodnight on her birthday, watching Boston and Greyson excel in sports, teaching the girls to swim, holding Bella at church—these are things he would have done too.

As I held Bella and thought of Troy, I thought of my role as the children's dad. I know God has called me to be their dad in the same way He gave me Nic and Anthony, but sometimes it is hard to feel like I belong in this role. I know Troy was their dad, and even though I adopted them all legally, I remain sensitive to Troy's legacy. When Andrea and I adopted Anthony, one of the court requirements was that his birth father relinquish his parental rights as Anthony's dad. Troy did not choose to leave them. He never signed away his rights as their father. When I watched the recorded video Troy had made for the kids just days before he died, I saw a man who loved his family more than anything. That is why we talk openly about Troy and Andrea in our home. Neither of them left their children by choice. They did not relinquish their role as mother or father. In fact, they did the opposite. They loved their kids to their last day on this earth. That is why Ginger and I work hard to keep their memories alive in our home. It's important to Ginger and me that we continue to reinforce the memories of Troy and Andrea with the kids. It's why at moments like this particular Sunday, when I feel the joy of being their parent, I especially think of Troy. And it's why I think of Andrea when I watch, with pride, the successes in Anthony's and Nic's lives.

As I stood singing and worshipping with the kids, this verse came to me:

> What, after all, is Apollos? And what is Paul? Only servants, through whom you came to believe—as the Lord has assigned to each his task. I planted the seed, Apollos watered it, but God made it grow. So neither he who plants nor he who waters is anything, but only God, who makes things grow. The man who plants and the man who waters have one purpose, and each will be rewarded according to his own labor. For we are God's fellow workers; you are God's field, God's building. (1 Corinthians 3:5–9 NIV)

This verse helped me see my role as the kids' father.

The day Jim adopted all five kids at the New Braunfels Courthouse. The boys, of course, kept Gilbert as their last name. The Girls added Ravella and made Gilbert their permanent middle name like Ginger did. May 22, 2009

Troy planted. I will water. Together we will raise them. While our roles are different, the goal is the same: to teach the kids to love the Lord and to grow up to be godly men and women. So as I held Bella, I held her as her dad, praying I would live up to the task I have been called to do. I pray I will make Troy proud. I cherish the time I get to spend with the kids, knowing how fast time flies. I don't think of caring for them as a chore. They are my kids and a joy to raise.

Later that afternoon, our girls went to a birthday party. Each came home with a helium-filled balloon. The next morning, the girls were drawing and coloring while the boys and I did chores. (We had to have the house clean for when Mom got home!) As I was working, Bella asked me if she could write a note to God, tie it to the balloon, and send it to Him. Bella wrote hers and sent it to God, and then she wrote Aspen and Annalise's for them, tied those notes to the balloon, and brought it to me. I wanted to read Bella's note, but I felt it was personal. I wish I had after reading Aspen's. Aspen's said, "Hello, God. How is heaven? What do you wear? How is Daddy? Tell him we said hello." Tears filled my eyes. When Annalise brought me her note, I decided to take a picture of it.

Below is Annalise's note, penned by Bella:

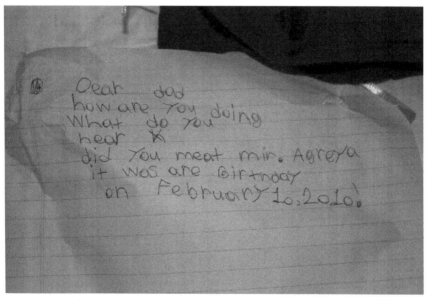

Annalise's (age 3) note about Andrea, which reads as follows:

Dear Dad,

How are you doing? What do you hear? Did you meet Ms. Andrea? It was our birthday on February 10, 2010.

Our family has suffered tragic losses. There has been a lot of pain, anger, disappointment, confusion, sadness, and guilt on our journey to each other, but God has made us a family. It is a family neither Ginger nor I sought or desired, but it is a family God called us to be. We have but one purpose, to use our talents and time for God's glory, no different from Troy or Andrea, our fellow workers who have received their reward. I look forward to seeing them again and talking all about the joy of our shared purpose. Some plant and some water, but we all share in the bounty of the harvest.

It's true that our circumstances do not define our God. But if you look closely, you will see Him *in* your circumstances, rejoicing with you in your successes and compassionately loving you in your trials. We know the feeling of not being able to see the other side of a stormy sea, where the waters are calm. When your world is rocked and you find yourself tossed about with doubts and fears, you might just be hanging onto the edge. When life suddenly shifts and does not meet your expectations, you might simply be trying to remain steady on your feet. But those moments do not define how or if God loves you. He can't do anything else but love you. You're His creation. He is not only in the boat with you but also waiting for you on the other side of your storm or mountain. He draws you closer. He whispers peace. You aren't alone.

Chapter 3 *Discussion Guide*

1. Ginger recalls that in the months that followed Troy's death, she verbalized to God her greatest desire was for God to give them another loving husband and father. She expressed her reluctant willingness to wait upon God and even to accept that His answer might be a "no". Have you ever had to wait for a prayer to be answered? How did you deal with the wait? What lessons did you learn?

2. Jim describes feeling guilty for being happy again. Have you ever felt "survivor's guilt"?

3. If something in your life has not turned out the way you planned, how did you react? Was it how you would have predicted you would have reacted? How do you want to react in the future? What were some of the parallels? What were some of the changes you noted in yourself by the end of your journey?

4. Jim and Ginger learned the cost of loving someone deeply is equal to the depth of grief they faced when they lost them, yet, still, they chose to love again. Loving people can obviously hurt us many different ways, such as divorce or abuse. Have you ever been afraid to trust or love someone for fear of being hurt again?

5. On their first Christmas holiday, Jim describes their blended family by comparing the two Christmas trees - one seemed perfect, while the other was visibly flawed. Are you hesitant to present to the world anything other than an image of perfection? How do you deal with the pressure of today's digital life to present yourself as perfect? God asks us to be authentic and real to show others His power. Discuss a way you can be more transparent and then note others reactions as they see you doing that. Jim and Ginger have found many people have been helped simply by them being open about their struggles.

6. Ginger and Jim's story was highlighted by the popular Christian author and pastor, Max Lucado, during his series *"The Sacred Home"*. Max introduced their story with a question to the large church audience asking, "Maybe the phrase *"This Sacred Home"* surprises you. You don't think of the home as a sacred place, but God does. Because the home is where God does His best work. Even when the home takes turns we never expect. The Ravellas can tell you, few families have experienced the changes that theirs has. But through it all God has been at work." What do you think the term *sacred* means? Does your home feel sacred?

Chapter 4

Questioning God

For we do not have a high priest who is unable to empathize with our weaknesses, but we have one who has been tempted in every way, just as we are—yet he did not sin. Let us then approach God's throne of grace with confidence, so that we may receive mercy and find grace to help us in our time of need.

—Hebrews 4:15–16 (NIV)

Jim

One of the most confusing and difficult weeks I've experienced happened in 2006. Andrea's condition had taken an unexpected turn for the worse. The week started with Andrea's having to restart two of the harshest chemo drugs. That in itself was difficult, because Andrea would lose her hair for the fourth time in four years. However, these were chemo drugs Andrea had taken twice before, so we thought we knew what to expect. Turns out we were wrong. That week of restarting all of Andrea's chemo, I did not understand what we were going through or why we were going through it. Andrea seemed excessively tired. She basically slept from Wednesday until Friday afternoon. She was very groggy. Her speech was weak and she was hard to understand. She also had several other symptoms, including shortness of breath, severe stomach pains, and swelling of her left hand. It was all so unexpected since Andrea had never had these side effects when she took the drugs in the past. I had some questions for God. Why on earth was Andrea having to go back on chemo, and why did our prayers seem unanswered? It was these thoughts that led me to John 11 and the story of Lazarus.

Of course I had read the story of Jesus's friendship with Mary, Martha, and Lazarus, and Lazarus' miraculous resurrection from the dead. But one of the things that makes reading the Bible so vital to our faith is, depending on what you are experiencing, God can speak to you in different ways as you read the same scriptures over and over again. I believe that even as some of you read *Hope Found*, the scriptures we reference may speak to you in ways that you have never experienced before. Even if you know the story of Lazarus, I suggest you avoid the temptation to skip over the parts you "know." Read it as if it is your first time reading the verses. You may find yourself drawn to something new.

> Now a man named Lazarus was sick. He was from Bethany, the village of Mary and her sister Martha. This Mary, whose brother Lazarus now lay sick, was the same one who poured perfume on the Lord and wiped his feet with her hair. So the sisters sent word to Jesus, "Lord, the one you love is sick." When he heard this, Jesus said, "This sickness will not end in death. No, it is for God's glory so that God's Son may be glorified through it." Jesus loved Martha and her sister and Lazarus. Yet when he heard that Lazarus was sick, he stayed where he was two more days. Then he said to his disciples, "Let us go back to Judea." "But Rabbi," they said, "a short while ago the Jews tried to stone you, and yet you are going back there?" Jesus answered, "Are there not twelve hours of daylight? A man who walks by day will not stumble, for he sees by this world's light. It is when he walks by night that he stumbles, for he has no light." After he had said this, he went on to tell them, "Our friend Lazarus has fallen asleep; but I am going there to wake him up." His disciples replied, "Lord, if he sleeps, he will get better." Jesus had been speaking of his death, but his disciples thought he meant natural sleep. So then he told them plainly, "Lazarus is dead, and for your sake I am glad I was not there, so that you may believe. But let us go to him." Then Thomas (called Didymus) said to the rest of the disciples, "Let us also go,

that we may die with him." On his arrival, Jesus found that Lazarus had already been in the tomb for four days. Bethany was less than two miles from Jerusalem, and many Jews had come to Martha and Mary to comfort them in the loss of their brother. When Martha heard that Jesus was coming, she went out to meet him, but Mary stayed at home. "Lord," Martha said to Jesus, "if you had been here, my brother would not have died. But I know that even now God will give you whatever you ask." Jesus said to her, "Your brother will rise again." Martha answered, "I know he will rise again in the resurrection at the last day." Jesus said to her, "I am the resurrection and the life. He who believes in me will live, even though he dies; and whoever lives and believes in me will never die. Do you believe this?" "Yes, Lord," she told him, "I believe that you are the Christ, the Son of God, who was to come into the world." And after she had said this, she went back and called her sister Mary aside. "The Teacher is here," she said, "and is asking for you." When Mary heard this, she got up quickly and went to him. Now Jesus had not yet entered the village, but was still at the place where Martha had met him. When the Jews who had been with Mary in the house, comforting her, noticed how quickly she got up and went out, they followed her, supposing she was going to the tomb to mourn there. When Mary reached the place where Jesus was and saw him, she fell at his feet and said, "Lord, if you had been here, my brother would not have died." When Jesus saw her weeping, and the Jews who had come along with her also weeping, he was deeply moved in spirit and troubled. "Where have you laid him?" he asked. "Come and see, Lord," they replied. Jesus wept. Then the Jews said, "See how he loved him!" But some of them said, "Could not he who opened the eyes of the blind man have kept this man from dying?" (John 11:1–37 NIV)

As I read John 11, I was drawn to Martha's response when Jesus arrived: "If you had been here, my brother would not have died. But I know that even now God will give you whatever you ask." And Mary's response was the same: "Lord, if you had been here, my brother would not have died."

They had sent for Jesus when Lazarus was ill, knowing Jesus had healed others and would surely come quickly to someone He loved, to His friend. So as I read this verse, I related to the questions being asked and the unspoken words between the lines. I could relate to the confusion in the sisters' words and their underlying disappointment in and anger at Jesus for not doing for someone who deeply loved Him what He had done for strangers. We all have certain expectations of God's love for us. I am certain those who actually walked the roads of Jerusalem with Jesus had even more. Jesus delaying His arrival until after Lazarus died did not seem to make sense to the sisters—much like my trying to understand why Andrea was in such pain no matter what I prayed. I wondered if I wasn't finding the right words to connect to God. Or worse, did He not care? To me, the only obvious answer to my prayers was for Andrea's pain to stop and her body to be healed instantly. Neither of those things had happened.

I was also drawn to the reaction of the Jews who commented, "Could not He who opened the eyes of the blind man have kept this man from dying?" You know, Mary and Martha probably heard these comments. They most likely began to ask the same question as doubt crept in the through the doorway of misunderstanding. We can all relate to Lazarus's friends. We see others being "healed" while we wait for our turn. How can God not help me, a Christian? Don't we deserve healing more than some? That's what we think when we look to humankind's knowledge to try to understand God's ways. The two do not equate.

Jesus knew the result of His delay in coming to Lazarus's side, and He even explained to the disciples why: "Lazarus is dead, and for your sake I am glad I was not there, so that you may believe" (verses 14–15). He told Martha up front, "Your brother will rise again" (verse 23). Jesus knew this had to play out, that Lazarus had to die for the Father's will to be done. As painfully hard as it was, the sisters just had to trust. Jesus certainly displayed His love for them in His own grief over their sorrow. "When Jesus saw her weeping, and the Jews who had come along with her also weeping, he was deeply moved in spirit and troubled" (verse

33) and "Jesus wept" (verse 35). This verse always intrigued me. Why would Jesus weep over Lazarus's death when He knew He was about to bring him back to life? It wasn't because Lazarus died. It was because he saw Mary and Martha's pain and was moved to tears. Even though He knew hope was around the corner for them, He was saddened to see their sorrow. So I realized, how could I think the Lord didn't care about Andrea when I read firsthand about His compassion?

Soon those who loved Jesus would have to draw on this deeper faith when He Himself was given over to death. How was He going to raise Himself? They did not need to know the how. They just needed to remember He could. Jesus's miracles were used to point to His deity— His ability to do what only God could do—not just for that moment, but for eternity.

This is what spoke to me. I did not understand why, but I knew I just needed to trust. God may have seemed silent to me that week when Andrea was in terrible pain, but that is only because I was listening with my human ears instead of my spiritual ones. I'm not saying I expected the same events to play out in our life as they did in Lazarus', but I am saying that God's character and His love were the same. I began the week questioning God and ended it with a reminder that He is timelessly trustworthy.

Ginger

Since November 27, 2006, I've learned a lot about compassion and empathy from how people showed both these things to me and my family. As a result, I've become much more aware of the hurting of others around me. I've realized that my life, untouched by real tragedy before that fateful day of Troy's death, had scarcely seen heartache, which had made it harder for me to recognize heartache in others.

I also began wrestling with God. "How could He," I kept asking, "inflict such suffering on me, His beloved child?" I had entrusted my life to Christ when I was nine years old. I had seen Him as a loving daddy, ready to rebuke but also always ready to embrace. All of a sudden I felt He had slapped me, not embraced me. I felt He did not open His arms to me but turned His back on me. Then I asked, "Isn't it shameful at best, or blasphemous at worst, to be thinking these things about my heavenly Father?" But I couldn't help it. I couldn't hold it back. The waves of anger swept over me time and time again.

I knew many people were changed because their perspective was changed. That's the nature of tragedy befalling someone you love. It's death brushing up next to you that makes you appreciate life. I would recall all of the people who began a relationship with God at Troy's memorial service. I was greatly moved when I thought of how God had worked in their lives. My head knew this, but my heart was brittle at the edges—so sometimes the fact that others had been saved at Troy's memorial service only served to frustrate me. My all-powerful God, after all, could have used any means to save souls for His kingdom, so why would He choose to ruin six lives to better the lives of those other people? It didn't make any sense at the time. I would have many more months of wrestling with God, arguing about His plan, and letting go of my own before I finally understood that I didn't have to understand and that, instead, I had to submit and let go of my demand for answers. "Why, God?" might never be answered; I had to try to make peace with that.

Wendy Killian wrote a book titled *To Have Loved* that I highly recommend. In it she states, "Jesus stands ready to help us, but His help is contingent on our absolute total obedience to His Word, whether or not we agree with it or understand it. His help is delayed and His power is bound and His glory is hidden as long as we stand around in disobedience and argue!" [3] Being totally obedient to His Word isn't instant or at all easy. In fact, relying on our power alone, it is impossible. But with the power of the Holy Spirit in us, it is not only possible but also probable.

I couldn't see the probability of it in my life for a long time because I truly felt as if the half of me that had become one whole when Troy and I were married had now died. I was walking the earth as an emotional

---

[3]   Wendy Killian, *To Have Loved* (Mustang, OK: Tate Publishing & Enterprises, 2009), 50.

cripple. I think I had always relied more heavily on Troy than I ever did on the Lord, so I was a woman fumbling and directionless in an out-of-control life. I felt like a failure as a Christian. Weren't Christians supposed to be stronger than this?

Following is one of my prayer journal entries. I wrote it about four months after Troy died.

> I am at my rope's end. I am hanging on for dear life. Life doesn't seem so dear, and I wonder what is the use of hanging on anyway? My energies are spent. I have slept hardly at all. Everything is pointless. I can't fall asleep or stay asleep. I am rarely hungry. I long for Christ to show up and do something big to help me out, or for Him to just show up and take me home. What have You done with me, Lord? How do You expect me to raise five children with no sleep? I wish I could scream at you, God, but I would wake the children. I was so comfortable in my pretty Christmas-card-picture life. Now I live in a cold and lonely world that is simply gray. Please hear my cry. I want to run away. I want to run to You, Lord, and away from You all at the same time. I feel empty. So empty. Like a carved-out pumpkin. Please make something beautiful out of these ashes. I am so angry with You for messing with my life. My head hurts. My body hurts. My soul is torn. My heart is crushed into bits. Though I know I don't have a chance in this world of making it without You. I need You to hang onto me, Lord. Please keep me from checking out. I could write all night, but then I see the sunlight coming and daring me to face the same things again for another new day.

I would like to say that this was written on just one really bad night, but those words reflected so much of what was consistently swirling around in my thoughts from morning to night. I think we are afraid to express our anger at God, certainly in public as professed Christians. But (surprise!) He is omniscient, already knowing everything. You might as well confess to Him what He already understands so He can come alongside you and help you. He longs for you to share your heart with Him. He is big enough to take our hurting pleas and shaking fists.

> Yet the Lord longs to be gracious to you; therefore He will rise up to show you compassion. For the Lord is a God of justice. Blessed are all who wait for Him. (Isaiah 30:18 NIV)

I would encourage anyone who is suffering to write down your struggles, feelings, and frustrations in the form of an outcry to God. Writing it down helps you pinpoint your real struggles and pain, and later helps you see how the Lord carried you through it. The book of Lamentations in the Bible is just that: a book of outcries to the Lord. If you need a format, David can give you an example or two in the book of Psalms. David knew what it was to feel God's blessing and favor, and only a short time later to feel the Lord's absence and denial of his pleas to return him to his previous "good" life. David got mad at God. David got sad. David got desperate. Yet that didn't change David's love of God.

> How long must I struggle with anguish in my soul. With sorrow in my heart every day. Turn and answer me, O Lord my God! Restore the sparkle in my eyes or I will die. (Psalm 13:2–3 NLT)

Like David, I begged the Lord to turn His face to me. I pleaded with Him to give me hope, strength, and the desire to continue to raise my children in the manner I always had. I asked for rest and reprieve from the arduous journey. I fought to accept my new life, when all I really wanted was to return to my old life. When I finished raging at God, I felt guilty, very frail, very weak, and very immature in my faith. Yet I felt the Holy Spirit's strength keep nudging me forward, even as I dug my heels in. I love this quotation from Jim Cymbala, pastor at the Brooklyn Tabernacle:

> I discovered an astonishing truth: God is attracted to weakness. He can't resist those who humbly and honestly

admit how desperately they need him. Our weakness, in fact, makes room for his power.[4]

As we read the following verses, we must remember that David, of all the people in the Bible, is the only one called "a man after God's own heart."

> I love the Lord, for He heard my voice, He heard my cry for mercy. Because He turned His ear to me, I will call on Him as long as I live. The cords of death entangled me; the anguish of the grave came upon me. I was overcome by trouble and sorrow. Then I called on the name of the Lord. O Lord, save me! The Lord is gracious and righteous; our God is full of compassion. The Lord protects the simple-hearted, when I was in great need He saved me. Be at rest once more, O my soul, for the Lord has been good to you. For you, O Lord, have delivered my soul from death, my eyes from tears, my feet from stumbling, that I may walk before the Lord in the land of the living. (Psalm 116:1–9 NIV)

This spurs the question, "How can one be a man or woman after God's own heart?" For the answer, we must look to God, who humbled Himself when he came to earth in the form of Jesus. During His thirty-three years of life, Jesus felt everything we feel. On the cross, He even briefly felt God's absence. Yet, He always knew who His Father was and trusted His plan, even in the pain.

The more I studied the Bible, the more I saw great men like Abraham, Moses, and Job referred to as heroes, such as in the "Hall of Faith" in Hebrews 11. At some point, they all came to the end of themselves and went to beg the Lord for a way out of their trials. Sometimes they faithfully waited like Job. Sometimes they regretted taking matters into their own hands like Abraham. Sometimes they asked multiple times for God to rescue them, only to find that the rescue really was just to watch God faithfully journey with them through the

---

[4]   James R. Cymbala, *Fresh Wind, Fresh Fire: What Happens When God's Spirit Invades the Hearts of His People* (Grand Rapids, MI: Zondervan, 2003), 13.

trial. Paul is our perfect example of this. He was a dedicated follower of Christ, a missionary before anyone knew what a missionary was. Yet God allowed some serious affliction in his life.

> Therefore, so that I would not become arrogant, a thorn in the flesh was given to me, a messenger of Satan to trouble me—so that I would not become arrogant. I asked the Lord three times about this, that it would depart from me. But he said to me, "My grace is enough for you, for my power is made perfect in weakness." So then, I will boast most gladly about my weaknesses, so that the power of Christ may reside in me. (2 Corinthians 12:7–9 NET)

I've always wondered what the thorn was that Paul kept asking the Lord to remove, but I think the point is that we can easily replace his thorn with our own thorn or trial. Our reaction should ultimately be that of Paul—boasting gladly in our weaknesses rather than being resigned to the fact that God stuck us with the problem. (This is much easier said than done, I know!) We just have to trust that eventually the rose will be more noticeable than the thorn.

When I didn't know what else to do in my moments of despair, I would journal. It was cathartic to put my feelings down in words. That is why Jim and I wrote on our blog for so many years. Yet the benefit comes even later as you look back on what you wrote. I can read those harsh words and be filled with thankfulness and wonder for all the ways God came to rescue me out of that pit. I read my journals and remember His steadfast faithfulness, and that He set me free once and will do it again.

There are some books that leave a lasting impression of inspiration. When I read Ann Voskamp's small but powerful book *One Thousand Gifts*, it opened my eyes to the critical key that unlocks real peace and lasting happiness—thankfulness.

Ann's journey out of the bitterness that could have very easily choked out the joyful life God had planned for her began with the small act of writing down a few things she was thankful for and ended with an eye-opening journey of discovery. She says, "The act of sacrificing thank offerings to God—even for the bread and cup of cost, for cancer and crucifixion—this prepares the way for God to show us His fullest salvation from bitter, angry, resentful lives and from all sin that estranges us from Him."[5]

She highlights the ultimate truth: "When I realize that it is not God who is in my debt but I who am in His great debt, then doesn't all become gift."[6]

> He who sacrifices thank offerings honors Me, and he prepares the way that I may show him the salvation of God. (Psalm 50:23 NIV)

In my darkest moments, I fervently prayed that the Lord would take my children and me to be home with Him. We would get on an airplane and I would think, *Maybe this will be the day we meet Jesus!* These are common thoughts for people suffering from depression and anxiety. Previously, I had never understood how someone could be in such a dark place, but in my desperation, I wanted the earth to swallow us up whole. I was searching for a way out instead of a way through. However, as awful as those days were, I think I needed to feel those feelings in order to better see the brokenhearted all around me. I now have a compassion for others that I honestly didn't have before. I am now able to counsel grieving people and can say with confidence, "I do know it feels easier not to go on. Going on is the hardest part, but it's also brave, beautiful, and essential to the plan God still has for your life."

If you are reading *Hope Found* and find yourself in that dark place, please share your feelings with a trusted counselor or wise friend. I did. My friends and my counselor reminded me to keep pressing on, pushing through. I remember my sweet Mom saying over and over again, "It won't feel this way forever. I promise." A huge lie the Enemy tells is that our dark secrets, worst fears, or shameful regrets are best kept private in

---

5   Ann Voskamp, *One Thousand Gifts: A Dare to Live Fully Right Where You Are* (Grand Rapids, MI: Zondervan, 2011), 13.
6   Ibid., 94.

the dark corners of our souls and that the way we feel will never change. But God has a hope, a plan, and a future for all of us! He promises it. Unlike humankind, God never once has broken a promise.

> "For I know the plans I have for you," declares the Lord, "plans to prosper you and not to harm you, plans to give you a hope and a future. Then you will call upon Me and come and pray to Me and I will listen to you. You will seek Me and find Me when you seek Me with your whole heart. I will be found by you," declares the Lord, "and will bring you back from captivity." (Jeremiah 29:11–14 NIV)

This scripture was written to the Israelites when they were stranded in exile and awaiting rescue and hope, yet the message is the same for all of us because this passage is about God's character, which hasn't changed one iota in all of these years.

In the months after Troy was gone, I had run out of my own strength. I found that no matter how much I tried, I couldn't heal myself. The strategy of letting time heal the wounds did not seem to be working. I felt like I was running in quicksand, wasting a lot of energy and yet still drowning in the end. On a lighter note, this is how I feel trying to keep up with the laundry of seven people—what an effort in futility!

I wrestled a lot with the Lord and realized that, despite my wishes, my rescue wasn't coming in the way I thought it would. God was not, in fact, sending a tsunami to Arizona to wipe us off the planet. In my heart of hearts, I knew I wanted more than just survival, more than simply existing. I wanted all of us to thrive. I wanted to still have a life of purpose. I wanted to *really* live again. Troy and I had never accepted mediocrity; I didn't want to disappoint either of us. I knew that the only way to find life again would be to throw myself at the feet of Jesus. I had to lay all of my hopes, dreams, and plans on the altar of acceptance. Then one day, I realized God was saying a loving but firm no to my daily prayer request for an escape hatch. It looked like God must have something left for us here on earth.

So I gave Him my raw soul and my bone-thin, sleep-deprived body. He was the One who loved me first, but I knew reconciliation with Him was a two-way street. I had to get on board. I continued reading my Bible, praying constantly, making my four-by-six notecards of scriptures, seeking out wise counseling, listening to volumes of uplifting Christian music, going to church even when I didn't feel like it, and reading a tall stack of Christian books about grief and God's sovereignty.

One of the best books that lays out a great road map to recovery and that helped me understand the role *I* had to play in my healing process was written by my dear friend Marlo Peddycord Francis. It's called *When Casseroles Cease.*[7]

The responsibility of my potential triumph over tragedy wasn't solely on the Lord's shoulders. I knew I had to be a willing participant. I searched for joy and found a little each day along the path of thankfulness. Trusting God again was a process, and I found that faith was a choice—more of a verb than a noun. I had to decide that even though I neither saw nor heard direct answers from the Lord, I would obey Him, as I'm instructed to do in His Word. While we don't get to choose what path our lives will take, God holds the map and the compass as we drive on, often in the blinding storms of life. The only way we find our way back and out of the shadows is to seek the Light. I had to choose whether I was going to marinate in my own pity, going it alone, or to trust that Light, Jesus Christ, to help me persevere. It took a lot of prayer and loads of patience, which I'm still working on.

> And we know that God causes everything to work together
> for the good of those who love Him and are called according
> to His purpose for them. (Romans 8:28 NLT)

As I worked through the long and lonely process of grieving, a friend told me he could picture me walking through the desert (pulling my leopard-print suitcases behind me, of course). He said, "I know you fall down, but as long as you keep getting up and walking, you are still

---

[7] Marlo P. Francis, *When Casseroles Cease* (Mustang, OK: Tate Publishing & Enterprises, May 27, 2008).

showing the Lord you are willing to do the work." That was a challenge like none other. Today, I better understand these scriptures:

> There is wonderful joy ahead, even though you have to endure many trials for a little while. These trials will show that your faith is genuine. It is being tested as fire tests and purifies gold—though your faith is far more precious than mere gold. So when your faith remains strong through many trials, it will bring you much praise and glory and honor on the day when Jesus Christ is revealed to the whole world. (1 Peter 1:6–7 NIV)

> Now faith is being sure of what we hope for and certain of what we do not see. (Hebrews 11:1 NLV)

Faith is not required nearly as much in times of prosperity. Hearing God's voice isn't as crucial when the music of life is a sweet melody. There is a hauntingly beautiful song by Andrew Peterson called "The Silence of God." It's about the doubts and anger we have when we don't feel that God is listening to our prayers. We are often afraid to even whisper those thoughts for fear that if He is listening, He might decide to stop. Even when God remained silent, I had to make the choice not to turn my back on Christ—because He did not turn His back on me at the cross. That certainly would have been the easier choice for Him. All the near-fatal blows that came from Troy's death didn't kill me like Satan had planned for them to do. I am stronger now because of the suffering. I seek to see this life in a new way, knowing that all its trappings and wrappings don't matter in comparison to the treasures we have in our families, our friends, and our health.

It's oh so easy to slip back into the imbalanced swing of life in the modern-day United States. We fall into the trap of believing that more is always better. I love beautiful things, flowers, furniture, homes. I admit it. When I was a little girl, I designed my own Barbie houses using real miniatures. I mean, how could Ken read the morning paper if it was plastic? My passion for good design is the reason I majored in interior design at Texas Tech University. I regret now, though, all the times I complained to Troy that we needed a bigger and better house. He worked very hard to provide for us. I was mostly a stay-at-home mom and didn't contribute much to the income. Admittedly, however, I contributed to the debt. We had some financial issues that constantly weighed on both of us. I remember thinking that if only we were financially stable, then I would be happier. Yet when the life insurance money came in and all the debts were paid, the house could be bigger, the car newer, and the clothes from better stores - I found myself pining for my old life. I would have happily given it all back to have Troy home again.

> Do not store up for yourselves treasures here on earth, where moths eat them and rust destroys them, and where thieves break in and steal. Store yourselves treasures in heaven. ... Wherever your treasure is, there the desires of your heart will also be. (Matthew 6:19–20, 21 NIV)

As I reflect on my purpose, I think my spiritual gifts have always been related to encouragement and hospitality. I've been a fairly good "cheerleader," but now what I have to share comes from an infinitely deeper well. Maybe I'm here to help someone see there is still hope. I know that my oldest son, Boston, feels that calling on his young life. When Boston was in high school, he mentioned that a friend from school had pulled him aside in the hall and asked Boston to pray for him as he struggled with severe emotional issues, namely, suicidal thoughts. In isolation, this boy was profoundly hurting on the inside. Boston sees others struggling and actually cares enough to love them through the tough days. At the age of sixteen, Boston began stopping at city bus stops to sit, talk, and pray with whomever he found waiting for a ride. I can't imagine being so spontaneously compassionate to strangers at that age. But I know where it comes from, a place deep inside of him that has felt that same compassion from others. I hope I am never too comfortable in my life, too selfish, or just too plain busy to stop, listen, and show compassion like Boston does.

Maybe my purpose is simply to tell someone to keep walking in their desert, to keep getting out of bed in the morning even when they don't want to. Whatever it is that God has for me to do, I know I must follow Him or else I will wander forever.

Though He slay me, yet will I trust Him. (Job 13:15 NKJV)

Years after that tragic day that changed my life forever, the Lord continues to tell me, "Choose this day whom you shall trust." I may never know why He allowed such trauma in my life, and I certainly don't know what lies ahead, but the one thing I do know is I must choose to trust and follow Him.

Now I know my life is not ruined as I once thought it was. It's a life with deeper roots from weathering the storm. I'm not better in terms of being more competent or able, but I now know who I am and what I can overcome as a member of Christ's family.

We now have this light shining in our hearts, but we ourselves are like fragile clay jars containing this great treasure. This makes it clear that our great power is from God, not from ourselves. (2 Corinthians 4:7 NLT)

Jim

I went through the normal emotions when you hear the word *cancer* spoken about yourself or a loved one. I was mad, angry, confused. I felt this was unfair and felt cheated as I tried to comprehend what was happening. However, I doubt I surprised God or disappointed Him in my reaction, because He is well aware of our struggles.

I realize as I write *Hope Found*, farther down the road of healing than our readers might be, that I had four years to learn what it meant to trust Him in affliction, thousands of days to work through how to reconcile God's will versus my own desires. I don't think what I write today will convince you or give you total peace if you are dealing with these matters. It is not an easy process or something you grasp in a moment. I believe it is a journey that you must walk yourself. I just pray my words will give you hope as you struggle with understanding why bad could happen and how God could allow it. As you work through your trial, there will be times you will question God. I want you to know that is okay. God is big enough to handle our questions and anger.

During Andrea's treatments, there were days we were so exhausted from the fight that getting out of bed seemed impossible. However, hardships rarely give you time to lie in bed, so we had no choice but to press on. Like a solider frozen by fear, knowing death awaits in the charge, we were scared but fully aware there was no safety in staying put. This describes the struggle we faced when we heard the bad news that Andrea's cancer had spread to her liver, lungs, and bones.

The physical reality crashed over me. Andrea's shortness of breath, the pain in her back and chest, her constant cough, and the changes in her vision were a constant reminder of cancer's relentless pursuit. Yet, God was giving us a peace that comes with knowing that He is in control, a peace that is not based on an outcome or a promise of healing but rather on what we already had obtained, salvation. We had to learn to trust Him and abandon ourselves to be used for His glory. It makes me stop and think there was a time I would have been afraid to type those words. I would have said it sounded like I was giving up and accepting Andrea's death, which was the last thing I wanted.

I remember an imaginary scene forming in my mind. It was as if she and I were standing on a cliff and before us was a valley, deep and wide. In the distance was a wall of water headed our way. I could hear it. I could see it rushing toward us. I was afraid because it seemed more powerful than me. The ground that seemed so secure before became inadequate as I began to doubt the ability of the ground I was standing on to withstand the oncoming water. There was nothing between us and the water but the valley and the ground we stood on.

I wished the water would turn away, but it kept coming. Andrea and I were on the cliff, high above the valley floor, holding onto each other. Then the water hit, crashing into the cliff, shaking the ground beneath our feet, spraying our face. It was scary as the physical impact of the water began to erode the sides of the cliff.

The water turned brown from the eroding soil. Chunks of earth fell away. Some of the soil disappeared. My fears were being confirmed; the ground was no match for the water and soon we would fall in. Maybe this is where the expression "waves of doubt and fear" comes from. The power of the water was incredible! Should we turn, abandon our stand, and make a run for higher ground?

The water finally settled into a constant, steady flow as it filled the valley below. There was a new sense of peace, as the water seemed less threatening. Yet when we looked down, we still saw the soil under our feet being washed away. So it went, periods of peace and confidence amid periods of doubt, worry, and anger.

Soon the water was all around us, and we stood isolated on our pillar of ground. There was no escape now. We thought, *Lord, how much more can the ground take? Should we just jump in and go with the water?* The Lord said, "No, stand your ground and trust Me." We argued back, "But Lord, look, the water is flowing over our feet." He said, "I created the water; it does not flow without My approval. It only goes where I allow it." I saw our friends across the way standing on the opposite bank, wanting to help. I saw the desire in their faces, their anguish. They were asking, "God, why are You doing this to them? It seems unfair." He told them the same: "Trust me. Trust me and see my strength in Jim and Andrea's weakness."

When we looked down, we were surprised to see the soil had been washed away, which exposed a solid rock beneath us. The water now flowed around the rock, powerless against the solid granite. We suddenly felt safe. Our circumstances had not changed, but our perspective had shifted. The water no longer threatened us. We stood on a single pillar of stone. That solid rock was Christ Himself.

The ground that we had first placed our faith in was our own abilities, doctors, medicine, and knowledge. However, what seemed so safe had turned out to be no match for the wall of water and its constant erosion. We learned that our strength and foundation was so much more than we could see, even though He was always there, right under the surface.

He is before all things, and in Him, all things hold together. (Colossians 1:17 NIV)

I learned how futile it is to doubt God. Andrea and I had grown stronger for having lost all of the loose soil, which exposed the solid rock underneath. I had covered the rock with the soil of my own selfish hands. The soil represented my prideful faith in myself and my own "goodness." The soil was my legalistic view that I was somehow capable of withstanding life's trials on my own if I simply went to church and prayed enough. It was smooth and had the appearance of strength, but it was a nothing more than sand. It had to be washed away for us to remember that our strength came from God. Rather than think how strong we must have been to face this wall of water, we saw how weak we really were. We did not "pick ourselves up by our bootstraps" and "tough it out." We took our struggles to the Lord. At times I was afraid we would let our friends down and that Andrea's death would be seen as if our faith was lacking. I dreaded the thought of others saying, "See, there is no God," if she died. But if her healing depended on our faith, then that would place the power in our hands and not in God's, which I knew was not a belief consistent with the Word of God. God. We realized it was God who drew people to Him through His display of power and not by our perceived strength. Many came to know the Lord because God shone in Andrea's weakness and her unwavering faith to the end. Only the Holy Spirit's indwelling power could allow Andrea to endure the torture she did while shining so brightly.

Where does your security and strength rest? Is it in your bank account? your job/career? your family? your church attendance? your good works? There are so many things in this world that we use to pack the soil around the foundation of our faith. It's all just fill dirt and won't hold up. After years of self-reliance, we easily forget the moment we first believed in Christ, the moment when we knew we were helpless and asked God to save us. A trial has the effect of stripping away our pride to show us as we really are, inadequate and in need of a Savior. Without admitting our need, we will continue to pack the dirt to build up our defenses. However, as with a sand castle on the beach, no matter how big you make the walls or how deep you dig a moat around the castle, the waves will overcome your efforts. All evidence of your work will be seen for what it is: temporary, with its magnificence seen only at low tide.

The moment I realized I was not the source of my strength was one of the most emotional events I can remember. I was listening to a Casting Crowns song called "East to West."

These are the lyrics of one verse, which to this day make me cry when I hear them:

> I know You've washed me white, turned my darkness into light.
> I need Your peace to get me through, to get me through this night.
> I can't live by what I feel, but by the truth Your word reveals.
> I'm not holding onto You, but You're holding onto me.[8]

After my anger, my sense of unfairness, and my pride finally left, I saw myself unable to alter the events playing out before me. I was in need of God to be God. This song spoke to me in my weakness. Those lyrics are the last words that stripped away my pride. I was not holding onto Him, but He was still holding onto me.

Even after I had learned to let go, God was not done with me. I would soon face the reality of what I could only imagine. From the time I began to fly, the last thing I would say to Andrea whenever I left for work was, "See you in a little bit." Andrea and I adopted this phrase instead of saying good-bye. Those words encompass the truth of our faith. This life is fleeting, and we can spend eternity with God in the perfection of heaven. So our good-bye, if necessary, would not be forever, because I knew I would see her in a little bit.

> Whereas you do not know what will happen tomorrow. For what is your life? It is even a vapor that appears for a little time and then vanishes away. (James 4:14 NKJV)

> And now, dear brothers and sisters, we want you to know what will happen to the Believers who have died so you will

---

[8]   Mark Hall and Bernie Herms, Casting Crowns, "East to West," 2010, 10-02T01.

not grieve like people who have no hope. For since we believe that Jesus died and was raised to life again, we also believe that when Jesus returns, God will bring back with Him the Believers who have died. (1 Thessalonians 4:13–14 NLT)

That's why the Bible tells us not to grieve as those without hope—not that we will not grieve, but that we have an underlying hope that puts life in a different perspective.

According to the *Merriam-Webster Dictionary, hope* is defined as "to desire with expectation of obtainment, to expect with confidence."[9] We need hope in our life no matter how slim the chances of our prevailing over any given dire situation. On December 17, 1927, a US submarine was accidentally rammed by a coast guard destroyer off the coast of Massachusetts. Six sailors survived the impact and were trapped in the sub. As their oxygen was running out, they tapped a message in Morse code on the hull of the submarine. The message they sent: "Is there any hope?"[10]

I could relate to those six men facing impossible odds but just wanting to know if there was any hope, any chance they would survive, any reason to hang on to. Even though in the end Andrea and those six sailors did not survive, our hope was not in vain, because our true hope as believers lies in Christ. If we stand on a foundation of faith in God, we are on solid ground despite the waves. He is in fact the one who calmed the seas and winds. As my wife was slowly taken from me, I learned of God's faithfulness as I studied how the psalmist could cry out to God in one verse and praise Him in the next.

That said, there is only so much you can do to prepare for death's blow. I can say it hurts, but that is terribly inadequate. It hurts so deeply that it is debilitating. It is the pain of your soul being ripped apart. My prayer is that you never feel this pain, the ache of longing to hear a voice, feel a touch, just one more time, the wailing from your innermost being

9   *Merriam Webster.com*, s.v. "hope," https://www.merriam-webster.com/dictionary/hope, accessed November 28, 2016.
10 Joseph A. Williams, *Seventeen Fathoms Deep: The Saga of the Submarine S-4 Disaster* (Chicago: Chicago Review Press, 2015).

when you realize your loved one will not come back. It was in these moments that I cried out to God, "Why have You forsaken me?" Jesus could relate all too well.

It was almost impossible for me to walk into our home without seeing Andrea walking alongside me. I tried to relive each moment with her when I looked at a place I knew Andrea had been, a place I knew she had stood, even a photograph of her in that exact spot. This pain is not a onetime event, though my type A personality wants me to see it as if it's a box to be checked off. It's certainly not that simple. The hurt and sadness are forever a part of me.

In time, the depth and frequency of the pain will lessen, but it will never be completed in this life, which leads me to my next question: what do we do with pain? My only escape from the sorrow was to remember what I had learned through four years of facing Andrea's cancer. I preached to myself that God is faithful, worthy of my trust, and always with me. The lessons I learned with Andrea would be the same ones I needed to face life without her.

I made the decision to place my trust in what is to come, the promise of everlasting life with our Savior and gifts of greater value than any earthly possessions.

> Do not conform to the pattern of this world, but be transformed by the renewing of your mind. Then you will be able to test and approve what God's will is—his good, pleasing and perfect will. (Romans 12:2 NIV)

Our humanness desires to avoid all difficulties. We would never go through life seeking out pain to prove our faith. When I was a kid, my family lived in the Philippines. I remember that on Good Friday, men would reenact Christ's walk to Calvary. They would carry a real wooden cross with their backs covered in "blood" from being whipped. God does not ask that we prove our faith by seeking acts of suffering, but we can't spend our life avoiding trials as if they were evil. The cross is the greatest gift, but it is also calls us to pick up our own cross and follow Him. We can't seek the good things God can give us yet be unwilling to serve Him in suffering. It is the adversity that draws us from our human desires and helps us conform to the image of Christ. The worse the adversity, the more we must abandon ourselves to God's will, and the more we must conform to the image of our Savior, Jesus Christ.

As I dealt with pain and suffering beyond anything I had ever experienced, I found an amazing comfort when I laid this burden down at the cross and told my Savior, "I cannot do this alone. I need You to make it through the next minute, the next hour, the next day." It helped me take my eyes off of my circumstances and look at God's love shown on the cross. God was using my pain for His glory. Humbled by the cross, I wanted to offer myself back to Him to be used. When we reach this point, God is ready to use us in ways we cannot imagine. Count it a blessing if you are able to see the results in this lifetime.

Recently, I met a friend who only knew us in the last four months of Andrea's life. She told me, "I know God because of you and Andrea. As I watched her wither away, she had such a joy that I was drawn to you both. I started going to church and gave my life to Christ." This is the best example of the power of God working though our brokenness. Andrea told me one day that if one person became a believer because of her cancer, then she would gladly give her life. Later, I found that same thing written in her prayer journal. She didn't just say it; she meant it. I know Ginger heard from many people who came to Christ because of Troy's example. God did not have to give us this confirmation of His sovereignty, but in His goodness, Ginger and I have been given this gift. It does not tell us why our loved ones died. It tells us God is able to use a life laid down for His glory, and that He does make beauty from ashes. When I looked at the spiritual side of the battle, I found purpose. In that moment, I felt the strength of my Savior as He lifted me from the pit and planted my feet on solid ground.

555th Fighter Squadron, Aviano AB, Italy, after Troy
gave Ginger a taxi ride in his F-16, July 2003

Randolph AFB - Jim's Air Force retirement ceremony, Aug 2012

Jim, Ginger & Nic at Anthony's High School Graduation May 2010

(Left to right) Gary Sinise, General Rand and Chief Dearduff
at Troy's Place, a rest and relaxation tent named after Troy
for the deployed troops at Balad AB, Iraq, Spring 2007

Dallas National Golf Course, Labor Day weekend 2011
Ginger and the kids meet President Bush. A week later he
sent a meaningful handwritten letter to Ginger.

Chapter 4 *Discussion Guide*

1. When in your life have you questioned God or been angry with God? Describe your feelings then. What about now? Has your perspective changed?

2. Have you ever felt like God was being silent and not listening to your pleas? Discuss the idea of "unanswered prayer." Are prayers truly unanswered, not answered the way that we want, or not answered yet?

3. If you've been in a position to support a friend who was questioning God, describe your experience. How did they respond to you? What encouragement could you pass on to them now, after reading *Hope Found?*

4. Where does your security come from? Your family? Your job? Your abilities? Have you ever come to the end of your rope and had to rely solely on God for your strength and ability to get through the day? Please share with the group what you took from the experience.

Chapter 5

The Contract

Trials challenge our view of what we think God owes us.

We are pressed on every side by troubles, but we are not crushed. We are perplexed, but not driven to despair. We are hunted down, but never abandoned by God. We get knocked down, but we are not destroyed. Through suffering, our bodies continue to share in the death of Jesus so that the life of Jesus may also be seen in our bodies.
—2 Corinthians 4:8–10 (NLV)

Jim

As Ginger and I discussed our initial responses to the news that our lives were not turning out how we had planned, we both admitted feeling somewhat cheated. We thought we had done our part and therefore were owed something by God. We went to church, taught Bible studies, and raised our children to know Jesus. In return, we wanted God to give us our desires and take away any hardships. Of course, we drafted our "invisible contract" from carefully selected scriptures and on our assumption that God's sole desire was for us to be comfortable and happy. We signed it, filed it away in case of emergency, and went off living. But when our plans fell apart and we took out the contract, we noticed God had never signed next to His printed name. He did offer us a contract, but it read quite differently. It was filled with His love for us, yet it was expressed in much different ways. It did have promises of joy and rewards for a faithful life, but it was written with an eternal focus, whereas our contract was solely focused on this life. And therein lies the rub.

After Andrea passed, I remember the overwhelming feeling of being lost, unable to focus on work or life. I found comfort in what I referred to as the "pit of despair," which was a time to sit in my self-pity—something I thought I deserved after all the years of fighting cancer and watching my wife suffer.

I had, after all, kept the faith. But now it was over. I had my answer, and it was not what I had requested. Now God owed me my time of grief, and I was going to take it. I definitely was going to cash that in. However, grief without truth and hope can begin to consume us, smother us, and ultimately will only take our eyes off God. Taking our eyes off God eventually leads us down a path of bitterness and resentment. I began to use my grief to strike back at God for allowing Andrea to die. I wanted to stay in the pit. Maybe it was my form of rebellion. I thought I had the right to give into the gut-wrenching sadness. My depression grew, and I was shocked by how easy it was to sink into total despair. It was comfortable, like a warm blanket on a cold night. I knew it would be far harder to climb out of the pit than it was to fall in. Even though I gave myself some grace and felt there were times I had to go there, I also had to make a conscious decision that I would not stay in the emotional abyss. The grief is the price I was required to pay for loving and losing Andrea. It wasn't a blank check.

There were many days when I had a knock-down, drag-out fight with grief. I came out with a sore and bruised heart, but God never left me. He was just calling me to trust Him as I walked a path I did not want to walk. Andrea had faced her battle, but this was mine. For those of us left behind, we are the ones who deal with the loneliness, fear, resentment, and anger. Our loved one's trial is over, but we start realizing ours has just begun. We see that somehow our loved one got out of all this mess while we are left alone to deal with kids, cooking, cleaning, bills, paperwork, and life on top of our loss. I wanted to escape. Ginger wanted to escape. But that was not God's plan for us. So, as we went on living, we found God with His hand outstretched. He was saying to me, "Come on, my precious son, it will be okay. I feel your pain and I love you. Are you ready to trust Me even more now? I have great plans for you on the other side. It's time for you to trust Me on your own, without Andrea." Truthfully, I was afraid to do anything on my own. Was I up to the task? Andrea and I had been a team; I was unsure if I was ready to face life without her. I was not ready to move forward. I wanted to hit rewind in hopes this was not reality. I wanted to hear Andrea tell me about that retirement home she wanted with the big porch from which to watch the sunset. I wanted to see her walk in the house with dirty hands and sweat on her brow from working in the yard. I wanted to hold her and tell her it would all be okay. But life in the past no longer existed. The harsh truth slapped me in the face when I walked into an empty house every day after work and the first thing I saw was my favorite photo of Andrea. With her beautiful blue eyes, she greeted me in a place that wasn't home without her. I went into my room and cried until I fell asleep.

The silence was deafening. It was just Anthony and me, unable to find the words to comfort one another. Then came the packing of Andrea's clothes, the sorting through her personal things, the empty side of the closet. Andrea's friends helped me through this most difficult time. It was like discarding our most intimate moments, an almost unbearable thing to do. Through it all, I wailed as I never have in my life.

I couldn't listen to my iPod without crying, even in public. It made me wonder how often I'd sat next to someone on a plane or in a public place completely unaware of the pain they were enduring. In my greatest moments of despair, I no longer wanted to be a witness of faith. I just wanted to go back to life before August of 2003.

The days began to run together. I lost track and didn't know if it was the weekend or a weekday. I wondered where the time went. I didn't seem to accomplish much all day, yet I had no time to do anything. Strangely, church offered little comfort in those early days. It had been a place where Andrea and I found our strength and grew together. As expected, my first day at church alone was not easy. For the first time, I felt out of place in God's house. All I saw was an empty place next to me. With couples and families all around, I felt even more alone.

While everyone else's lives went on, I was suspended in suffering. I was drifting away from the God who had sustained Andrea and me all those days before—those days of disease and disappointment, those days of waiting and wasting away. It was becoming easy to forget how faithfully He had carried us.

Everything about my life up to that point had involved Andrea. My days consisted of working and coming home to take Andrea to lunch. On those days, I might find her just getting out of bed. Or if it was a nice day, she'd be sitting on the porch reading. I would get her out of the house so she could feel the sun on her face or have some time away from the sofa. Otherwise, the only other reasons we went out were for endless doctor appointments, church, or occasionally the grocery store. Andrea had been my reason for living. Cancer drove every decision we made. Until after her death, I didn't realize how much of my life cancer had consumed. I spent four years and five months fighting for Andrea. Now I had no one to fight for. It was one of the strangest side effects of losing her. My feeling of hopelessness was overwhelming, but I had to remember God was with me. He had a plan for me and for my future. My love for Andrea was a blessing, and being her caretaker was a privilege. Burying her was not an option, but it somehow fit into God's plan for us—God's plan for me. The same God who gave her to me had the right to take her away. But that was very hard to accept. I needed the same relief He had given us during Andrea's battle. My war looked different now. It would be a battle for my heart to remain soft, just like Andrea's always had.

Ginger

The weeks that passed following Troy's service were a blur. I felt a dread and heaviness as Christmas approached. Holidays always seem to highlight your feelings; I found there was no holly or jolly to be found, only an empty chair at the Christmas dinner table, an empty stocking hanging on the mantle, and an unopened gift—a sweatshirt I had bought for Troy in California the last day I spoke to him. Somewhere in the crevices of my mind, it still seemed like he was just deployed and come January would be home.

Months passed. The numbness of the initial shock wore off, and then reality set in. The hurting was not going away. In fact, it was getting monumentally worse. I found it true for me, and common for others I counsel now, that some of the most profound depths of misery are reached at about three to six months after a catastrophic event. This is the time everyone else goes back to their normal lives, and the realization that your life will never be the same again squarely hits you between the eyes. Often, my thoughts were rampant with hopelessness. I wondered if my cries to heaven were just falling on deaf ears.

After Troy's death and before I married Jim, the kids and I moved into a rental house. I had the biggest master bedroom and closet I'd ever had. The bedroom shared a wall with the guest room, which was often occupied by one of the many people who stayed to help us during this time.

Since I had insomnia for months on end, I would be up many nights crying, listening to music, talking on the phone, or talking to God. I am certain this was annoying to the person trying to sleep on the other side of our shared wall. Even in the daytime, there was always commotion from the children and seldom any quiet in the house. There was no place for me to go and be alone in my pain.

I did one of two things. My first choice was to get in my car and drive to an empty parking lot to weep. I imagined just driving forever, hoping I could leave all the heartache and burdens behind. If leaving the house wasn't an option, I often disappeared into my bedroom closet, shut the door, and lay on the floor. Those who know me well will attest to my tendency to be a little messy, so imagine clothes or shoes being shoved into every corner and me having to dig my way in for a spot. It was in that closet I could pour my heart out to Jesus. I remember when the times of grief were so engulfing and overwhelming that I would lie on the floor and wish I could sink into the floor, clawing my way a little deeper. The thought of being below ground level oddly seemed comforting and befitting of how I was feeling. It was an unusual thought, one I had never experienced. Often, I cried so hard that I would hyperventilate. I battled with constant nausea. Occasionally, I would lose feeling in my hands and face. Sometimes my vision would go blurry. At first, I thought it happened because of all the tears running into my eye makeup, but then I noticed it happened when I wasn't wearing any. Like a broken water faucet, my tears didn't shut off for months. I remember thinking one day about five months after Troy's death that I had finally gone through one whole day without crying. That was a first. It unnerved me a little because I'd become so used to the tears.

> Our hearts are sick and weary and our eyes grow dim with tears. (Lamentations 5:17 NLT)

I let my children see me cry. While I didn't want to scare them, I also did not want to hide healthy grief reactions from them. Boston fought the tears for a long time, even into his high school years. I almost rejoiced on the rare occasions he would cry because I knew it was something he needed to do. I think he felt weak, maybe that if he cried he wasn't being the man of the house he had promised his dad he would be. In any event, I knew I felt better after crying, and I hoped for the same relief for my son, for all my children. Bella would often ask me, "Mommy, why are you crying?" My response was always the same—"I miss Daddy." Part of me hopes my children remember their mother crying from a broken heart over losing their father. I hope they correlate the amount of tears to how much I love and miss him.

> You keep track of all my sorrows. You have collected all my tears in Your bottle. You have recorded each one in your book. (Psalm 56:8 NLT)

I like to think that Jesus will show me the bottle of my tears someday. I think His hands will lovingly open a beautiful journal with all the dates and times of—and reasons behind—each tear I wept. He's a good God who takes our grief and makes it both valid and valuable. I believe that Jesus, in His tender mercies, wept with me at times. I don't think

He would have told us to mourn with those who mourn if He wasn't going to do it Himself.

> Rejoice with those who rejoice; mourn with those who mourn. (Romans 12:15 NIV)

Jesus will meet you on the floor of your closet or the driver's seat of your car as you hunch over the steering wheel, tears falling on the dashboard. Even the times when I didn't feel the Lord's presence, I knew He was with me because of this promise to us in the Bible:

> But when you pray, go into your room, close the door and pray to your Father, who is unseen. Then your Father, who sees what is done in secret, will reward you. (Matthew 6:6 NIV)

After Troy's death, I received a letter written to me by a fellow soldier of Troy's in Iraq. He told me that he hadn't known Troy well but that each time he struck up a conversation with him in the chow hall, Troy always mentioned that he missed the kids and me. The man wrote that he had passed by Troy's desk and noticed the many photos Troy had posted of us. He also wanted me to know that even though his encounters with Troy in the middle of a war were brief and few, it was evident he was a man who loved his wife and children very much. I put the letter aside and lay on the floor of my closet that night and thanked the Lord for giving me a husband who openly loved us very much. I also earnestly prayed that He would give me that again someday, or at least allow me to be content to live with only the memory of it.

> The widow who is really in need and left all alone puts her hope in God and continues night and day to pray and ask God for help. (1 Timothy 5:5 NIV)

One night in the closet, I called a woman I didn't know. Her name was Marlo Peddycord Francis. She had reached out to me via e-mail after an Air Force chaplain shared my story with her. It was a night when I needed to talk to another widow, someone I thought might understand. I remembered her e-mail from the month prior. I felt God saying, "Go ahead and call this woman in North Carolina. I know she's a complete stranger to you, but she's not going to be for long. Don't be afraid. Go into your closet. I will be there too." I cried to a stranger that night on the phone, with my Father beside me. To this day, Marlo continues to be a wise and loving sounding board, someone who has been in the trenches before me and with me. She is a person who will steer me in the right direction. Since then, I've thought of soldiers in foxholes, children in hospitals, women in shelters, and homeless people on the streets, all those who have no closet to go to when they need time on their knees in private. I think of the ones who don't have someone to call late at night. I appreciate my closet and, of course, my good friends, but I know I have much more than a mere physical place to seek refuge. I have my Savior, Jesus Christ, the true refuge from the storms of life, and I know He is with anyone who calls upon His name.

As I mentioned earlier I went from being a great sleeper to a virtual insomniac. When I did fall asleep, I would have often have nightmares. In them, Troy would be alive, wounded, and far away, somewhere I couldn't get to him. Sometimes we would be running together, hiding from the enemy. I still dream about him to this day, as I know Jim still dreams about Andrea. The nights were the longest, hardest, and loneliest times. I was at my most vulnerable and would pile pillows all along Troy's side of the bed so it didn't feel quite so empty. Many people would tell me that the Lord would wake them at all hours of the night to pray for me. I do the same for others now, knowing how critical it is to pray for those who are at heartbreaking points and trying to get through their own long nights of anxiety and depression.

With the prodding from friends, I came to the conclusion that I needed medical help and medication. I had taken some things to fight off the insomnia and anxiety but was afraid to commit to long-term medication. As I contemplated all this, I wondered whether taking medication meant my faith wasn't strong enough. Drained emotionally, my physical body was beginning to fail. At nearly 5'8", I weighed only 107 pounds. My skin was broken out, and I lacked the energy, strength, and patience to take care of my children. I also came to the conclusion that I was clinging to some pride. One of my pastors at church who had struggled with bouts of depression explained to me the occasional need for medications. If your body, mind, and spirit were a beautiful cathedral crumbling from decay, you would need to deploy some scaffolding to help support it during the rebuilding project. He said a pill certainly wouldn't fix my problem but that it would serve as one part of the restoration process, alongside the more important aspects of prayer, study, and wise counsel.

God's power is not limited. We must pay attention to the warning signs inherent in dangerous thoughts. The Devil is always at his strongest when we are at our weakest. This is because when we are weak, we are more likely to let lies drown out the truth.

We are all told to follow our heart, trust our feelings, and go with our gut. I will tell you that when you are beaten down by depression and the heaviness of life, it's next to impossible to think clearly. Feelings come and go, and if you start basing your decisions on your feelings, they will take you down an even rougher path. I can tell you from the searing pain of grief, the haze of sleeplessness, and the desire to feel some relief that I was looking for a way out. However, many of the roads out would have led to nowhere. Had I listened to the lies of the Enemy, the one who wants to kill, steal from, and destroy us all, it would have only led to complete disaster and heartache, as well as lifelong repercussions for my children and my ministry. With many voices in my head telling me who or what could be my escape, my rescue, even my revenge, none of them were of God.

> My dear children, you belong to God and have defeated them, because God's Spirit, who is in you, is greater than the devil, who is in the world. (1 John 4:4 EXB)

In the years following those early days, the hurt and the grief would still sneak up on me. I was surprised by the deep sadness that washed over me on the day that would have been Troy's and my twenty-first wedding anniversary. He had been gone eight years. I was happily married to Jim. The sadness came without warning. The morning of the anniversary, I was looking through old photographs and found one of Troy and me when we first began dating, visiting the Riverwalk in San Antonio on a day trip from college. As I studied the photo, I clearly saw my own teenage boys in that teenage boy looking back at me. I was struck by the way Troy's hair and eyes shone so handsomely, the way he draped his arms around me, and even the timeless black T-shirt he wore. Such similarities were impossible to ignore. All served as reminders that our boys were growing into men without his being here to see it. As I wept, I had the idea that maybe I could take a break from my day's calendar of obligations and go find those steps. That Riverwalk was the nearest I could get to somewhere Troy and I had once been together. I couldn't resist the pull.

As I walked along the winding San Antonio River under the heavy canopy of old oak trees, I searched for the spot where the photograph was taken. Once I found it, I sat in the middle of those steps, letting people walk around me. I thought if anyone knew my loss, they would think my God had certainly abandoned me. But I knew better. I felt His comforting presence and peace despite the pain I felt. I recalled all the ways He provided for me and for the kids. I knew my God prevailed. He rescued me from the sinking sorrow of the past. Don't get me wrong, I still feel all the broken places in my soul, but they do not define my days and leave me hopeless.

As I passed a number of tourist couples snapping photos of one another along the landmarked trail, I stopped several times to ask them if they wanted me to take a picture of them together. All but the very last couple refused. I wanted to tell them, "No, really, let me take it! Someday you might just wish you had captured this moment."

The Lord lifted my head during that week, and I came to see how He never once abandoned me. He never broke His covenant. And He's keeping His promise to hold a spot for me at His divine dinner table. Until that day comes, I must keep walking down our beautiful, broken road.

He will wipe every tear from their eyes. There will be no more death, or mourning, or crying, or pain—for the old order of things has passed away. (Revelation 21:9 NIV)

Jim

We don't go through life with a placeholder in our schedule for a tragedy. By nature, trials arrive on their own timing. It's up to us to adjust to them. We tend to be creatures of habit, so we even make a trial try to fit into our schedule. Andrea and I quickly built our schedule around cancer because we wanted to feel we had some control over what was happening. But Andrea's cancer had different plans, and the detour caused a disruption in our faith.

We experienced several earthquakes when we lived in Turkey and Alaska. It felt quite unsettling to have the ground beneath my feet shimmy and shift. I've been through tornados in Texas and hurricanes in North Carolina, but those do not compare to an earthquake when the floor of your home starts to move. Hurricanes and tornados bring wind and rain, but the floor and walls of your home are not supposed to shake and sway. That's the way it felt when Andrea and I woke up to cancer one morning. It was startling, to say the least. When what you thought was impossible happens, your life suddenly feels out of control. You find yourself asking questions you never thought you would ask:

- God, are You real?
- Is the Bible just a made-up story?
- How can God love me and let this happen?
- Why me?

> Delight yourself in the Lord and he will give you the desires of your heart. (Psalm 37:4 NIV)

As humans, we quickly make comparisons and determine how unfair our situation is. Our desired outcome and release from the trial becomes a test of God's existence and love, thinking that if He is real, then this will end. When we take this approach, we make this life the focus of our faith and our desire the validation of God. We use what is meant for eternity and apply it to a temporal life. However, the outcome of our trial cannot be a litmus test for God's love. God desires for us to seek Him in our daily life. When life's course changes from the path we have planned or hoped for, it does not mean that what we believed is thrown out the window.

> But God demonstrates his own love for us in this: While we were still sinners, Christ died for us. (Romans 5:8 NIV)

This is the true contract we have with God. This is the one He actually signed—with His own blood. We were sinners, and He sought us and gave His only Son to reconcile us to Him. This is how I know He loves me. His love for me is not based on me getting a new car, a new house, or a new job.

As a mature Christian, I knew enough to know those things were not what truly mattered, so those were easy for me to let go of if God's answer to my request for them wasn't yes. But asking for the mother of my children to be healed? That seemed only fair. He owed that to us, right? I would have given up anything in the world for Andrea to live. It was the only desire of my heart. So how does Andrea having cancer fit into my faith?

I related to Jesus's night going into the garden of Gethsemane as He struggled with dread of the next morning's cross. My time in the garden happened often in those four years and four months that Andrea was sick. In those times, I still prayed and tried to utter the words, "Not my will, but Yours." Here is an excerpt from a blog entry I wrote on September 27, 2007, during Andrea's final year, titled "Just Faith, Please":

> Andrea and I trust God no matter the outcome of this cancer. Whether my last entry into this journal is Andrea's healing or her death, we trust God. We trust God to give us all we need in either outcome. Trust me, I have written both these entries in my mind many times. I have lain awake at night or awakened early in the morning thinking what I

would do the moment after I kissed Andrea good-bye. I have walked down that path and thought about what would life be like far too many times. I have also, on more occasions, thought through the moment a doctor says the term we long to hear each visit, NEOD—no evidence of disease.

Having come to a point where I could say, "Not my will, but Yours," was not giving up on my ability to ask and believe for Andrea's healing. I always believed that God allowed me to come before Him and lay my requests down. Yet I could not come before God and give Him the ultimatum, "Either you heal Andrea or I do not believe." My desire could not be a demand. God is God; I am not. I knew I couldn't see the bigger picture, because the only picture I could see had Andrea in it.

In those moments, however, my struggle to trust continued. It was hard for me to be honest about how hard it was, because I usually didn't share my intimate thoughts with others. God showed me that He could handle my honesty and that I could talk about it, as it might even help others who were struggling like I was. The thought of losing Andrea weighed on me. There was one moment I will never forget. It was January 2007; Andrea had just been released from ICU. We walked into her new room on the hospital's seventh floor. I shut the door. We were alone for the first time in four days. The previous four days were the hardest days I had gone through. I was brought to the edge of everything I dreaded, and anticipated the grief of suffering I knew would follow. However, we had a break for now. Andrea had pulled through. I put her in the chair by the window because I wanted her to enjoy the beautiful blue sky and feel the sun on her back. As I tucked a pillow behind her, I happened to look out the window and see a hearse backing in. I knew what it was there for. I was just very thankful it wasn't there for us. I will never forget that moment as I looked out the window over Andrea's small frame as she sat facing me in that hospital chair and I knew God had given us one more day.

Knowing my wife would suffer through the pain of cancer's final days was hard for me to take. Seeing her hurt and struggle while I was unable to do anything to stop it was without a doubt the most difficult part for me. We had always had a hope of healing and believed the suffering was bearable because it would be relatively short in duration. Yet when cancer makes its final push, when you know what the outcome will be, you can only wait for cancer to do its ugly work. I dreaded it. Every time we drove to Andrea's doctor's office in North Carolina, we would have to drive by the hospice as we entered the hospital parking lot. I would try to look the other way, but I always seemed to stare at that sign. My eyes would be drawn to it while my mind willed them not to. There was no escape from Andrea's battle to maintain her weight or the constant noise of the oxygen machine in the house; the fifty-foot hose that tethered Andrea to the machine felt like an intruder in our home. I hated coming in the front door and following the hose to find Andrea. Having to carry the oxygen bottle everywhere we went felt like carrying a leash. The fifteen pill bottles on the bathroom counter, the tissues from her bloody noses, the scarves, the wigs—all accessories to the crime that was robbing me of my wife. And every day I looked for strength from God to look past it all and trust Him unconditionally.

Praise God, He was faithful to give us the strength we needed to make it through those days. Cancer could not take away the hope we have in Christ because cancer's battlefield is physical. It won the battle, but it had already lost the war. Of course I wish we could have been spared the pain, but this was our trial, our cross, and our conflict.

The most important battlefield is the one within your mind. For me, I had to constantly fight thoughts of jealously as I watched couples walking past, laughing and carefree. Those feelings were very real but could only lead me to resentment. There's no relief found in resentment. Andrea and I had to accept our new normal. For us, my stopping the car on the side of the road for Andrea to vomit, having to buy wigs, making constant trips to doctors, having night sweats, and picking up endless prescriptions were part of our everyday life. I couldn't compare and covet what others had. Those around us were having their own struggles; our struggle just happened to be more public.

As a fighter pilot, my wingman was trained never to be too far from my aircraft in combat. That isn't always what happens, but it's always the plan. God, however, never left us to fly alone. He has proven

Himself faithful, by being our strength when we are weak and to calming our fears when we are shaking.

God's Word is full of encouragement and hope. It takes your eyes and mind off this world and helps you enjoy an eternal perspective. What seems so overwhelming will soon seem insignificant to you. When you read God's contract, you will see it is filled with promises that are everlasting. Hold fast to the Word and the things of this earth will grow strangely dim.

> I lift up my eyes to the hills where does my help come from? My help comes from the Lord, the Maker of heaven and earth. He will not let your foot slip he who watches over you will not slumber; indeed, he who watches over Israel will neither slumber nor sleep. The Lord watches over you the Lord is your shade at your right hand; the sun will not harm you by day, nor the moon by night. The Lord will keep you from all harm he will watch over your life; the Lord will watch over your coming and going both now and forevermore. (Psalm 121 NIV)

Does this take away the grief of losing Andrea? Even Jesus, part God, part man, grieved. Are we to assume we are somehow immune from grief? Do the promises spoken in the psalms infer we will not suffer or grieve? No, I think they say just the opposite. Psalm 121 would never have had to be written if our lives were free from trials. Why would we ever need to read, "Where does my help come from?" Life can throw all sorts of difficulties at us, but God is our shield. Life can take away, but God gives back. Life can bring fear, but God brings peace. Life can cause worry, but God gives joy.

> He is your shield and helper and your glorious sword. Your enemies will cower before you, and you will trample down their high places. (Deuteronomy 33:29 NIV)

> My God is my rock, in whom I take refuge, my shield and the horn of my salvation. He is my stronghold, my refuge

and my savior from violent men you save me. (2 Samuel 22:3 NIV)

As for God, His way is perfect; the word of the Lord is flawless. He shields all who take refuge in Him. (2 Samuel 22:31)

But you are a shield around me, O Lord; you bestow glory on me and lift up my head. (Psalm 3:3 NIV)

The Lord is my rock, my fortress and my deliverer; my God is my rock, in whom I take refuge. He is my shield and the horn of my salvation, my stronghold. (Psalm 18:2 NIV)

We wait in hope for the Lord; He is our help and our shield. (Psalm 33:20 NIV)

No matter how much we think we deserve an easy life, God never promised us one. Faith is forged in the fires of our trials. A life without difficulty is a life without faith. Wishing difficulties away or trying to hide from our struggles will only leave us unprotected, unprepared, and unable to find the healing power of hope. So as we look to God's Word and to the wisdom, the love, and the protection we find in its pages, our needs are met when life becomes more than we can handle alone. Ginger's friend who suffered her own tragedy in life once said, "May you be strengthened by your weakness."

Chapter 5 *Discussion Guide*

1. What "silent contracts" do you have with God? For example, "Lord, If you will do this for me, I will do this for You."

2. What do you secretly hope that God will not ask of you?

3. What do you think God's actual contract is with you?

Chapter 6
Walk by Faith

The only thing worse than being blind is having sight and no vision.

—Helen Keller

Therefore, being always of good courage, and knowing that while we are at home in the body we are absent from the Lord—for we walk by faith, not by sight.

—2 Corinthians 5:6–7 (NIV)

Jim

The following is Andrea's journal entry on the topic of trusting, written April 19, 2007:

> Today I met a wonderful woman and her husband who are breast cancer survivors for two years. We talked about our common experiences. At times there were tears in her eyes just recounting all she and we had been through. I looked at her and thought how marvelous it must be to be two years out from treatment. Her hair had grown back and was beautiful. There was no exhaustion in her eyes, but cancer had still left its mark. The possibility it could come back, the dread of facing treatment again. That look is only shared by those who have heard the doctor say you have cancer and have faced the chemo chair, the months of sickness, weakness, hair loss, vomiting, and countless side effects of drugs meant to randomly destroy life. But they

are also the ones who have the chance to experience the joy of trusting God when life hangs in the balance, to fall back in faith and be caught in the arms of God, to strip away the meaninglessness of life, to feel the love of the body of Christ. I count it all joy to have suffered for Christ.

When you find yourself in a situation that was not part of your plan, you find yourself having to trust something (well, someone) bigger than you. However, we humans are led by what we see, feel, touch, and smell. Our senses give us balance in life, and we learn to rely on them. I discovered early in pilot training that these senses could mislead me. In fact, many pilots have been killed by what is called spatial disorientation. It happens when you cannot reconcile what you feel the plane is doing with how the plane is actually moving. When you are unable to tell if you are climbing or descending, turning right or left, it can lead to deadly consequences. One of the more famous cases of this was when John F. Kennedy Jr. was killed flying his private plane to Martha's Vineyard. The investigation showed the following:

> Kennedy's mind started playing tricks; the instrument panel and his head were telling him different things. Kennedy lost his bearings, then lost control of the plane. This is being called a "disorientation accident." Kennedy seems to have had a sudden attack of what pilots call "vertigo:" a three-way disconnection between reason, instinct and reality, even an inability to tell the difference between up and down.[11]

When flying through a clear sky, your mind balances what you see with what you are feeling. When you enter the clouds, you no longer have that visualization to confirm what your other senses are telling you. This can lead to confusion and vertigo, where you are unable to tell which way is up—a very deadly situation for a pilot. To counter this, pilots are taught to rely on our instruments. The cluster of round dials that display what the plane is doing, how high the aircraft is, how fast

---

[11] Ed Vulliamy, "Why Kennedy Crashed," *The Guardian*, https://www.theguardian.com/world/1999/jul/25/kennedy.usa, accessed January 20, 2017.

it's going, and if it is descending or climbing are all vital to flight. The main instrument a pilot uses is called the attitude indicator.

The attitude indicator (ADI), a simple half-blue, half-brown circle, represents if the plane you are flying is going up or down. In between the two colors is a horizontal line that shows when you are in level flight. When you go into the weather, fluid in your inner ear can make you feel like you are turning right or left or going up or down even though you are in level flight. So the solution is to focus on the attitude indicator regardless of what you feel. You have to force your mind to believe what it sees on the attitude indicator.

I trained many hours to build the habit patterns of trusting my instruments, because it was a matter of life and death. As a fighter pilot, if you become very disoriented you can ask a wingman to talk to you. Your wingman can tell you the attitude you are in, in hopes that what you see on the instruments and what you hear will override what you feel. The next option is to fly formation off your wingman and let him or her lead you through the weather. You then use the other aircraft as your attitude indicator as you descend out of the clouds and land. If a fighter pilot cannot reconcile what he sees with what he feels, he will be unable to continue flying and then may be forced to eject.

Flying on instruments is how I like to picture walking by faith. Much like when flying through clear skies, life is easy when we can see what lies ahead. Then, when a storm comes and we enter the clouds of the unknown, we have to rely on our spiritual instruments in the way that I relied on my plane instruments. Our eyes must remain fixed on Christ, our only truly steady horizon. We do that by praying and by reading the Bible, which tells us who God is. That is our "horizon line" to lead us in life, despite what we feel. When we take our eyes off of Christ, we feel lost and adrift. It takes a conscious effort to keep our eyes on Christ in the midst of a trial, because a trial is like the clouds to a pilot; you lose all sense of where you are or where you are going.

> Now faith is confidence in what we hope for and assurance about what we do not see. (Hebrews 11:1 NIV)

How do we experience this confidence the Bible speaks of? We must "see" with our spiritual eyes by personally knowing the God we serve and His character. We learn this by repeated reading of His Word, much like I practiced flying over and over again in the simulator. It was not sufficient to practice one time, nor is it sufficient to read the scriptures every once in a while. I would write verses on note cards that Andrea and I referred back to when life was tossing us to and fro. Also, I listened to sermons and exclusively Christian music because they fed me the truth and gave me the strength to press on despite what a doctor said or what a CT scan showed. Confidence also came from spiritually mature believers in our church community, who helped point us to the spiritual horizon. While Satan will try to convince you to sit in your pain and surrender to your feelings, I encourage you to focus on Christ when the storms come. Never think you have to go it alone. Many pilots have died trying to do this, and many believers have been spiritually lost in the same way. Don't let pride keep you from asking for help. Remember that others have been where you are. There is no shame in admitting you have lost your horizon. Life, like piloting, can get out of control in an instant. Build your habits now and know when it's time to call for help.

Ginger

For most of my life, I have struggled with extreme nearsightedness. "Blind as a bat" pretty much sums it up. Several months after I married Jim, I underwent PRK (photorefractive keratectomy), also known as corneal surface ablation. When I made the decision to have the procedure, I didn't think about how much pain there would be in the process. My main focus was on my hope that I would be able to open my eyes and see something past the end of my nose once all was said and done. Jim said, "Won't it be amazing to see again?" I responded with, "Actually, it will be seeing clearly for the first time!"

My extreme nearsightedness had been my way of life for as long as I could remember. I actually had planned on getting the surgery when Troy returned from Iraq. I put on my first pair of glasses when I was seven years old and remember being stunned by all the individual leaves on the trees as I walked outside! From that day on, I was never without glasses or contacts. In junior high, before I got contacts, I became very self-conscious about wearing glasses, even though I desperately needed them. As a kid, this caused me great strife in the summer, because summers involved swimming and swimming isn't conducive to everyday eyewear. My stick-skinny body, big teeth, and thick glasses didn't help me win any swimsuit competitions.

I would occasionally ditch the glasses while swimming and lying out poolside in my effort to be more "cool." Yet the next day at school, my friends would say, "You are so stuck up, Ginger! I waved at you at the pool and you just stared at me!" The truth was, I never even saw them. My plan to be the popular beach babe backfired.

I gave it one more shot. Every summer, our extended family went to a campground in west Texas for our annual Wiman family reunion, where some of my best childhood memories were made. The summer after my eighth grade year, we made the familiar trek to camp, where there happened to be another gathering going on. Even better, it was with boys who were not relatives. My girl cousins and I decided we would "take a walk" to check out the other campground. We found some cute boys in the distance. Feeling self-conscious, I got the brilliant idea that I would try to meet them without my glasses on. I remember us all sitting under the pavilion, talking and flirting.

As the afternoon heat forced everyone else back to their camp or the swimming pool, a sweet boy and I stayed behind to talk under the shade of the pavilion. We exchanged addresses as pen pals and hoped to see each other again before going home. This whole plan of mine was working great in my mind. The only hitch was that I wasn't quite sure what he looked like! We wrote back and forth a little. I enjoyed my summer crush despite my best description of him being, "He has brown hair and is a little taller than me." No surprise, something was always missing in the relationship. I guess that something might have been that I would not have been able to pick him out in a lineup. In hindsight, I imagine that he probably wouldn't have recognized me either, wearing my Coke bottle glasses and all. Talk about a blind date!

As I think about that story, I am reminded that we never see with complete clarity on this earth. We only catch a glimpse of God's face. We see a little bit of what He is doing, but we can't see the big picture yet. For me and Jim, the question of why He took Andrea and Troy when their lights were shining so brightly will always be there. Such is the case not only for anyone who has had to let go of a beloved long before they were ready but also for those who are victims, outcasts, alone, sick—afraid of what tomorrow holds because today looks bleak. The Lord knew we would struggle without answers and without His physical presence, so He left us with the Holy Spirit and this command:

Walk by faith, not by sight. (2 Corinthians 5:7 ESV)

Though we wrestle with the hardest questions of why God lets bad things happen to His people, He still asks us to trust Him. "Trust the Master," as my Auntie Faye says. God knew this would be the most difficult thing for us to do. Jim and I know we may never, this side of heaven, understand the full extent of His divine plan or get answers to our questions—not that there haven't been a million times I pounded my fist and asked the questions anyway. Life gets blurry from our perspective. Humankind will forever struggle with seeing God's bigger picture because we look at our own suffering or the injustices of this world through personal filters of grief, lenses of bitterness, and the nearsightedness that comes with being human. At best, life doesn't make sense. At worst, we can lose faith in a God who truly loves us.

Just as I used to fumble for the light switch to find my glasses, I have fumbled through some seriously emotionally foggy days—dense, gray ones. Feeling that my life was over after Troy died, I couldn't comprehend God's love being tethered to this atrocity. Straining and squinting, I couldn't picture what our lives would look like without Troy in them. Those were the days the depression would sink in. Thankfully, my human shortcomings were no match for my Father's mercies. The Lord asked the kids and me to remain faithful in our fellowship, rest in our relationship, and hold onto His hand in the dark despite our "blindness." I clung to this promise:

> I will lead the blind by ways they have not known, along unfamiliar paths I will guide them. I will turn the darkness into light before them and make the rough places smooth. These are the things I will do. I will not forsake them. (Isaiah 42:16 NIV)

We are still called to lay our lives and troubles at the Lord's feet. Then when He walks, we are to follow, even blindly at times when we don't understand, just because He's asked us to—and even when He walks us down a road we aren't familiar with. He helps us leap over hurdles when our knees are weak and our faith is weaker. As a child must hold the hand of a parent when the surroundings are unfamiliar, even dangerous, so must we hold onto God's hand tightly and march on. You can go it alone, but ultimately you will not find your way out of the bottom by yourself—something King David knew well when he begged God as follows:

> Do not cast me away from Your presence, and do not take your Holy Spirit from me. (Psalm 51:11 NIV)

After Troy died, I struggled with being a single mother, carrying the burden of grief and sadness for me and all my children. I felt my heart actually breaking into bits inside my chest and could not imagine life ever being good or worthwhile again. That is when others came along and reminded me I had to choose to trust a good God who can only give goodness because that is His nature.

Though the long tunnel of misery is in my rearview mirror, I have no guarantees of what lies ahead. Uncertainty is the only assurance. We live in a fallen world with a hazard around every corner. Jim and I don't always know what our next step should be as we strive to continue to unify our blended family. We don't know the places, either the physical ones or the spiritual ones, that the Lord will take us. I must remember with thankfulness how God led us out of that desert time in our lives. Otherwise, I can still get carried away by sadness or fear. I still find myself at times collecting anxieties—worrying about the kids' futures, their faith walks, sickness, losing Jim—and lining them up like colored glass on a windowsill. In such times, I am trying to control and forgetting to let God go before me. Old sins die hard. That's the slippery slope of living in a world that was never meant to be our home—only a place to pass through.

After my eye surgery in the fall of 2008, I found that my outpatient procedure was a bigger deal that I'd initially thought. Pain, double vision, the inability to focus, and dry eyes were a constant battle. Yet miraculously, my vision went from 20/800 to 20/40, and eventually 20/20. Since the ability to focus clearly took a while, I had to be a *patient* patient.

Whether the wound is on the outside or inside, the Healer is at work and the clouds will part. He will take care of us if we ask. I have to choose not to be afraid of the future even when I know the terrors of the past. One day, we will all join God in eternity, where there will be no sleepless nights, no tears, no bits of our heart falling all over the floor, and no pain—forevermore! How awestruck Troy and Andrea must have been when they reached the gates of heaven and saw everything clearly for the first time. The Lord must have told them why they were put on earth, what His purpose was for their early deaths, and where He was taking those of us they left behind. What a glorious day that must have been!

> Now we see things imperfectly as in a poor mirror, but then we will see everything with perfect clarity. All that I know now is partial and incomplete, but then I will know everything completely, just as God knows me now. (1 Corinthians 13:12 NLT)

Jim

Before having global positioning systems (GPS) in our cars and phones, the risk of getting lost was certainly much higher. Of course, even with GPS, getting lost is still a possibility (though I'm not naming names because she co-authored this book with me). When Andrea and I got an assignment to Alaska in 1992, one of the first things someone told us was to buy was a *Milepost*. For those of you who may not remember, there used to be paper maps you physically carried in your car. But this map of Alaska was unlike any other map. The *Milepost* map not only had all the roads but also listed everything along the way, including a dirt road at mile 24.5 or a gas station at mile 112.3. Everything along that road was marked by mileage. Because the environment is so remote and harsh in Alaska, it was important to always know where we were. Getting lost in Alaska can quickly turn a scenic drive into a life-and-death situation.

When you listen to someone give you directions, it always helps to have landmarks listed. Rather than hearing "take the third left," hearing "turn left after the Wal-Mart" simplifies the process and gives you more assurance that you are going the right way. The longer the distance you have to go, the more "markers" it helps to have. The *Milepost* was like that because we could always look at the map and find out exactly where we were. If we were in need of food or gas, we knew exactly how far it was until the next restaurant or filling station. It gave us a sense of security.

As Andrea and I started our journey on the road with cancer, I did not always know where we were or how far we had to go until the end. Like running a race without knowing if it's a 5K or a marathon, we found it hard to pace ourselves. Now, imagine running that same race without any idea of the course you are running. We were in the dark, trying to find our way to where God was leading us. First, we had to find out our destination. We approached this from an earthly view and prayed for physical healing. We did not know how we would get there or how long it would take. But the more I sought and trusted in God, the more I found that our true destination was already set. We were actually heaven bound. Healing from cancer was not the end; the cancer was an opportunity to allow God to shine through us, independent of the earthly outcome. Although healing was still something we believed could happen, it had taken a backseat to our desire to serve the God who already had given us a gift we could never repay Him for—our salvation. Once we knew the destination, the route was not as critical. Our journey was not cancer but our calling to use the resources God had given us for His glory, in response to our salvation. I realized God provides us "mileposts" in our lives to remind us we are not lost.

> Your word is a lamp for my feet, a light on my path. (Psalm 119:105 NIV)

I found that godly mileposts came in many forms: a verse in scripture during a silent prayer, the voice of the Father through a sermon, a word of encouragement through a phone call, letter, or song—all simple reminders that He was with us and we were heading in the right direction. There are no limits to how God can speak to us if we choose to listen and be spiritually attentive.

I also found that sometimes God does not give us directions to the end point but to an intermediate point, many times not very far ahead of where we are. It is like standing in total darkness with the path lit only as far as God wants us to walk. For Andrea and me, there were times when we saw only a few steps ahead. Then, we had to trust and wait for further illumination from God. When all I wanted was to take off and get over the trial, the slow pace pointed us to the fact that God cares deeply about *how* we get to our final destination. Because of His loving kindness, the milestones He provides also help strengthen our faith. Much like encountering roadside rest stops full of shade, shelter, rest, and drinks to quench your thirst, there were times during Andrea's battle, usually when it was most difficult, when one encouraging person or message gave us the ability to "get back on the road" and keep going. On the other hand, we sometimes had to rely on remembering past mileposts to keep our faith strong. Mileposts teach us to trust. They are a reminder that God had been with us before and that He is still there in the silence and madness of our trial. We have His Word to hear his voice. He is the same today, yesterday, and tomorrow. Therefore, we can wait in the darkest of times and know that He is still with us.

Mileposts become the bricks and mortar to the foundation of our faith. We can stand on all the past promises and answered prayers, which help us trust through today's trials. Even though the future is not clear, even if the path that lies ahead is in total darkness, we can trust that our Father sees it all. There is no darkness to Him.

When the Lord is leading us, we are on the right path. It's not about us picking the one and only correct path. It's about trusting Him on the path we are on. In my vanity, I had come up with the "perfect path" several times. *Yes, Lord, I can see it perfectly clear. The next treatment and then we will be done*—as if to say, "Now that I learned that lesson, we are ready for Your healing. Yes, Lord, just over that next hill." But that was never how it worked out. There was another bad scan, a higher tumor marker, or an unexplained pain, followed by more chemo, more side effects, and more pills. I didn't know what we were fighting, cancer or side effects from the drugs that we were hoping would heal Andrea. You get so deep into the problems that you're not sure which way is up. Then it happens: God sends you a milepost and clarity returns to your life.

Suddenly, the gift of Christ's sacrifice is sweeter and more humbling, and you find yourself not asking what God will give you, but what can you give to God. You started by begging for healing, and you end up laying down your own life and desires to a loving God. That is the miracle of His kind of love. It takes our eyes off of ourselves and puts them where they belong. It takes away our selfishness.

> All of us have become like one who is unclean, and all our righteous acts are like filthy rags. (Isaiah 64:6 NIV)

It makes you realize there is nothing you have done or will do to deserve salvation. It makes this temporary life be seen for what it is: vapor. There were some very dark days, but God always provided us with a milepost, a gentle, loving reminder that said, "I'm right here."

Ginger

> But we have this treasure in jars of clay to show that this all-surpassing power is from God and not from us. We are hard pressed on every side but not crushed, perplexed, but not in despair, persecuted, but not abandoned, struck down but not destroyed. We always carry around in our body the

death of Jesus, so that the life of Jesus may also be revealed in our body. (2 Corinthians 4:7–10 NIV)

What a descriptive picture of what our place is on this earth! Our treasure is the power of Christ and His Word, which is still just as alive today as ever. He chooses for His Holy Spirit to dwell within us. We, however, are those pitiful little clay jars trying to hold Him in. Being an interior designer, I have seen a few jars in my day. I am always attracted to a pretty urn or vase. But I am guessing that the type mentioned in this foregoing scripture are those plain terra-cotta ones. They are more than a little rough around the edges and have no adornment whatsoever. No matter how cute we think we might be, even on a good-hair day, we are all still plain, dirty, and unattractive vessels. The beauty we have comes from Christ in us.

Among the flood of emotions that overcame me as I sat on my three-year-old's bed and listened to a general methodically tell me that my Troy's plane had gone down, I felt my life slip down the drain. I felt unable to stop it, just like the last of the bathtub water. Troy and I never sat down and planned for how one of us would raise them alone. Believe me, I wish we had. There were many days and nights when I would long to hear Troy's wisdom and advice about what on earth I was supposed to do.

My definition of loneliness was parenting alone. With every soccer game or school function I attended without Troy, it became clearer that he was really never coming back. In those first months after he died, I would lay in bed and think of all the milestones in our children's lives that I would now see alone, everything from Aspen's and Annalise's first steps, to Boston's high school graduation, to Greyson's shooting the big buck, to Bella's father–daughter dance at her wedding. Those were just some of the thoughts that tormented me by night. From the six of us sitting at the dinner table and looking over to the empty chair where Troy should be sitting, to filling out the first school form and not knowing what to write in the "father's name" blank, simple tasks became difficult. What if his name somehow ended up on a sign-up sheet to drive for a field trip because I couldn't bear not to write in his name?

> He is a father to the fatherless and an advocate for widows.
> (Psalm 68:5 NET)

My children were wrapped in love and protection from the harsh winds of change that blew into their precious lives. So many prayers were prayed for them, and God showed up big time. He has given our children an eternal worldview, a greater sense of compassion, and a soulful maturity that is unrecognizable in other kids their age. Even though, no doubt, they each will continue to face insecurities, obstacles, and fresh grief, they know there is nothing Jesus won't help them through. I have battled my own insecurities as their mother. Am I loving them enough? Am I making sure they always know who Troy was and how crazy about them he was? Am I too tired, too distracted, too busy, to notice when their hearts hurt? I've spent many years asking myself these questions.

Though my heart overflows with thankfulness for Jim walking the parenting journey beside me now, I still struggle with how hard it all is at times. The parent that I once was has had to evolve. I admit to looking at all seven of our kids and wondering if I would ever be enough for each of them. I felt like I should join every parenting support group that was out there. But the source I knew I had to turn to every day, every hour, was my heavenly Father. The Word says this:

> I can do all things through Him. (Philippians 4:13 NKJV)

I was never equipped to handle this on my own, and God wasn't asking me to. Our weaknesses simply highlight His strengths. He was fully aware of my need for Him. The fact was that I needed to be aware of my need for Him. He knew the plans He had for all of us, because Christ is the one holding the other half of the map. There couldn't be a better Guide.

I lift my eyes to the hills—where does my help come from? My help comes from the Lord, the Maker of Heaven and earth. (Psalm 121:1 ESV)

Jim

When Andrea and I lived in Turkey, there was a destructive earthquake with a death toll of over seventeen thousand.[12] Andrea, the boys, and I went with some friends to a village that was hit very hard. Our friend, who was a missionary, was helping get trailers to the people who lost their homes. We went along to hand out candy to the kids and visit with the families. I remember driving around and seeing all the houses and apartments that had collapsed. But strangely, many of the homes, even those that had survived, were surrounded by blue tarps— makeshift tents. I asked my friend, "Why the tents?" He told me it was because the people were too afraid to live in their houses. They were so afraid of going to sleep in their home and the walls coming down on them that they would rather sleep outside on the wet ground. And who could blame them? They had just experienced the earth shake; there was no certainty in life for them. Their home was stripped of its protective qualities; what was once seen as their shelter and protection had turned into their greatest fear. Isn't that just how we are at times in our life? I've thought of all the times I allowed fear to force me away from the security of my faith. We choose to live in a tent when we have a home. We allow our fears to make what is secure seem insecure. We allow fear and worry to cast a doubt on what God has promised. We become suspicious of God's greatness and His promises. We allow Satan to convince us that God cannot be trusted, that God is too good to be true, or that God simply does not care about our life.

And so we live in a tent just outside the palace. Lord, help us to live fully inside the security of Your all-encompassing love for us.

---

[12] *History.com*, "Deadly Earthquake Strikes Turkey," 2010, http://www.history.com/this-day-in-history/deadly-earthquake-strikes-turkey, accessed November 14, 2016.

Chapter 6 *Discussion Guide*

1. Ginger states: "At best, life doesn't make sense. At worst, we can lose faith in a God who truly loves us." Can you think of a time when circumstances caused you to lose faith? How did you overcome your doubts and learn to trust God again? If you are still in a period of doubt and fear, how can those around you come alongside and walk with you during this time?

2. On a scale of 1 to 5, how much do you trust God? Consider 1 as "I can call on God when I need Him but I essentially believe in being self-reliant. I've got this." and 5 as "God's got this and I submit that I don't. He will shape an outcome that He intends for my family and my future and I believe it will ultimately be for His glory and my good."

3. Jim talks about the Milepost Map. What are some mileposts in your life when you saw God tangibly at work? Do you use those mileposts to remind yourself or others of God's faithfulness? How do you recognize new mileposts?

Chapter 7

Hold On

What God does in us while we wait is as important as what we are waiting for.[13]

—John Ortberg

> Though the fig tree does not bud
> and there are no grapes on the vines,
> though the olive crop fails
> and the fields produce no food,
> though there are no sheep in the pen
> and no cattle in the stalls,
> yet I will rejoice in the Lord,
> I will be joyful in God my Savior.
>
> —Habakkuk 3:17–18 (KJV)

Jim

Unlike the warrior who knows the hour and the day of his battle, we find that life rarely comes with a set schedule of predictable events. The military does a remarkable job teaching pilots to be ready for the unknown. First, you are taught the basics of the aircraft systems. You learn the "operator manual" long before you ever fly a plane. The understanding of how the plane works is what prepares you for when things break down. In most cases, if you have an emergency, you have time to analyze the situation and make a decision about how to get the

---

13   John Ortberg, *If You Want to Walk on Water, You Have to Get Out of the Boat – Leader's Guide* (Grand Rapids, MI: Zondervan, 2003).

plane back on the ground safely. There are some emergency procedures that you have to memorize, because if that emergency occurs, there is no time to pull out your checklist and read what to do. You just have to react based on your training and your instinct. The most critical steps of an emergency are printed in bold text, which is called "boldface."

As a trainee, I took a boldface test every week. I and my classmates had to write the steps to the emergency procedures. If we left out a word or even a letter, then we failed and were grounded until we passed. Each day, a student was given a simulated emergency with the class watching. If that emergency required the boldface, the trainee had to say the steps exactly as they were written without looking at the checklist. It was a pressure-filled environment, but that was intentional to help replicate the pressure we would feel in an actual emergency. In those cases, there was no room for error. This technique of preparing inexperienced pilots to fly was proven effective many times over when a pilot made it home.

As I thought of how my training had prepared me for emergencies, I thought about how I had been preparing my spiritual life to handle the "emergency" I was in with Andrea. Initially, I felt unprepared to face Andrea's cancer and the possibility of losing my wife. I realized it was because I didn't know the critical truths in my operators' manual, the Bible. I had been sitting back and going to church, not putting the Word in my heart. Suddenly I was in catch-up mode, trying to learn His Word, His boldface.

> Do not merely listen to the word, and so deceive yourselves. Do what it says. Anyone who listens to the word but does not do what it says is like someone who looks at his face in a mirror and, after looking at himself, goes away and immediately forgets what he looks like. But whoever looks intently into the perfect law that gives freedom, and continues in it—not forgetting what they have heard, but doing it—they will be blessed in what they do. (James 1:22–25 NIV)

James is telling us to know our biblical boldface, to take the Word and make it part of who we are and how we think. In the military, we use the term "forcing function," which describes an event that causes us to act even if we think we are satisfied with where we are. An example of that happens every time we move. Military families know the best way to get the house unpacked and cleaned is to schedule a party. When you have hundreds of boxes to unpack, you can rationalize not unpacking as a way to spare yourself the trouble of packing for the next move. Once you schedule a party, it forces you to make a house a home, to refuse to settle for living out of suitcases and boxes. That is a forcing function. Cancer was my forcing function. I could no longer settle for being a hearer of the Word. I needed to be a doer of the Word. I needed God, and I needed to know His character and His promises based on His Word. Otherwise, I was more susceptible to one of the greatest lies, which is the thought that I could take care of my own needs. Isn't that what Satan used to tempt Jesus?

> Then Jesus was led by the Spirit into the wilderness to be tempted by the devil. After fasting forty days and forty nights, he was hungry. The tempter came to him and said, "If you are the Son of God, tell these stones to become bread."
>
> Jesus answered, "It is written: 'Man shall not live on bread alone, but on every word that comes from the mouth of God.'"
>
> Then the devil took him to the holy city and had him stand on the highest point of the temple. "If you are the Son of God," he said, "throw yourself down. For it is written: 'He will command his angels concerning you, and they will lift you up in their hands, so that you will not strike your foot against a stone.'"
>
> Jesus answered him, "It is also written: 'Do not put the Lord your God to the test.'"
>
> Again, the devil took him to a very high mountain and showed him all the kingdoms of the world and their splendor.

"All this I will give you," he said, "if you will bow down and worship me."

Jesus said to him, "Away from me, Satan! For it is written: 'Worship the Lord your God, and serve him only.'" Then the devil left him, and angels came and attended him. (Matthew 4:1–11 NIV)

Jesus showed us the way to respond to trials; Jesus knew His boldface.

We are naturally prideful and want to run our own lives. Then, once we find life is too hard to handle alone, we cry out, asking God, "Where are You?" His answer: "I'm where I have always been, right by your side. Now that I have your attention, let's talk."

Ginger

I am still confident of this; I will see the goodness of the Lord in the land of the living. Wait for the Lord; be strong, take heart and wait for the Lord. (Psalm 27:13–14 NIV)

While I often felt like I was wandering with no sense of direction, the Lord was patient and loved me unconditionally. Freedom happens when we are at the end of ourselves, and it becomes all about what the Lord can do. Jim and I have discussed the topic of patient submission at length. There was nothing Jim could do to heal Andrea. There was nothing I could do to make life return to normal for me and the kids. Surrender was our only viable option, so the sooner we started to let go, the better. Waiting, clinging to hope for dear life, healing, doesn't happen overnight. Much like the marks on the doorframe with our kids' names, dates, and the inches they grow, emotional healing and spiritual growth are measured in tiny increments.

Before I became I mom, I had time to quilt. I would piece small fabric squares together for days on end, never imagining the quilt top would actually look like something worthwhile in the end. Then one day I would run the last seam, flip it over, and there it was—my piece of art. That's how I feel about our new family. We're like a patchwork quilt crafted by the Lord. Fragments of my old life with Troy, scraps of my brokenness, and now pieces of my newfound sunshine with Jim and his story—all stitched together. It is a whole new creation far prettier than anything I could have ever imagined. If you are waiting on a rescue at this moment, waiting to see what the other side of all your broken pieces will look like when God rearranges everything, pray for perseverance and patience. I begged for the ability to sit, be still, and just wait on Him. He gave it to me; He will also give it to you. God loves all His children with the exact same love. I pray the light of the Son will shine upon your face and call you forth to live with a waiting hope in our living hope, Christ Jesus.

> Yet the Lord longs to be gracious to you; He rises to show
> you compassion. For the Lord is a God of justice. Blessed are
> all who wait for Him. (Isaiah 30:18 NIV)

I can't say that I have physically felt the presence of the Lord quite like I did one afternoon in the spring of 2007. I was deeply weeping, facedown on the carpet of my bedroom. Suddenly, I felt Him. I felt the presence of Jesus on me, covering my whole back with His arms stretched wide and around me. He was weeping with me. It was as if I could hear his sobs mixed with mine. I knew His very breath was near. I will never forget it. Tears still sting my eyes at the memory. It was like a blanket of comfort, shared pain, and abiding love. I was not alone. He was there with me in my pit, like He was with Joseph in that well; like He was with Paul in the deep bowels of that tiny prison cell; and like He was with Andrea and Jim in the hospital.

God loved me and had the power to resurrect me from my despair.

Jim

> The Lord is my light and my salvation whom shall I fear?
> The Lord is the stronghold of my life of whom shall I be
> afraid? (Psalm 27:1 NIV)

As a caregiver, I found that one of the hardest things to do was watch cancer beat up on Andrea. It is a desperate feeling to see someone you love suffer while you are helpless to stop it. As we settled into a long battle with cancer, I felt as if we were suspended by strings and seemingly helpless to control life's events. We would swing closer to death, and then swing back to life at the last moment. The cycle continued as we sought to trust a sovereign God.

I saw two choices in the storm: run from God or run to Him. I knew if I ran from God, having lost my faith in Him, I would only find myself alone and helpless. On the other hand, with God I would find a shelter under His wings. By choosing to run to Him, I found Him faithful, not because He made the storm go away, but because He showed me I don't have to fear the storm.

> That day when evening came, he said to his disciples, "Let us go over to the other side." Leaving the crowd behind, they took him along, just as he was, in the boat. There were also other boats with him. A furious squall came up, and the waves broke over the boat, so that it was nearly swamped. Jesus was in the stern, sleeping on a cushion. The disciples woke him and said to him, "Teacher, don't you care if we drown?" He got up, rebuked the wind and said to the waves, "Quiet! Be still!" Then the wind died down and it was completely calm. He said to his disciples, "Why are you so afraid? Do you still have no faith?" (Mark 4:35–40 NIV)

You may be in a place where you trust in God but find yourself waiting on Him. Your trial is not over—maybe it is unchanged or getting worse—and you find yourself just holding on. I encourage you to keep holding out your hands to your heavenly Father, knowing that He will never let go of you.

Ginger

I received a letter in the mail one day, maybe a few months after Troy died. I don't remember whom exactly it was from or how she got my contact information but I remember very well what she wrote. She told me she had lost her husband when she was younger, in her thirties like I was. And that she, too, was left alone to raise their five children. She was now probably in her late 50's. Her children were now grown. Recalling the time after her husband died she flash backed to how she worried so much about the emotional and spiritual health of her young children. Would they grow up deficient? Rebellious? Resentful? Insecure? Would they be empty? Angry? She remained single their entire childhood. She raised them alone in one sense. However, she told me that without a doubt, the Lord God raised those kids with her. That He carried them. Protected them. Covered them. She told me their ages now – all in their twenties. She beamed about their graduations, careers and families of their own now. Each child was a successful, kind, and most of all godly adult. None had walked away from their faith.

As I poured over this stranger's letter to me, not even being surprised that God would somehow give this woman my story and my information, I was still overcome with emotion. She wrote exactly what I was praying for. What I was on my knees over – my kids and their futures. Their Dad was never supposed to not be a part of their stories; their weddings, their own babies, their hiking trips, their soccer games, their dance recitals.

In my mind, the nest that Troy and I had so painstakingly, lovingly, prayerfully built had fallen to ground; forever torn apart. The storm that I felt had destroyed each gently-placed tuft, twig, fine strand of leaf, and blade of soft green grass that we built it with seemed too scattered to patch back together, certainly not by myself. I was flying alone now.

However, that was not the truth. God wasn't asking me to rebuild our nest without His mighty help. I wasn't flying alone. Here was a stranger I never had and never will hear from again who was being used by the Lord to remind me of His love for us.

I read a story about the weaver bird, also known as a weaver finch. They are small birds with strong beaks and are known for their elaborate and sturdy nest building. These homes aren't traditional cup-shaped nests. They are highly complex and almost fully enclosed with only a small opening for them to enter; almost like a bee hive hanging from a tree. It's a fortress of safety from predators and weather, mostly built by the male of the species. Our Almighty God equipped this small bird to build an intricate yet sturdy shelter for its' family. There is even a species called a "widow weaver", known for her long black plumes.

I had to remember that Troy and I learned how to build our nest from the ultimate Weaver, our Savior. That foundation was still there even in my doubts and waiting. Our own hanging nest may have fallen in the storm but it did not break apart in a way that Jesus could not put it back together. He is omnipotent. Nothing is beyond His ability to rescue, recover or repair.

Years later as I write this book, my children are not quite in their twenties yet, like the kids of the woman that wrote to me all those years ago. But they are in their teens now, and Boston will be 20 years old this year. Yet I could still write a letter to a young widow today and tell her the same thing that woman wrote to me. God's promise has held true.

> "He is a Father to the fatherless; He gives justice to the widows, for He is holy. He gives families to the lonely, and releases prisoners from jail, singing with joy." (Psalm 68:5-6 TLB)

People who meet my kids and then find out our story are often astounded to see "how well they turned out". I know, without a doubt, that they have made the choice to be thankful for the many ways God has provided and have allowed Him to mold them into His image. His image is full of grace and gratitude, beauty and bravery. They are wise beyond their years. They had to grow up faster than I was ready for. They know about great evil in the world. They know deep sorrow. Yet they know how it feels to be rescued. I watch each of them have such compassion for others. They have been comforted and are sensitive to help others.

> "Praise be to the God and Father of our Lord Jesus Christ, the Father of compassion and the God of all comfort, who comforts us in all our troubles, so that we can comfort

those in any trouble with the comfort we ourselves receive
from God." (II Corinthians 1:3-4 NIV)

The nest that Troy built for us, with the Lord's help, is today hanging back on the branch. God also helped me learn that it's ok if my nest looks a lot different than the one I had planned. I never wanted to be a "blended" family. I never wanted the photos of Troy to not age with him. The dreams and the home we built look different now. Jim's too. Of course Jim has been a nest builder himself not just for his own family but now for ours too. There is a specific of type of weaver bird that builds its' nest in a colony of others. That's us; a group of those round hanging nests clinging on to the Tree of Life. It's the best real estate - the ultimate place to find ourselves, even when it would seem ridiculous to the world. We've seen the Great Weaver's work. He can be trusted. He will rebuild your nest. Just hold on.

Chapter 7 *Discussion Guide*

1. Jim describes the pilot's term *"Boldface"* and how he applied that to his life. Are you spiritually training to handle suffering in life? If not, how can you start to "learn your biblical boldface?"

2. Are you in a season of waiting? What are you waiting on and how is God using the waiting in your life?

3. Have you ever reached out to offer comfort to a stranger, an acquaintance or a close friend that is grieving? What have you learned about "being there" for those that are hurting?

Chapter 8
Sovereignty

Nothing takes God by surprise.

For as the heavens are higher than the earth, so are my ways higher than your ways, and my thoughts than your thoughts.

—Isaiah 55:9 (KJV)

Jim

As I traveled to Washington, DC, on business one day, my plane had mechanical issues, causing me to arrive three hours late and miss my meeting. As a result, I decided to go to another meeting, one I had not been able to fit into my schedule during past visits. The meeting venue was section 60, site 8525, of Arlington National Cemetery, where I would finally introduce myself to Troy. I had thought about this day many times, not knowing what I would say.

As fellow fighter pilots, Troy and I shared a love of flying, which gave us a unique bond. Therefore, it was humbling to kneel at Troy's grave and know that although we had never met, we shared so many moments—both professionally and now personally. We shared the love of Ginger. I had watched Boston play for his first club soccer team; felt the touch of Greyson, as a young boy, as he sought stability in his life; drove Bella to her first day of school; and heard the twins say "Daddy" for the first time when they looked at me. I was now raising another man's children, and I needed to "meet" that man. I wanted to talk to him and tell him the kids are doing fine and that Ginger still misses him. I needed to tell him I promised to love and care for his family, to stand in the gap he left behind. It was an odd feeling to say all of this at Troy's grave, but I left never feeling closer to a man I had never met. Somehow I knew him more than I have known few others in my life.

Whenever I see a United States flag, I remember that Troy died defending that very flag. When you serve in the military, it's so much more than just a flag. It is the banner under which you serve. It's the symbol of the country you are defending. When you are deployed, it is your link back to your own family and home.

There's a lot of pride to see the US flag painted on the tail of your aircraft. It serves as a constant reminder of those who have gone before us in battlefields all over the world, as well as those who were left in the fields of foreign lands. We never forget those like Troy who gave the last full measure. They are those who looked past their own safety and placed the best interests of others above their own interests.

The desire to live drives our instinctive response to life. When Troy heard that fellow Americans were calling for help in a life-and-death situation, he had no time to weigh the options. If he didn't respond quickly, they were going to die. For him, the decision was simple. In that moment, Troy decided his purpose was to defend men he had never met. All that mattered was that they wore the same flag on their uniform, the same flag that adorned the tail of his F-16. That is what drove his decision to give his last breath so that others may live. That is why I choose to honor Troy whenever I see our nation's flag or hear the national anthem.

Ginger had a similar experience. I took her to Ft. Sam Houston National Cemetery, section 110, site 699, where she knelt and met Andrea for the first time. It was a very emotional moment as I left her alone and watched from the car as they "talked." Neither I nor Ginger thought we would find ourselves in the position of being widowed. My plan was to grow old with Andrea, as Troy's was to grow old with Ginger. God's plan was different from both of ours.

Ginger

I wrote the following words on September 3, 2008: "As of today, it's been exactly two years since I last saw Troy, since I last touched him, held him, kissed him."

It was not the last time I felt loved by him, as I know he loved me until he took his last breath, but it had been two years since our last good-bye at Phoenix International Airport. We had experienced many deployments, but that was the first time I had to send my man to the "front lines." I became a pseudo single parent that day. Thinking back to that Sunday morning in September, I have tried to retrace our final farewells. The kids were sitting at our kitchen table eating breakfast, and Troy went around to each one and spoke soft words of love and encouragement. I watched him hand each of the bigger kids a small silver F-16 pin to put on their school backpacks.

To Boston, he assigned man-of-the-house responsibilities. As a mom, I found that hard to hear. Boston was just a little boy, but I knew he would take this instruction from his dad very seriously. I remember standing in the kitchen and crying over the stovetop. In one moment of comic relief, Bella looked up at Troy, who had tears streaming down his face, and, giggling, told him he was being a crybaby. Bella's toddler insensitivity made us laugh and eased the tension of the moment. Today, Bella has matured into a compassionate, loving young woman who would make her dad proud. Often, Jim and I will find an encouraging note from Bella on our bedside table when we are having a bad day. She's that kind of thoughtful. God knew that Troy and I needed her witty side on that September day. She was very matter-of-fact at that age. One day not long after Troy died, Bella came in from playing outside. I asked her what she had been doing. Without hesitation, she said, "I have been talking to Daddy." It sent a message to me that the children would each communicate with Troy in their own ways.

When it was time for Troy to head to the airport the morning he left for Iraq, some friends took the bigger kids to church, and another friend, Heidi, came over to sit with our babies. She gave up her own Sunday morning to give me the precious gift of being able to park at

177

the airport, go inside with Troy, and enjoy the last meal we would ever share together on this earth.

I kissed him good-bye at the security gate and went to the airport bathroom to cry. I thought I had put all my faith in God's corner, placing my husband and my heart into His hands. Despite all evidence otherwise, I look back and realize I was gambling with God a little. I was betting on Him but believing that my husband and my family would be off-limits. They belonged to me, right?

There is an element of control we all have in the daily decisions of life and over the direction we would like to go. However, we must give all those decisions prayerful consideration, seeking God's wisdom and listening to the Holy Spirit's whisper to our hearts. The more personal the request or the more difficult the road we are traveling at the time, the harder it is to let go and let God be God. If our first desire is to live with the trust and confidence that God is in control, then the only place left for our desires is the backseat. My kids really hated the backseat when they were younger. Everyone was always jockeying for the highly desirable "shotgun" seat up front. Once all five met the legal requirements and no longer needed to ride in car seats or booster seats, it just boiled down to pecking order when it came to who rode where. Oldest in front, youngest in back was how we rolled. Their desires made sense, though. The view is clearer from the front. The stereo is within reach. The cacophony of a thousand voices behind you is dulled. They wanted to help make decisions and have one-on-one conversation with me, the driver. Isn't that just like us as God's children? I want to be up front with Him. Maybe if He would just let me be copilot, then I could try to help. I dislike not seeing over the back of His headrest, yet that is exactly where He often places me, smack dab in the backseat. Could I hop over the console and forcibly squeeze in to call the shots? I could try. We all have free will and the ability to accelerate the pedal and steer in the direction we think is right. However, poor decisions we make at that point generally take us down the darker, longer, more difficult road.

Sometimes when we don't understand the road we are on, we find it easy to start questioning God's will. The distrust of God's supreme authority and sovereignty began in the Garden of Eden when the Devil planted seeds of doubt about God's intentions for Adam and Eve. The innocent have been affected ever since humankind chose to listen to themselves over the commands of God. Yet, just like in the Bible stories of the garden, the desert of Jesus's forty-day temptation, the garden of Gethsemane, the Egypt-to-Israel wilderness walk, and all of those places where people, even Jesus Himself, cried out to God for His guidance, the Lord has always had a plan of redemption. In your own dark valley, He has a way out of the wilderness for you. You just need to wait for the light to shine through the trees and onto your path.

Often, we cannot feel God's presence and cannot see any possible way He could craft value and victory out of desolation and defeat. It is in those weak moments that Satan begins to challenge our perceptions of God's abilities. He knows better than to mess with God, so he begins to mess with God's people. Satan preyed on my mind day after day, night after night, after I lost Troy. Initially, it was about the decision Troy and I had made for him to volunteer to go to war. Satan whispered, "You know you could have stopped this. He could have said no. You could have said no. You could have crafted some way to get him out of it. You know God could have stopped this if He really loved you. Maybe He doesn't love you as much as you thought." Those were lies, but it was very easy to believe they were truth.

During one desperate point when I was lying awake trying to rewind the hands of time, I recalled that I had accidentally broken a decorative military figurine just a couple of months before Troy deployed. That day replayed in my head. I had innocently purchased a collectible of a woman holding a folded flag. I thought it was patriotic, but Troy reminded me there was more to it—she was holding the flag she had received from the casket after losing someone in battle. I felt foolish for buying the figurine. Then shortly after Troy mentioned what it was, it fell and broke. Could this horrible tragedy have all spawned from that omen? I tossed and turned.

I called our pastor in a panic, asking if Troy would still be alive had I not broken the folded-flag figurine and if Troy hadn't ever deployed. Was "jinxing" a real thing? I knew the answer deep down, but Satan was attacking me. My only weapon to fight back was the Word of God. My pastor, Steve, gently reminded me of solid biblical truths.

> I know that You can do all things; no plan of Yours can be thwarted. (Job 42:2 NIV)

Pastor Steve had once asked similar questions himself. When he was newly married and in seminary, his young pregnant wife began feeling ill. They went to the doctor, and she went into an early labor. The delivery room became a trauma room. Suddenly, she developed eclampsia and died quickly after childbirth. He was left alone to raise his baby son. He wondered if he had done enough or could have altered their course, questioning whether he had missed some early signs or chosen the wrong doctor. Even as a pastor, he wrestled with God, but he found peace through the same scriptural truths he was now telling me. He said he had to have ultimate faith in God's supreme authority.

> A man's days are numbered. You know the number of his months. He cannot live longer than the time You have set. (Job 14:5–7 NLV)

> All the days ordained for me were written in your book before one of them came to be. (Psalm 139:16 NIV)

These verses remind me that from the beginning of time, God's plan was to take Troy home on November 27, 2006, whether it was in the cockpit of a jet or the cab of his pickup as he drove to the grocery store. I found an e-mail Troy sent to me while he was deployed in Iraq. It was dated October 5, 2006, just six weeks before he was killed. He wrote this:

> I am, in general, very impressed by most of the personnel here. Their sacrifice, like ours, is huge, but all are doing it with great attitudes and a strong sense of pride just to be able to serve our great nation. It especially hits home when you visit the hospital and realize the real sacrifices made

by our soldiers and Iraqi soldiers and police alike. I truly realized, as I have over and over again, what we are blessed with, what so many Americans have and continue to take for granted each and every day. I tell you, not one person who walks through the hospital takes anything for granted anymore. Whenever I go there I have to continually say a prayer to remind myself that I serve a sovereign God who is in control of everything and is ever faithful. He is in control and is impacting/touching so many lives for His cause, even in the face of such tragedy/sorrow. That reassurance comes from the good news stories that are generated each and every day at that facility by the men and women who serve outstandingly there. That reassurance does not come from the blessed life He has given me, because I truly understand that can all end in an instant. I've truly realized that His sovereignty and power, rather my true belief in it, should have nothing to do with and doesn't have anything to do with the blessed life He has given me. It (the blessed life) comes from His Word, His promise, His Son's blood—faith, my dear. Faith, regardless of what happens to me, to you, to our children. Faith in the face of tragedy. I am so thankful I, we as a family, have Him to lean on. Many here do not. For many, the hospital is a place that shakes their faith … hard to understand at first, 'til you see it firsthand. I am comforted to know that regardless of the outcome, God *is* in control.

As I read his words, my heart beat faster. Troy's faith had been put to the test. The decision to trust a loving God had already been made. How could I read his message and not know those words were written for me in the painful months that lay ahead?

Even if this isn't similar to your circumstances, even if your loved ones didn't die doing something they were passionate about or with an assurance of faith beforehand, there is still healing that can be found for you and for your situation under the merciful shelter of our Lord. Your loss may have come from critical illness, senseless crime, suicide. Whatever your story, it can still be God's story and your victory. Brokenness can bring about wholeness. Good emerges out of bad.

Weakness becomes strength. I want to worship a God too big, too powerful, and too wise for me to comprehend. Sometimes when I am sharing our family's journey, I can scarcely believe the events I'm talking about are my story. I am in awe and humbled that, with the Lord's help, I get out of bed each day and have peace, knowing that no matter what the day brings, He's got us in His hands. Our house is built upon the Rock that is higher and mightier and stronger than I could ever build on my own.

Each Veterans Day, we honor and remember all who have chosen the narrow and difficult path of service above self. Military life is bittersweet. I have never gained more or lost so much because of any one thing. Yet, my hope is not in our nation or even those who serve dutifully to protect it. That is the sand. It will be washed away, one way or another. Because the Lord is Lord over all, my pain is not pointless. My misery is also my miracle, just as yours can be, too.

> He is before all things, and in Him all things hold together.
> (Colossians 1:17 NIV)

Jim

On the one-year anniversary of Andrea's passing, my plan was to be at Andrea's grave at 1:07 p.m., the exact time she went to be with the Lord. I dreaded going to her grave, but I went there about every three weeks.

When I approached the gravesite on that particular afternoon, I saw fresh flowers on Andrea's grave. On top, I found a card from Ginger. I brought my own flowers, which I added to Ginger's. I also brought a picture of Andrea because I wanted anyone who saw her tombstone to see her as more than a name. As I watched the time tick closer and closer to 1:07, I thought through the events of December 17, 2007: finding Andrea unresponsive, calling Nic and telling him to get Anthony out of school, reaching out to family and friends while I waited for Andrea's oncologist to arrive and confirm what I knew I had to do.

I stayed at the grave to talk to Andrea and found myself thinking of

Andrea's mother, June. It's hard to imagine what it must be like to lose a child. It's as unnatural as losing your spouse at such a young age. I thought about Andrea's sister and niece having lost a sister and mentor. So many people were affected by Andrea and her life, a life that was cut way too short. As I left, I looked back again at Andrea's picture with a new type of feeling, something that I hadn't felt before. It was the end of a year of reflection marking the first of everything without Andrea. Afterward, I met Ginger for lunch. As I sat waiting for her, I saw the door open. Then in she walked. At that moment, I saw my wife in a whole new way. I saw not just my wife but also my life. I saw her smile at me from across the room and felt her love and her excitement to see me. I told her, "Nothing about what happened to Andrea changed because of you, yet everything about my life since that day has changed because of having you in my life." In Ginger, I now saw my future. And in that instant, I didn't feel the guilt I'd struggled with the entire past year—guilt over being happy while I was also still sad. It was a relief to finally have the feeling lift.

Together, Ginger and I both know that Andrea and Troy await our arrival. I'm happy when I think of Andrea in heaven, where she always wanted to be. Andrea once wrote in her journal after a Chris Tomlin concert that she felt the evening of worship was a little like being in heaven. She had asked God if she could leave earth, but God told her it was not yet her time. It is the same for Ginger and me today: it is not our time to go. Until it is our time to go, it's our job to serve God as Troy and Andrea demonstrated to us, with all of our hearts, souls, and minds.

Ginger

> Now to Him who is able to do exceedingly abundantly above all that we ask or think, according to the power that works in us, to Him be glory. (Ephesians 3:20–21 NKJV)

> For the eyes of the Lord search the whole earth in order to strengthen those whose hearts are fully committed to Him. (2 Chronicles 16:9 NLT)

The Lord says, "I will rescue those who love me. I will protect those who trust in My name. When they call on me, I will answer; I will be with them in trouble. I will rescue and honor them. I will reward them with a long life and give them My salvation." (Psalm 91:14–16 NLT)

Since the day I answered that heartbreaking knock at my front door, I never stopped praying for the miracle of Troy's remains to be recovered. On Friday, November 22, 2013, almost seven years to the date of his crash, I was called into the commander's office at Randolph AFB. By God's design, General Robin Rand, Troy's last commander, mentor, and personal friend, met with me face-to-face. He took my hand and told me there was news of Troy's remains being recovered. A small portion had been returned to the US Embassy via the country of Jordan, which had received them from Iraq. Tears filled my eyes. Though it was not his total remains, it was monumental and miraculous. I always knew the search was akin to looking for a needle in a haystack or a grain of sand at the beach, but we knew there was nothing beyond God's reach.

Lord, you have seen what is in my heart. You know all about me. You know when I sit down and when I get up. You know what I'm thinking even though you are far away. You know when I go out to work and when I come back home. You know exactly how I live. Lord, even before I speak a word, you know all about it. You are all around me. You are behind me and in front of me. You hold me in your power. I'm amazed at how well you know me. It's more than I can understand. How can I get away from your Spirit? Where can I go to escape from you? If I go up to the heavens, you are there. If I lie down in the deepest parts of the earth, you are also there. Suppose I were to rise with the sun in the east and then cross over to the west where it sinks into the ocean. Your hand would always be there to guide me. Your right hand would still be holding me close. Suppose I were to say, "I'm sure the darkness will hide me. The light around me will become as dark as night." Even that darkness would not be dark to you. The night would shine like the day, because darkness is like light to you. You created the deepest parts of my being. You put me together inside my mother's body. How you made me is amazing and wonderful. I praise you for that. What you have done is wonderful. I know that very well. None of my bones was hidden from you when you made me inside my mother's body. That place was as dark as the deepest parts of the earth. When you were putting me together there, Your eyes saw my body even before it was formed. You planned how many days I would live. You wrote down the number of them in your book before I had lived through even one of them. God, your thoughts about me are priceless. No one can possibly add them all up. If I could count them, they would be more than the grains of sand. (Psalm 139:1–18 NIRV)

When the experts confirmed the remains were Troy's toe bones (phalanges), I asked for the specifics of both these new remains and the remains from the original crash site. The medical examiner (ME) explained to me that what was found at the crash site were skull fragments, the very top portion of Troy's skull. The latest were the phalanges from the tips of his toes. After the ME answered my question, I sat in silence for a moment as the tears streamed down my face. I replied, "So, am I correct in saying that all we have of Troy is the top of his head and the tips of his toes?" He answered, "Yes, ma'am." Immediately I knew that was a clear message to me from the Lord. He wanted me to know, "Don't worry. Troy is mine. I have him from the top of his head to the tips of his toes. I have never left him or forsaken him. Nor have I left or forsaken you. Remember this." It was humbling to know the God of the Universe would care enough to send me that kind of big, powerful, unfathomable love in such a small earthly package.

Though we may not always see it and certainly don't deserve it, our God does everything with a purpose. He is intentional with the way He cares for us. My favorite number is seven, because I know it is a number rooted in biblical significance (and also the number of children Jim and I have together). I believe the Lord allowed seven years to pass between Troy's crash and the recovery of his phalanges as a reminder of His perfect love for us and so there was practically enough time for the children to mature and remember the moment. The number seven is mentioned 287 times in the Bible: seven days to create the earth, seven colors in the rainbow, seven trumpets. Seven, seven, and more seven. When I found myself standing on Troy's grave once again as we buried the new remains weeks later, my mind was clouded with sorrow. My heart was heavy with grief as I stood on the once-again fresh grave at Arlington. Yet on that day, I stood thankful for what I had: Jim by my side; children who are emotionally whole, physically healthy, and walking with the Lord; a vast number of loved ones still surrounding us; the heroic efforts of the great men and women who serve our country and my family; and people who were not able attend Troy's first service but were now able to celebrate his life with us. One of the doctors Troy had befriended, who had written to me about him, came to the service. Afterward, he told me he struggled with spiritual things. Having known Troy, he wanted to pursue faith for himself now.

Troy's heart was a heart after God. I loved him more than life itself and always will. However, I falsely believed his heart belonged solely to me. He was, in truth, never really mine. God always loved him more than I ever could. As I stood there that day, I knew God still loved us. He had never abandoned us. He longs to show us all He does for us. God never wastes our pain.

Arlington National Cemetery December 11, 2013.
Exactly seven years after Troy's first funeral, a small
casket now held newly-recovered, partial remains.

Chapter 8 *Discussion Guide*

1. What does the word "sovereign" mean to you? How does your definition relate to the phrase, "God is in control"?

2. Have you ever experienced something that you believe could have only been orchestrated by a God "too big, too powerful, and too wise … to comprehend?" Please share with the group what happened and how it impacted your view of God's sovereignty?

3. What is your view of suffering in this life? What examples can you think of – either in your own life or in this book – of God not wasting our pain if we allow Him to change us for the better?

Chapter 9

Perspective

We can complain because rose bushes have thorns, or rejoice because thorn bushes have roses.

—Abraham Lincoln

Fixing our eyes on Jesus, the author and perfecter of faith, who for the joy set before Him endured the cross, despising the shame, and has sat down at the right hand of throne of God.

—Hebrews 12:2 (NASB)

Jim

While she was taking a drive one day in Alaska, Andrea told me, she stopped by a river and got out to sit in the grass. It was so soft and inviting that she lay down. And when she did, she noticed that when she focused on the tall grass right in front of her face, the mountains in the background were blurry. Yet when she focused on the mountains, the grass in front of her was blurry. She came home and told me how life is like that. We see clearly what we choose to focus on. She could focus on the difficulty of cancer and her faith would be blurry, or she could focus on her God and allow this life's hardships to blur instead. She said, "It is all in how you look at it." I have thought about the wisdom in her words many times, and how they helped change my understanding of what Andrea was going through during one of her chemo treatments.

Ever since the beginning of the battle in 2003, I was amazed by Andrea's constant strength. How she faced the chemo treatments, the doctors, the tests, and the blood draws was beyond me. I participated as much as I could as a caregiver, but I knew I could never fully understand what she was facing. I understood the medical aspects of Andrea's treatments, but my understanding was shaped by my viewpoint. Then one day in 2006, God allowed me to see from a different angle what my wife was dealing with.

She had already been diagnosed with terminal cancer at that time. We had returned to the chemo room for a second round of treatment in North Carolina. Andrea had finished her initial treatment and radiation, but the cancer had again returned. Following is a journal entry I wrote in October 2005 while at one of Andrea's treatments:

> The chemo she's taking is called Abraxiene, and it's been hard on Andrea. Although she is relentless in her fight, it's still difficult to see her sick. Andrea is so strong, so I know when I see her break down, I realize how demanding it must be. Andrea does not want to stop or give in, and she rarely shows how hard this is on her. When I see her cry over the pain, and I see her express how much it hurts, I gain a little understanding. It is difficult as her husband to see her hurt and know there is nothing you can do to take away the pain but to ask God to have mercy on her.
>
> As we waited for our turn in the chemo chair, we talked and laughed, trying not to notice all those around us who looked one step away from death. In the back of our minds we hoped we would escape before we were in their shoes. I wondered if they looked at us and thought, *Just wait. I was once like you before chemo took its toll—full of life and naive to the reality of cancer; hoping against all hope I could win.* Everyone in the room knew the odds: that only a few of us would win the lottery and the grand prize, which was leaving this room and returning to normal living. In the cancer world, the term is "in remission." We all hoped we would hear those words one day.

By this time, we were veterans of the chemo room, and sadly it was becoming routine. It was always the same. Andrea would sit in the La-Z-Boy chair, the nurses come in with the bags of chemo and hook her up, and I sit and watch it go into her, drip by drip. I had seen far too many people sitting in a La-Z-Boy facing death all alone. My promise to Andrea was she would never be alone in the chemo room. I knew that even though I physically went with Andrea to every appointment, there always came a time when Andrea had to go where I could never go. This feeling came when they took her away for surgery. I could only go so far with her, and then I had to let her go. It was hard, very hard to do. I wanted to be there for her, to hold her hand and comfort her, but I could not go those last steps. It reminded me that no matter how hard I tried, I could never fully understand what Andrea was going through.

This day was like all the others. I sat in my chair facing Andrea while we chatted to pass the time. Andrea sat in the La-Z-Boy, a place reserved only for her. But on this particular day, I got closer to her world and what she was experiencing. I only moved three feet, but I went miles in understanding what my wife was dealing with.

I met Andrea and our friend Lisa at the chemo room. I arrived one hour into an expected three-hour chemo session. It was Tuesday after a holiday; the chemo filling station was packed and behind schedule. Treatment days were long. It was not uncommon for us to be there over six hours. Andrea got up to go to the bathroom. I walked with her and then returned to sit with Lisa. For some reason, I sat in the La-Z-Boy instead of my chair and began to talk with Lisa. In that instant, just from changing my perspective, I could feel the enormity of Andrea's battle.

I had stepped closer to where Andrea has gone, where she had to go alone. Only she could sit in that chair and experience all that came with it. I felt closer to Andrea as I sat there. I felt closer to what she must have felt every week. I felt closer to the struggle she went through. I felt closer to the fight she was fighting. I felt closer to the fear she encountered every time she sat down in that La-Z-Boy. The anguish of remembering just how sick the treatment would make her. Knowing you are bringing yourself closer to death just to have a chance at life. I felt closer and farther away at the same time. The distance reminded me that this seat was Andrea's. I felt the space between us. I felt sadness that she had to go there. I wished we were not here. I felt the enormity of the task before her. I felt the weight on her shoulders. I felt the dread of what was coming. I felt sad for my wife. I felt sad she had to go to such a place. I felt the loneliness of the La-Z-Boy.

Andrea returned to the chair and stood before me with her beautiful smile as if to say, "What are you doing in my chair?" I looked up from the La-Z-Boy, and all I could say was, "I'm sorry."

Only two measly words were all I could find to say, but I knew what I meant. I'm sorry you have to sit here. I'm sorry you have to face this. I'm sorry you are sick. I'm sorry you are scared. I'm sorry you have to go here alone.

Andrea was tired, but she was a fighter—and that, combined with her faith, was her greatest asset and our greatest hope to eventually leave behind the La-Z-Boy. I loved her so much, and she inspired me by her drive to keep life normal. When she put mascara on those last few eyelashes, she showed her determination to hold onto life. Those of us around her were challenged in our own lives by her example. When Andrea went out, she was always put together, matching her scarves to her outfits. I think people were surprised. I think people expected to see Andrea beaten down, but she was not. The La-Z-Boy reminded me of the difficult road Andrea had to walk, and I was more humbled by her with every passing day.

Ginger

This may sound odd, but I finally found the strength to toss away Troy's contact lenses. They were among his personal belongings shipped to me from one of his lockers in Iraq. When I opened his travel kit and saw them, I cried. Then I stored them. I moved them across three states and stored them again. I realize they were just slivers of latex, but they had once touched his amazing green eyes. Throwing them away meant that he was never coming back to wear them.

Troy had the prettiest eyes. They were green or hazel depending on the day and what he was wearing. They were a perfect match to his green flight suit. Such warm, kind eyes. They were the first thing I noticed about him when I met him my sophomore year in college. In his eyes was a hint of both mischief and romance.

He did not need vision correction until he got a little older and spent a lot of time on the computer and flying airplanes. So several years after his death, I sat with his contacts in my hand, uncertain of what to do. I started to put them back in the cabinet, but I thought that maybe this was the day I should throw them away. He certainly didn't need them anymore. So why would I? There are many of Troy's things that I have set aside and saved for the children or for myself, but I decided the contacts could go, which unexpectedly became a turning point of healing for me.

Troy's eyesight was made perfect the second he died and went home to be with Jesus. Andrea's frail body was no longer ravaged with cancer when she took her last breath that day in the hospital. No more imperfections. No more illness. What a glorious day for them!

> They will see His face, and His name will be written on their foreheads. (Revelation 22:4 NIV)

> He will wipe every tear from their eyes. There will be no more death or mourning or crying or pain, for the old order of things has passed away. (Revelation 21:4 NIV)

But we have this treasure in jars of clay to show that this all-surpassing power is from God and not from us. We are hard pressed on every side but not crushed, perplexed but not in despair, persecuted but not abandoned, struck down but not destroyed. We always carry around in our body the death of Jesus, so that the life of Jesus may also be revealed in our body. (2 Corinthians 4:7–10 NIV)

The treasure we have is that He would choose to dwell His Holy Spirit within us while we are still walking the earth. Although I knew that truth, I didn't feel treasured or pretty anymore after Troy died, and I knew I looked a little worse for wear. Troy always made me feel beautiful, despite the stretch marks, extra baby weight spilling over my jeans, and some dark under-eye circles—things motherhood bequeathed me with. He and I had aged together, but I knew he still saw me as the youthful girl I was in college. However, now I suddenly felt vulnerable and judged by the world's standards. Without even realizing it, I found that being such a handsome guy's wife had made me feel pretty. So without him, I felt very plain. In my loneliness, I struggled to see myself from another perspective. Inside my heart, I also felt ugly from the jealousy I had as I watched other married couples go on with their lives. In that first year after he died, I struggled to regain my confidence and feel contentment. Then that day when I sat on the bathroom floor with Troy's contacts in my hands, I could almost hear Troy say, "Ginger, just throw them away. It's all going to be okay." He was free of the things he needed in this world. I had to let go of the thing I thought I needed to feel whole and beautiful—I had to let go of being Troy's wife.

If I truly believed God was in control, that my plans must sync with God's, and that my identity and worth were not solely tied to being Troy's wife, I knew I had to loosen the grip I had on my life. After all that had happened, it seemed reckless to trust the Lord, but it seemed fatal to do anything other than that.

Jesus's death certainly must have seemed unplanned to every person who lived with and loved Him. We see now that Jesus's death and resurrection was God's plan A all along. Since God raised Christ from the dead, certainly I would be a fool to doubt that He could resurrect this woman looking back at me in the bathroom mirror. I knew I had to choose to see that I was still loved, cherished, and beautiful, and that I had a future and a purpose, even without Troy by my side. We are beautiful because God calls us beautiful. Nothing could or can ever take away who we are in Christ.

> I will betroth you to me forever; I will betroth you in righteousness and justice, in love and compassion. (Hosea 2:19 NIV)

> "For I know the plans I have for you," declares the Lord, "plans to prosper you and not to harm you, plans to give you hope and a future." (Jeremiah 29:11 NIV)

Following are beautiful lyrics from the Chris Tomlin song "I Will Rise":[14]

> There's a day that's drawing near
> When this darkness breaks to light
> And the shadows disappear
> And my faith shall be my eyes.

When Troy met our Lord that November day, not only did he not need his contacts, but also he no longer needed his faith. His faith became his eyes! For those of us still on this side of heaven, the opposite is true. My faith must not be based on what I see, such as the absence of the man who loved me more than he loved himself. I had to throw those expectations away with the contact lenses. My faith had to be all about what I couldn't see, believing that God was going to restore my life just like He restored Troy's vision.

---

[14] Chris Tomlin, Jesse Reeves, Louie Giglio, and Matt Maher, "I Will Rise," *Hello Love*, CCLI 5183450, 2008.

> I will lead the blind by ways they have not known, along unfamiliar paths I will guide them. I will turn the darkness into light before them and make the rough places smooth. These are the things I will do. I will not forsake them. (Isaiah 42:16 NIV)

Jim

Back in 2005, when Andrea was battling stage IV metastatic cancer, we were growing spiritually. We spent many nights praying until sunrise. Yet the sickness remained. There were many days when Andrea hurt so bad she could hardly get out of bed. One day a friend came to Andrea and told her we should do Communion each day. At first I was resistant, not wanting to feel like it was something we were doing to gain God's favor. But over time, the thought of Communion continued to haunt me as something we needed to do. I talked to Andrea, and we made the decision to do it. It turned out those evenings of Communion would irrevocably change how we faced cancer in Andrea's last years.

As the cancer reports continued to be negative, it was obvious that our only hope was a miracle. There were many difficult days and nights, but we found a surprising comfort in our nightly time of Communion. As we passed the bread and the cup between one another, it brought us to the cross, where Christ suffered for us. In my mind, I knelt at the cross, my hands pressed into the blood-soaked soil beneath it. As I reached up, I felt the roughness of the wood. Then I looked up, seeing His beaten body, His head down, the crown of thorns piercing Him, blood dripping from His brow. With His head hanging, too weak to lift it, He slowly opened His eyes and looked down on me. In that moment, I understood the price that was paid for my salvation. I saw our trial in light of His suffering, and I realized I had no right to complain. Andrea and I would continue to fight and pray and hope, but also suffer, for Christ, our Savior and Redeemer.

> Dear friends, do not be surprised at the fiery ordeal that has come on you to test you, as though something strange were

happening to you. But rejoice inasmuch as you participate in the sufferings of Christ, so that you may be overjoyed when his glory is revealed. If you are insulted because of the name of Christ, you are blessed, for the Spirit of glory and of God rests on you. If you suffer, it should not be as a murderer or thief or any other kind of criminal, or even as a meddler. However, if you suffer as a Christian, do not be ashamed, but praise God that you bear that name. For it is time for judgment to begin with God's household; and if it begins with us, what will the outcome be for those who do not obey the gospel of God? And if it is hard for the righteous to be saved, what will become of the ungodly and the sinner? So then, those who suffer according to God's will should commit themselves to their faithful Creator and continue to do good. (1 Peter 4:12–19 NIV)

Ginger

Although Jim and I did not intend for this to happen, we first met on Christmas Day. It makes us smile deep down, because without even realizing it, we were given the most incredible gift that year: a chance at a new life. Through the years, Jim and I have taken turns being one another's rock to stand on, a place to land during the throes of sorrowful grief. There have miraculously been only a handful of times when we were both hurting so much that we couldn't be there for one another, but the Lord sustained us through even those difficult days.

Jim has always been saddened with me and my children over Troy's crash, the circumstances around it, and the hole that was left behind in our lives. He understood what Troy was doing on his mission that day and suddenly found himself taking care of Troy's wife and children. When Jim first mentioned marriage to me, I told him, "Don't marry me because you feel sorry for me. Marry me because you love me." He said he was marrying me not only because he loved me but also because he was confident that it was what God had called him to do. The Lord had sent me and my children another man to step in and "take the stick," as pilots refer to it, from Troy to continue to keep us on course as a family.

From how he imparts knowledge of Troy to our children to how he helps other fallen families with me, Jim has honored Troy and his sacrifice many times over. Since meeting me, he also began to pray for Troy's remains to be found whenever he heard "Taps" played, which happens on bases all over the country at 5:00 p.m. every day. So, as you can imagine, when I was told the news of the partial recovery of Troy's remains, Jim was right by my side with a heart overwhelmed with gratitude. As soon as the tears stopped flowing and we walked out of Baba's office, he began helping me make plans for Troy's service. He diligently helped me put together a second Arlington service in just three short weeks.

Unlike the 2006 service, in which others did the heavy lifting of planning and preparation, this time it was up to me, Jim, and the kids, who were now much older and able, to decide how we could celebrate Troy and the miraculous recovery. Jim made many phone calls, logistically planned our trip, meticulously made professional-grade programs, and offered loving insight to make Troy's service and reception a solemn yet joyful occasion. He understood that the service was a chance for the children to fully comprehend what their daddy being buried in Arlington National Cemetery meant. Only Boston truly remembered the first service at Arlington seven years prior. Greyson had been just six years old, so his memories were few. Bella attended, but she was only three. The twins had not been at Arlington at all, as the temperature had been barely above freezing and they were just babies.

The children all decided they wanted to say something at Troy's service. To help them choose what they wanted to talk about, I wrote down many of Troy's characteristics on small pieces of paper, words and phrases such as *strong leader, determined, caring, funny, loving.* I laid them all out on the coffee table, and the children selected which of their daddy's traits they thought they possessed. Then they wrote their own stories from there. Each was unique, was incredibly touching, and accurately described the similarities and connections they will always have with their father. Jim said he would like to introduce the kids at the service and wondered if it would be appropriate for him to say something in honor of Troy. I told him that of course it would be, if he felt that is what the Lord wanted him to do. Until Jim got up at the service, I didn't know what he was going to say. Then once again, he exceeded all expectations.

After briefly talking about his unique role to fill in the gap for Troy, Jim said he knew Troy's words were what he was meant to read on that very momentous day—words we all needed to be reminded of most. In some way, they were words from the grave for us to live by. Jim then proceeded to read the e-mail Troy had sent to me a few weeks before he died (see page 172) The same e-mail God used to give me confidence that He was in control had also given Jim the confidence to know that he was doing exactly what he was supposed to be doing as my husband and father to our children. After Jim finished reading Troy's words, he turned and proudly saluted Troy's small casket of remains. Troy's powerful legacy does not in any way cast a shadow on Jim. Their shadows stand equally tall, merging into one great covering for our household. A friend once shared a story from a sermon she heard where the pastor emphasized Joseph's unique calling to become Mary's husband and Jesus's earthly father. She said she was struck with the thought that my Jim was a modern-day Joseph. Why hadn't I ever thought of that? Joseph loved Mary and committed to her despite the detour of his own life's plan. Jim's full name is James Joseph Ravella. His parents couldn't have possibly known how much he would live up to his name someday. They passed away before I met Jim, but I have a feeling they would be very proud of their youngest child.

> When I consider Your heavens, the work of your fingers, the moon and the stars which You have set in place, what is man that you are mindful of him? (Psalm 8:3–5 NKJV)

Jim

When I used to read accounts of faith in the Bible, I always wished I could have faith like Moses, Joseph, or David. Finally, I realized I was focused only on the part of their stories where everything was made right—the happy ending, if you will. I went back and reread their stories in their entirety and wondered if I would have been able to make it through the same difficulties.

I want to be the Joseph who ruled, but am I willing to be the Joseph in prison? Am I willing to be the Joseph who forgave his brothers? I want to be King David, but am I willing to be the David in the wilderness? I want to be Paul, but am I willing to be Paul in chains? I want to be Peter, but am I willing to be martyred for what I believe? I want to be Daniel, but am I willing to be taken into captivity? I want to be faithful, but am I willing to endure suffering like Job? I want to be in a position of respect, but am I willing to wash the feet of others?

Although the Bible is complete, God is not finished writing stories to encourage others. The stories that remain to be told are stories like ours. "Ordinary people serving an extraordinary God," as Katie Davis, missionary and best selling author, refers to it.[15] But are we willing to endure difficulty to allow God's love to be seen by our children, neighbors, and coworkers? Are we willing to lay down our lives for future generations or those we will never meet? When Christ asks if we love Him, are we willing to stretch out our arms as He did and say, "Yes, Lord, I love you this much."

---

[15] Katie Davis with Beth Clark, *Kisses from Katie* (New York: Howard Books, 2012).

Chapter 9 *Discussion Guide*

1. What do you choose to focus on in your life - the positive or the negative? The challenges or the blessings? How does this impact you and those around you?

2. Jim describes a day when he sat in the chemo chair and his perspective changed. When has your perspective in life changed about something because of an unexpected experience you had?

3. How would you describe who you are in God's sight? How does this impact how you view yourself?

4. What earthly thing, person, or idea are you clinging to right now that you need to release to God and trust Him with?

Chapter 10
Scars and Jars

Christ's love is the key to healing and thankfulness.

Rejoice always, pray continually, give thanks in all circumstances; for this is God's will for you in Christ Jesus.
—1 Thessalonians 5:16–18 (NIV)

Jim

For better or for worse, trials will change us. What varies is how long the change will last. Will it be fleeting, buried under a busy life, a distant memory of pain that is fading day by day? Or will it forever alter who we are? What I'm learning is that the amount of change is not necessarily linked to how difficult a trial may be. It's more about our willingness to want to change. My prayer for you and me is that we learn from every trial, not waiting until we experience total devastation to turn our eyes to the hill from where our help comes from.

Andrea once asked, "Jim, what are you going to do when this is all over? Will your faith be as strong as it is today in the midst of all this?" She knew what drove me to abandon myself and totally depend on God was the daily struggle we faced with cancer. She gently explained, "This will end one day; either I'm going to be healed or I'm going to die, so I want you to keep the faith you now have when it's over."

> Brothers and sisters, we do not want you to be uninformed about those who sleep in death, so that you do not grieve like the rest of mankind, who have no hope. For we believe

that Jesus died and rose again, and so we believe that God
will bring with Jesus those who have fallen asleep in him. (1
Thessalonians 4:13–14 NIV)

Those who know Christ can face suffering with an eternal
perspective. That ability is one of our greatest tools we have when
we witness to a lost world. We all share the common experience of
suffering, but when a believer suffers with hope, it stands out.

While I realized this was Andrea's and my path to walk, I failed
to understand what our boys were going through. As Andrea and I
engaged in hand-to-hand combat, praying together late at night, we
grew together in gaining a heavenly perspective. It was not until three
years after Andrea passed that I realized my boys did not have the same
experience. While visiting Andrea's grave one day, the boys told me they
had not realized just how sick their mom was. In their minds, Andrea's
disease was serious, but they never saw any other outcome besides her
getting better.

I wondered if I had failed as a father. Should the boys have been
given more detailed information? Had Andrea and I lived in a fantasy
of hope that confused the kids? We were honest with them all along the
way, but Andrea had made the choice to continue with life as "normal."
She worked hard to achieve that, which, I guess, gave our boys a sense
that she was invincible. She did not hide from them how serious her
cancer was, but she did not want our kids to change the way they lived
because of it. In 2006, Nic was going to study abroad during his junior
year of college. When questions arose about whether Nic should go,
Andrea said something I'll never forget: "I want him to go because I
want Nic to live his life." By not changing the way we lived, Andrea
was telling cancer that while it might take her life, it would not define
how she lived that life.

Jim, Nic and Anthony at Nic and Kate's wedding, Pennsylvania, 2009

Each of us has the opportunity to dwell on all we've lost or reflect on what we were blessed to have. All seven of our children can take the memories of their mother and father to become better people—spouses, mothers, and fathers—or they can choose to allow it to stunt the growth God wants for them by becoming bitter. I pray my boys will be a light to the world just as their mom was—to the world that seeks answers, purpose, and meaning to life and that looks to faithful, hopeful, joyful sufferers to do it. I looked at Andrea every day, seeing how she lived facing death, and knew without a doubt it was because of Christ in her. She showed us how to balance trust in God with her own desires. When forced to choose, even near death, she chose her God and she chose life.

Ginger

Having grown up in a hub of Southern conservatism, I admit that I might have been a bit judgmental when it came to tattoos. More than that, I just never considered getting one. However, after losing Troy, I found myself considering a lot of things I had never considered before. When your world spirals into the land of the great unknown, life gets a little less black and white. As the one-year anniversary of Troy's death approached, it was a time for me to reflect on the challenges and the changes I had gone through the twelve months prior. Though many others walked with me, there were many times when it was a lonely sojourn as Jesus and I walked the broken road together. I knew He was the only one who really understood all the nuances of my suffering and the true enormity of my pain. He Himself had, long before me, gone through more hurt than I could have imagined. He suffered all the way to the cross, separating Himself from His Father, taking our sin upon Him so we would not have to spend eternity separated from God. After Troy's death, I completed a study on the ark of the covenant, a place that tethered God to His people, the Israelites. The ark contained the original Ten Commandments, a pot containing manna from the days God sustained the Israelites in the wilderness, the writings of Moses, and several other powerfully meaningful objects. There were many rules and regulations regarding the care of the ark, and no one could enter into the holy of holies but the high priest. To say the ark was sacred is an understatement. It encompassed God's promise to the Old Testament believers that His presence would always be with them. The ark is mentioned over two hundred times in the Old Testament. When Christ came to earth and atoned for our sins on the cross, He became our "ark," a promise that we can all forever be linked to the Almighty. He is our refuge and the only place we can go for real hope.

> God also bound Himself with an oath, so that those who received the promise could be perfectly sure that He would never change His mind. So God has given both His promise and His oath. These two things are unchangeable because it is impossible for God to lie. Therefore, we who have fled to Him for refuge can have great confidence as we hold to the hope that lies before us. This hope is a strong and trustworthy anchor for our souls. It leads us through the curtain into God's inner sanctuary. Jesus has already gone in there for us. He has become our eternal High Priest in the order of Melchizedek. (Hebrews 6:17–20 NLT)

Anchors serve the unique purpose of keeping a ship from drifting from the mainland, holding it safely in position. Much like an anchor, our hope in Christ guarantees ultimate safety. When the waves crash in and the storms of life threaten to take us away from the mainland, we can cling to Jesus, our anchor, who keeps us steady, planted, and firm. After losing Troy, I journaled about the feeling of sinking, drowning in the deep. It seemed to be the only analogy that expressed my feelings. Sadness and despair constantly threatened to pull me under. I felt chains were wrapped around my body, slowly pulling me below the water's surface or simply dragging me away from my lifetime of faith. When I heard this scripture in Hebrews, I clung to it as a promise directly from God to me. I didn't have to be hopeless, because He lived in me. No matter how battered my little ship felt, He was not going to let me drift, much less sink.

For many weeks I thought of the scripture and the anchor again and again, until one day I decided the image of an anchor would make a great tattoo, something that would be a constant reminder of Jesus holding on and not letting me sink into my grief. I wanted to mark our journey together with an outward sign of an inner scar. Even Jesus kept the scars on His palms after the resurrection. My tattoo combined the anchor, the cross, a heart, and the scripture reference of Hebrews 6:19. It's amazing how tattoos strike up conversations between people who have them. Most people have a meaningful story behind theirs, as it is a mark to show others what they themselves can never forget. Today, most people (even my parents) are accustomed to my ankle art, which is simply a physical reminder and testimony of what my hope looks like. In time, it may fade from my skin, but the real presence of my Savior will never fade.

Ginger's tattoo

Jim

During the spring of 2006, Andrea was in the throes of her third round of chemo. One night, she called me to come back to our room and asked me to pray for her. I knelt beside her, placed my hands on her, and began to intercede on her behalf, asking God to take away her queasiness and pleading with Him not to let her get sick. In the middle of my prayer, Andrea vomited all over the wall.

Angry with God, I was tired of seeing my wife sick and I was sick and tired of feeling helpless. I sat on the bed and lashed out at God. Lost in my self-pity, I failed to notice that Andrea had gotten up and was in the bathroom. I walked over to the bathroom door and witnessed the greatest act of worship I had ever seen. Andrea was sitting in front of the toilet, still vomiting, but raising her hands and thanking God for specific things He had done in her life. I felt ashamed of myself for my weakness. Andrea taught me once again what it meant to be thankful in all things.

We tell our children that showing our thankfulness to God is the biggest testimony we have as a family. We've sown plenty of tears, but we have also reaped much joy. The Lord did that for us. We planted a garden full of sadness and watered it with our tears, and He gave us a harvest of hope in Him.

Ginger

In the months following Troy's crash, occasionally an Iraqi terrorist group would air footage of Troy on the Al Jazeera website and Iraqi television channels. They might show his military ID, our family photos (which they pulled off the Internet), or even, horrifically, his dead body. They usually timed these media footage releases with some political event or antiwar protest in the United States.

I would then get a call or visit from our base commanders, informing me of what was going on. I stopped watching the news the day Troy died because it was either too depressing or extremely slanted toward someone's agenda. After seven months of receiving requests that I go on camera with a statement, I finally decided the time was right.

Maybe I found a little strength to fight back. Maybe I was fed up. Or just maybe I thought I could make a difference. Despite whatever political side one assumes, my point was to magnify that our brave volunteer military deserved the support of the American people. Our soldiers live and die in harm's way, so they should be supported for their selfless sacrifices. We, as the Americans they fight to protect, ought to have their backs, because most certainly they have ours. It's not a partisan decision. Fewer than 1 percent of our nation serves the other 99 percent. The men and women of our military fight not only for us but also for global peace and democracy. Being in a military community, we constantly heard inspiring stories from our friends in combat and the real positive changes that were taking place as a result of their efforts. On the home front, military supporters' heartfelt, patriotic acts of support were making a difference. But did the average American ever hear any of those stories?

The turning point in my patience happened one fall day in 2007. Another viewing of the insurgents' footage of Troy's body was released on the Internet, and the local Phoenix newspapers ran antiwar articles. The very same day, the children and I happened to receive a very special delivery, six very beautiful handmade quilts that had been crafted from Troy's clothing by the delicate elderly hands of a nearby town's quilting group. The newspaper reporters came to my house to cover the sweet story. The story ran in that small-town paper, but it never ran in the Phoenix paper as the story about the Al Jazeera footage had. To me, that just meant that bad news made headlines long before good news ever did. And that meant letting the enemy win. Troy did not let that happen on the battlefield, so I certainly was going to do my part to prevent that from happening in my own land.

I'm not sure how I thought I could singlehandedly reverse the cycle of negative media, but if I could succeed at doing it for just one moment, that was enough. I read my statement and finally gave the media the interview they'd been asking for since Troy's death. It was just a small local event, but a few days later it caught the eye of television journalist Bill O'Reilly. Already incensed about the latest Medal of Honor recipient's story being announced on the very back pages of the *New York Times*, he was looking for similar stories of combat heroism that weren't making headlines and invited me to appear on his program. Troy always loved watching O'Reilly's show, so I knew he would have been pleased for me to step out of my comfort zone and appear on that particular program.

Moving forward in the fight against negativity in our own home, Jim, I, and our children decided to start a "thankful jar" for our family, which was a tradition Andrea and Jim had practiced before. Sitting on our kitchen counter, the jar contains slips of blank paper and pens for each family member to jot down something God did for them that day or week. Reading the slips of paper at a later date or when facing new difficulties, we can remember God's faithfulness, answered prayers, and blessings. We reminded the kids that our thankful jar's contents would serve as a way to recognize God as the One giving them goodness, and not attribute it to themselves.

> Therefore, since we are receiving a kingdom that cannot be shaken, let us be thankful and so worship God acceptably, with reverence and awe. (Hebrews 12:28 NIV)

Back in 2007, I needed to understand what God was asking me to do with regard to being thankful in the midst of my nightmare. Was He asking me to be thankful for the fact that He had taken Troy? Well, I simply couldn't do that. Was I disobeying God by not thanking Him? As I studied the scriptures, I realized He was asking me to be thankful not *for* all circumstances but *in* all circumstances. So, each day after Troy died, no matter how mad at God I was, I always told Him thanks for something. Suffice it to say, even on the worst day, there was always something I could find to thank Him for. However, I found it quite difficult to reconcile my thoughts about the video propaganda. It seemed to be the highest form of cruelty and disrespect to human life, to my beloved heroic husband. Not to mention, how was I as a mom ever to keep the kids from researching and finding that footage someday? I needed to protect them. I also needed to model forgiveness for them. Many days I had to seek the Lord's help to obey His words to forgive, because I simply couldn't do it on my own.

> For if you forgive men when they sin again you, your heavenly Father will also forgive you. But if you do not forgive men their sins, your Father will not forgive your sins. (Matthew 6:14–15 NIV)

God provides me perspective, and I seek His help to forgive. Through Him, I've found that forgiveness actually lies more between God and me than between al-Qaeda and me. It lies between you and God more than between you and your offender. Sometimes, God allows us to see that He does take what was meant to harm us and use it for good.

But Joseph said to them, "Don't be afraid. Am I in the place of God? You intended to harm me, but God intended it for good to accomplish what is now being done, the saving of many lives." (Genesis 50:19–20 NIV)

Do not be deceived, my dear brothers. Every good and perfect gift is from above, coming down from the Father of the heavenly lights, who does not change like shifting shadows. (James 1:16–17 NIV)

Being confident of this, that He who began a good work in you will carry it on to completion until the day of Christ Jesus. (Philippians 1:6 NIV)

Jim

Not to us, O Lord, not to us but to Your name be the glory, because of Your love and faithfulness. (Psalm 115:1 NIV)

Shortly after we were married, Ginger told me that she finally felt happy—the first time in a long time. I told her I finally felt normal again. Losing a spouse involves much more than the initial blow of the loss. Andrea and I had done our best to adjust to cancer and make our life normal as it could be, but I had forgotten what simply living was like.

Then it hit me one day as I was coming home from work and I called Ginger to ask if I needed to pick anything up from the store. My life suddenly had a new sense of normalcy. I got up for work, took Anthony to school, and came home to Ginger, who was cooking dinner and doing things around the house.

Strangely it was the fact that my life with Ginger was wonderful that seemed to be the hardest thing for me to accept. I learned that this response was the result of survivor's guilt, which is fairly common. My survivor's guilt made the first year of our marriage bumpy at times. Ginger, who had experienced over twelve months of loneliness before we met, had dealt with her loss and was ready to move forward. On the other hand, I went from loss to joy in a matter of months. I learned that I did not have the time to grieve Andrea's death before I met Ginger. I know I did a lot of adjusting to losing Andrea during our four years of fighting cancer, but I hadn't taken that final step. As a result, my life was mixed with joy from having Ginger and the kids in my life and sadness and guilt for feeling that joy. I never doubted that God had brought us together as a family. I just never thought that being happy and living a "normal" life was going to be so difficult to adjust to.

So much of my identity had been found in who I was with Andrea and the engrossing life we had of fighting her cancer together. When that ended, I felt like I was standing in the front row of a concert venue with the music suddenly silenced. I could still hear the music ringing in your ears, but when I looked around, I discovered that everyone who had been standing next to me left without my realizing it. Life suddenly made no demands of me. I did not realize how consuming the battle had been until the battle was over. And the silence only reminded me of the price that was paid. Thankfully, God used Ginger to take away the silence and the emptiness of my life without Andrea. I had been loved the best any man could for almost twenty-five years with Andrea, but this was different. I never expected to feel loved again, because I did not think it was possible. It is not that Ginger's love is better or purer than what I had before in my life; it is just different. I had found in Ginger someone like Andrea whom I could trust with my feelings without fear of being hurt or taken advantage of. I also went into my new marriage with a greater appreciation for each moment. Since I knew only God could have brought us together, I knew that everything else would fall into place. The kids, all seven, were also part of this plan. This miracle was not for just Ginger and me, exclusively for our happiness, but it included each of us. I trusted God, knowing He would work out the details. I found a deeper understanding of God's greater plan.

Family picture of the whole "Gilbert/Ravella
Clan," San Antonio TX, December 2015

So as I drove home from the store that day, my life was vastly different, although it was also back to the way it had been before cancer. I could not help but reflect on all that had happened in my life. I turned down the radio and listened to the silence, not just the silence in the car but also the silence of life. There was no trial, no life-and-death pressure. Life was just normal. I listened for God to direct my next steps as I turned the page of a whole new chapter in my life.

Chapter 10 *Discussion Guide*

1. Ginger mentions the difference between being thankful IN all circumstances and not FOR all circumstances. Have you seen anyone demonstrate this in your life and what impact did it have on you and others?

2. If you're not already thankful IN all your circumstances, especially the most difficult ones, what are some tangible ways you can train yourself to shift your focus?

3. A thankful heart often produces a life of hope. Do you agree with that statement? If you do, how do think that happens?

Chapter 11

Surrender

Embrace the life God has given you.

In your heart you plan your life. But the Lord decides where your steps will take you.

—Proverbs 16:9 (NIRV)

Jim

Two days before Andrea passed, I was writing in my journal in the ICU. Across the room sat Andrea's nurse Irma, who was typing notes into the computer. As Andrea was sleeping, I asked Irma, "What do you think about faith, hope, and God's will for Andrea?" We talked for a while. Before she left the room, she said, "The presence of the Lord is in this room. I don't know what He has to say, but He is here." It was one of the few times I was alone with Andrea in her ICU room. Unsure what to do, I got up and knelt at Andrea's bed. As I prayed, this verse came to my mind:

> While Jesus was still talking to the crowd, his mother and brothers stood outside, wanting to speak to him. Someone told him, "Your mother and brothers are standing outside, wanting to speak to you." He replied to him, "Who is my mother, and who are my brothers?" Pointing to his disciples, he said, "Here are my mother and my brothers. For whoever does the will of my Father in heaven is my brother and sister and mother." (Matthew 12:46–50 NIV)

In my spirit, I felt that the Lord had come to be with His daughter, as if He were standing at the foot of her bed. This was a meeting between the Creator and his creation, between Andrea and her God. I had no claim on her as a husband. Earthly relationships were not important in that moment. Andrea was created to worship Him, praise Him, serve Him, and bring glory to Him. I could not stand in the way of that.

My relationship with Andrea was a blessing and a gift, but it was not the reason for which she was created. In that moment, I didn't even worry about whether she would be healed or not. There was something far greater going on. When I arose, my burden was lifted. Andrea was fulfilling God's purposes. That was all I really needed to understand, so I didn't need to worry. Christ was preparing a place for her. Even though her vital signs indicated that she was not completely present in that hospital room, I have no doubt she was meeting with her Greatest Love, and it was not me.

> As for man, his days are like the grass; as a flower of the field, so he flourishes. When the wind has passed over it, it is no more; and its place acknowledges it no longer. But the loving kindness of the Lord is from everlasting to everlasting on those who fear Him, and his righteousness to children's children, to those who keep His covenant, and who remember His precepts to do them. The Lord has established His throne in the heavens; and his sovereignty rules over all. (Psalm 103:15–19 NIV)

Ginger

Life can be consuming and chaotic, but sometimes God calls us to swim farther out into deeper waters to exercise the spiritual muscles He has provided us through the storms of life. Jim and I have a running joke that within seconds of sitting on the toilet, one of the kids is calling our name or knocking on our door, like there is some kind of transmitter connected to the kids' rooms. Whenever I tell anyone how many children we have, the guaranteed reply is, "My, you have your hands full." I nod and smile politely, but I think sarcastically, *Oh, really? I hadn't noticed.*

I've teased my children, saying that finding out I was pregnant with the twins while still having three little kids under foot sent me into therapy. At times there is more truth behind that statement than I would like to think. Having two babies at the same time is a challenge for most anyone. Years earlier, when Troy and I were discussing having another baby, we knew that having four small children would be taxing because we had seen many of our friends do it. We thought our family would feel crowded, but we also felt it would be complete. I remember that just weeks after I took the pregnancy test, Troy looked over at me and said, "I think you're having twins. You're getting bigger sooner than you did before." At the time, I thought that might be the craziest thing in the world that could happen to us and promptly told him he was nuts. No way were we having twins. The day we went to the ultrasound, I was the one who was shocked and crying uncontrollably when the technician announced, "It's twins!" Then followed a difficult pregnancy, five weeks of bedrest and a caesarean section. But then those two perfect little angels arrived and made our family complete.

When the twins were six months old, Troy said good-bye to his new baby girls. As it would turn out, they would never know their father. When Aspen and Annalise were toddlers, they were looking at a snow globe with Troy's picture inside. They exclaimed, "Look at the boy!" They had no idea who he was. It broke my heart.

More than once in those months following Troy's death, I locked myself in my room when the twins were crying because exhaustion and emotions rendered me unable to care for them well. My grief counselor told me I suffered from not only posttraumatic stress disorder but also postpartum depression and delayed bonding. As much as I hated to admit it, I think her diagnosis had some validity.

I journaled this around the time the twins were two: "It's been work, but the twins and I are building and strengthening the natural bonds between mother and child. They need to know they can trust me, and I need to trust God will give me the strength I need for each new day." I often turned to my own mother when I felt defeated and discouraged with how the process with the twins was coming along. That is when she read to me a passage from one of my favorite books, *Streams in the Desert*. I cried when she read the following:

> I longed to leave the common daily toil,
> Where no one seemed to understand or care.
> But Jesus said, "I choose for you this soil,
> that you might raise for Me some blossoms rare. [16]"

Aspen and Annalise are my blossoms rare. They are blonde-haired, blue-eyed identical twin girls who were never meant to know their biological father in the way most children do. All of their childhood memories will be of Jim being their father. He has now chosen to love, nurture, and father them in the ways Troy wasn't given the chance to do. The longer I live, the more I see that my God specializes in the rare. I see the twins together and observe a bond that goes beyond mere sisterhood. They share a room, sleep in the same bed, are in the same class at school, and do sports and pretty much everything else together. After I put them to bed, they *still* stay up talking and giggling. They have always been there for one another from the beginning. The nights when I didn't have the emotional and physical strength to care for them the way I had cared for the others—the time before depression and grief gripped me—God knew they were going to need each other. And in that, I realized their particular story was not about me at all—it was about them. Having Aspen and Annalise was nothing about what I needed and everything about what they needed. Each of my children has a separate journey, a unique ministry in their own circle, and their own story that must be told from their own perspective—all of which will compel others to have hope and know Christ. To find peace to the answers we seek, we must first realize that this life is not all about us.

> The fear of the Lord is the beginning of wisdom. (Proverbs 9:10 NIV)

---

[16] Lettie Cowman, *Streams in the Desert* (Grand Rapids, MI: Zondervan, 2008), 339.

Jim

When I think of surrender, I think in military terms. The battle has been raging on, and one side is hopelessly out of food or ammunition. Surrendering is not what they want to do, but they have no other choice. The other force is far superior. That is what I felt like on January 7, 2008, a particularly difficult day, as I tried to put words to the way I was feeling inside:

> I picked up Andrea's death certificates and removed her from the military system as my wife. I officially become a single parent in the eyes of the military. I'm sitting down, with the folder of the death certificates by my side. They are very official looking; they freeze in time a life once lived, now gone. They capture the facts of December 17, 2007, in unfeeling words, the smooth, cold paper only adding to the insensitivity of the words typed on the page. Immediate cause of death: respiratory failure, twenty-three days. Condition leading to the cause listed: metastatic breast cancer, four years. I'm struck that only the cancer gets recognized in the end, its final victory emblazoned forever by the state of Texas. No mention of who she was, what she meant, her family, her accomplishments, her faith, her laughter, her unending love for me and the boys. There is no block to check on these things, no scale to rate how much she meant to us. Those are left for us to carry on. Andrea June Ravella, age forty-five. Surviving spouse: James J. Ravella.

That sums it up, one of us deceased and one of us surviving.

Funny, when I read that word *surviving*, it seemed to capture what it's like after losing someone. You're not exactly living or loving, not going or growing—just surviving. You eat to survive. You sleep to survive. But I looked forward to living and not just surviving. I longed to find my purpose. In the end, my faith came down to trust, and I had to decide whether or not I truly trusted God. Once I made that decision, I received a new sense of purpose and finally started living again.

Faith is required whenever we seek God's will in our lives, but trust is needed when the answer to our prayers is not what we asked for. It is then that God looks at us in silence and waits for us to trust Him. He uses the time to see if we believe what we profess. He causes us to ponder if we only desire to embrace the gifts of the cross but flee from its requests of us.

This was Andrea's example to me: she had faith that could truly move a mountain. She had faith in the healing, but her trust was not tied to the outcome of her cancer. That is how she went back to chemo week after week and faced scan after scan. Each unfavorable outcome caused us to question the God she sought relief from. Yet there was a trust between Andrea and her Father that was built upon the God she had known nearly her entire life through countless hours of reading God's Word and spending time in prayer. It was a trust built upon a relationship started in a little girl about six years old standing at the altar of a small church on Thirty-Third Street in Wichita Falls, Texas. When God sent His Spirit to indwell the once little girl, she learned at an early age to trust Him always, which was expressed early in our marriage when we prayed for assignments. Andrea told her dad, "We are praying for a specific assignment, but if we don't get it, then we know God has something better for us." Those are seemingly simple words, but they paint a beautiful picture of having the faith to ask while also having the trust to accept whatever the outcome.

All of these memories triggered a concept that made much more sense to me—those of us who knew and loved Andrea carry the essence of the strength of her testimony. We carry her "life certificates." Her death certificates are for the official business of life, but her life certificates can actually change the way we live. Andrea's extraordinary example of faith and her rare example of trust are stamped on all those who were blessed to have met her. As I sat and looked over her death certificates, I felt God tell me the following words about trust. I typed as fast as the words came to me.

> I want you to fully enjoy the blessings of the cross. Its promises are true and its gifts are sure. But I also don't

want you to flee from what the cross asks of you. I do not ask anything more of you for your salvation than your faith in what was done on the cross. But I will ask of you to show your trust in Me so that I may reach others. Allow Me to bless you through the cross. Allow Me to grow you through life's difficulties. Enjoy the rewards of your faith, but don't flee from Me when I ask you to trust Me. You can do this when I abide in you. Andrea was small for a reason; I used her apparent weakness in the world's view to put an exclamation point on her example. I have plans to prosper you and not harm you. Do you trust those words? That is the question I have for you today. Think before you answer. I need people with faith, but more than that I need those who trust Me to be My witness. Will you trust me? If you take this step, you will find I will give you all you need. If you take this step and move from faith into trust, I will send you opportunities to show this trust to others. For there are so many in need of this lesson. There will be hard times, unanswered prayers, and events you do not understand. I will challenge you to move your relationship with Me from one built on receiving from Me to one built on laying yourself down for Me. I know this may scare you, but do you trust Me? Life will be difficult, not because I don't love you or have left you—far from it. I send trials so you can be all that I have planned for you, so you will realize the reason and purpose for which I spoke you into existence. Out of your faith, which can only be proven of worth in a trial, you will be fulfilled because you will be living in My will. And trust Me, there is nowhere else you would rather be. If you only knew what awaited, you would seek this with all your heart. If you knew fully what I have for you, there would be no need for faith or trust. I could reveal it all, but I choose not to. Do you trust Me that this is right? I'm asking you to believe and trust by faith. There is nowhere else you will feel such joy—not just happiness, but pure joy, free from circumstances and free from conditions. Then you will feel the comfort in the shadow of My wings. There you will feel the peace that surpasses all understanding. There you will find Me. You will shine to a world searching frantically for peace and happiness. The world is not looking for the answer to be found in Me, but you will point them to Me, because you will be "strange" to the world. You will be unexplainable. You will be like Andrea. People were drawn to her for reasons they did not understand. That was Me they saw. That was Me using a willing daughter to help others. That is My power made perfect in her weakness. Did you see it? Did you get a glimpse of who I am? I was shouting through Andrea's silence in the ICU. I was seen through her smiles in the chemo room. I was trying to get your attention through her gentle yet strong acceptance of the race I laid out for her. Do not be deceived. She was not forgotten, and I held her in My hand every step of the way. Now allow yourself the fulfillment of drinking from the well of Living Water. Allow yourself to experience My love in suffering or disappointment, for the words *suffering* and *disappointments* are fleeting. They cannot transcend to eternity; they will be left behind. Allow them to take you closer to Me and to eternal things. But you will have to first know Me, and then trust the One you know and not what you may see or experience. I know this is hard; did not My own Son struggle in the garden? But did He not choose what was eternal over what was temporary? Allow yourself to fall back in faith, trusting I will catch you. Won't you come to Me? Won't you allow Me to show you how great I truly am, how far above your thoughts and expectations I am, how deep and wide and tall My love is for you? Won't you allow me to show you the depth of love I expressed in My Son's death? Allow yourself to see My love for Andrea in her death. Yes, she is gone from you, but her example still tugs at you. It still calls to you because that is My voice you are hearing. I love you. I only desire you to see the truth of the world you live in, that it is just a flash, a vapor in the wind. There is a truth that exists beyond what you see, feel, taste, and touch. This truth is unseen yet so real. But you can only experience it by trusting Me when life's inevitable challenges come. Let your faith be your shield and the Word be your sword as you fight life's challenges.

Ginger

Each year at Easter, we celebrate Christ's victory over the grave as we scurry around stuffing jelly beans in plastic eggs, glazing the perfect ham, and making sure the hair bows all match the dresses. However, when we step back for a moment, we remember that Easter represents the foundation of the Christian faith. Good Friday and Resurrection Sunday both give us the ultimate answer to the question, "How can a fallible, sinful human being ever be invited to live with a flawless, sinless King?" At Easter, we receive the invitation to outdo all invitations. Can't you just picture it? Elegant calligraphy penned by the Master Himself on the finest of linen paper, brilliant white, to represent His purity. Signed in red with His own blood. Edged with a thin line of gold to hint at the glamour of the event's destination—heaven.

Have you ever just longed to be invited to that most special of events? When Troy and I were first married, we became friends with a group of people pretty far above our income bracket. They were young and newly married like us, but they were without any financial restrictions, always attending some sort of gala, ball, or fancy charity fund-raiser. They had the prestige and money to be "worthy" of the invitation. In my mind, they were in the favored position in society. Nonetheless, we were all friends, and occasionally they put us on the invitation list to the best parties in town. I longed for these invitations, as they made me feel included with the in-crowd. Troy was a good sport about going, although he didn't get caught up in popularity contests. I fretted over what to wear, whom we would talk to, and if we would feel out of place at the country club venue. Troy *worked* at the country club, and I *worked* for an interior design firm. The people we would be mixing with were our customers, not our peers. We knew how to fit into pretty much any social setting, but would someone question why we deserved to be at one of these swanky parties? While we ended up having a nice time, all I specifically remember was how desperately I tried to fit in. Isn't it wonderful that Christ's invitation, sent straight from the cross to us, isn't wrought with social implications and segregations? We are all invited, no matter where we come from or what we've done.

My precious friend Tami, the wife of our Phoenix pastor, always had a copy of the latest *Our Daily Bread* devotional in her purse or car. She encouraged me to read the short daily lessons when I didn't have the time or energy for much else—a "snack" in terms of Bible study. But all of us frazzled busy moms out there will take whatever spiritual vitamin we can get our hands on. On Easter Sunday, I grabbed one of these devotionals as I was leaving church. It was titled "Taking the Cross."

> He who does not take his cross and follow after Me is not worthy of Me. (Matthew 10:38 NIV)

> The cross. We see it today as the rough wooden instrument of death for Jesus Christ. But before His followers had even a faint idea that Jesus would die that way, He spoke of the cross. The men didn't associate the cross with Jesus' approaching death, but they knew what a cross signified. Crucifixions were a common method of execution. The disciples had a vivid picture of the agony, punishment, and misery that the cross represented. So why was Jesus promoting cross bearing? Because He wanted disciples who were willing to face the difficulties it would take to serve His cause. That's still our challenge today. Are we willing to take the cross and serve Christ in self-denial? The task is great—but it is eternally rewarding.[17]

>> Then He said to them all: "If anyone would come after me, he must deny himself and take up his cross daily and follow me. (Luke 9:23 NIV)

> He wasn't saying that we must all be crucified. The cross to which He was referring is the act of putting to death our own heart's desires [and dreams, I would add] and quietly

---

[17]   Dave Branon, "Taking the Cross," *Our Daily Bread*, March 29, 1997, https://odb.org/1997/03/29/taking-the-cross/, accessed January 20, 2017.

submitting to God's will [whether or not it makes sense, I would add]. Such dying is denying our earthly wants for more heavenly needs. It's easy to think if we only had larger homes, bigger bank accounts, more compliant children, more accommodating mates and were in the picture of perfect health, then dedication to God would be easier. Such dying is accepting unchangeable circumstances, unthinkable horrors, lack of physical healing or safety in the skies. Such dying is loving despite misunderstandings, hurts and broken relationships. Such dying is walking forward without your life's partner into a lonely world with only your children by your side. The devotion says. "Jesus said we must take up our cross daily. We are to rise each morning and cheerfully [not easy, Lord! I would add], bravely [even less easy, Lord! I would add] shoulder our load, because there is something else that is 'daily.' It is the continuous, sufficient grace of the One whose strength is made perfect in our weakness."[18]

Each of us has or will have our own cross to carry. Our prayer should be that God would give us the strength not only to carry it for the journey but also to willingly accept the burden of it. This is, of course, not possible if we are relying on our strength. But when we call on His strength, it absolutely is.

> I pray that out of his glorious riches he may strengthen you with power through his Spirit in your inner being. (Ephesians 3:16 NIV)

When I was nine years old and accepted Christ's gift of salvation, I had no idea what it would mean to take up my cross. Even if I could have imagined it would involve such a burdensome load as the one I was given twenty-seven years later, I, as a child, had total confidence that I would not go through anything alone. I knew Jesus would help me. It was a simple faith, and that simple faith was what I needed to

---

[18] Bill Crowder, "Dying to Live," December 28, 2007, *Our Daily Bread*, https://odb.org/2007/12/28/dying-to-live/, accessed January 20, 2017.

fall back on as an adult. Jesus had helped me through from the time when I had playground squabbles with my friends all the way through the loss of Troy and beyond. That promise was exactly what Jim and I told some new friends over dinner, after years of learning what it meant to surrender to God.

Our guests were Sarah and Brad Sullivan, part of our tight-knit F-16 Air Force community and the unifying body of Christ. They didn't know Troy or me, but they had prayed for me and the kids when they heard the news of Troy's crash while they were stationed in Korea. Now it was my turn to cry out to God on their behalf. Brad and Sarah, high school sweethearts, were newly stationed in San Antonio and beginning their life together as husband and wife. They hadn't even moved into their new home before Sarah found out she was expecting their first child. That same week, she was told she had stage II breast cancer.

Joy and sorrow. Excited expectation and disappointing dread.

As soon as Jim and I heard about them, we wanted to meet them to help them in any way we could. But we wondered whether they would be encouraged by us. Would we give them hope? Would we give them fear? We just wanted to love on them and encourage them, but they ended up teaching us more than we taught them. Sarah was already thinking of ways she could minister to those whom she knew she would be in treatment with. This is an incomprehensible thought to the world. But the world doesn't understand that her strength is not her own. Her strength comes from the Maker of heaven and earth.

Picking up her cross, Sarah entered the chemo room for the first time with their unborn baby still tucked inside of her. Brad stood next to her, praying for many miracles and asking that God would give her the strength to carry the baby, carry the cancer, and carry the cross He had asked her to carry. Everything in the world that was precious to him sat in that La-Z-Boy.

Months later, their precious baby girl, Chloe, was born unharmed from the chemo, perfect in every way. Tragically and very unexpectedly just two weeks later, Sarah died of a brain aneurism. The doctors speculated that the chemo had somehow weakened her blood vessels. She left behind Brad to raise their baby girl on his own. Pilot families did their best to love on him, but now he had to take up his own cross. Brad later met and married a widow, Jenny, and became the father of her children. She is now the mother of sweet Chloe. Together they also have a baby boy, Drew. This is another story of yours, mine, and ours, but ultimately it is a story of another family belonging to Jesus and following Him despite the cumbersome cross they have been asked to carry.

Each of us has or will have our own cross to carry someday. Our prayer should be not only that God would give us the strength to carry it but also that we will pick it up in the first place. Sometimes that point of decision is the where the rubber meets the road in our walks with Him. In Matthew, scripture tells us that even Jesus, knowing God's perfect plan and desiring to do the will of His Father, became "sorrowful and troubled" when thinking of the trial of suffering, humiliation, and agonizing pain God was asking Him to endure at the cross.

> Then He [Jesus] said to them [His disciples], "My soul is overwhelmed with sorrow to the point of death. Stay here and keep watch with me." Going a little farther, He fell with His face to the ground and prayed, "My Father, if it is possible, may this cup be taken from me. Yet not as I will, but as You will." (Matthew 26:38–39 NIV)

We can rest in the fact that Jesus paved the way before us. The deep groove in the road was carved out by the heavy weight of the cross He carried so we would have a clear path on which to carry our own. I picture Him walking with us, lifting the weight a little, and stopping when we stop, willing us to go on.

> "Never will I leave you; never will I forsake you." So we say with confidence, "The Lord is my helper; I will not be afraid. What can man do to me?" (Hebrews 13:5–6 NIV)

Chapter 11 *Discussion Guide*

1. How do you feel about the subject of prayer? The Bible says that prayer enlightens our eyes, renews our minds and transforms our lives.
   Reference:
   Romans 12:2-12
   Jeremiah 29:12
   Ephesians 1:18
   I John 5:14

2. Are there things you can be doing to strengthen your faith and give you a solid foundation to prepare you for the trials ahead?

3. The Greek word *"Kenosis"* is defined as self-emptying of one's personal will to be become entirely receptive to God's divine will. Jesus exemplified the ultimate act of kenosis on the Cross. Can you think of a time in your life that you have poured out your own will and desires and allowed God's will to fill you?

Chapter 12

Lost and Found

The memory of the righteous is blessed.
—Proverbs 10:7 (NKJV)

Jim

Memories can bring a smile or a tear when you have lost someone. A simple song can remind me of an exact moment with Andrea. There have been so many songs I can recall listening to over those years of battling cancer that expressed words when I was unable. Sometimes one would help me refocus my eyes on God. I think the most incredible thing about the power of music is it lets you know that someone else understands what you're going through. When Andrea was really sick, I would wake up on Saturday mornings, go into our office, and put Brooks and Dunn's "Believe" on repeat. When I hear that song now, I can see myself in our old house and feel the emotions of that time. For me, touching something that belonged to Andrea always has the power to awaken a memory.

From the day I met Andrea at the stoplight to the day I saw Ginger for the first time in her mom's Toyota 4Runner, I have often correlated cars to major events in my life. When Andrea and I returned from our tour in Turkey, we needed a second car. I remember the day she saw the brand new, metallic blue, 2000 Toyota Highlander at the dealership in Goldsboro, North Carolina and how much she loved it. She looked at me with her beautiful smile and asked if we could buy it. How could I say no? Sixteen years later it has quite a few scratches, some dents, and lots of miles—but most of all, a million memories. When Andrea passed away, I gave the car to Nic. When I go to visit Nic I always look forward to him picking me up in that Highlander. Hanging from the visor is a chain that Andrea put there. It's like a time capsule of memories for me. I feel closer to Andrea when I sit in that car. I can close my eyes and see her in it, smiling back at me with her beautiful blue eyes. That car matched her eyes.

There was one specific meaningful moment that occurred as we were driving home from Duke Hospital one spring day. Andrea heard of a new chemo drug that was having amazing results, so we had driven up to see if she could be in the treatment trial. I will never forget the young female doctor telling Andrea that she did not qualify to be in her drug trial because she had been on too many other chemo medicines. The doctor said, "I feel terrible because I have the power to save your life, but I can't." Can you imagine a doctor telling a patient with terminal cancer those words? Andrea responded, "It's okay. Don't feel bad. You don't control whether I live or die; only God controls that." On the drive home, I remember looking at Andrea singing along to a worship song, her eyes closed and her hands raised to God. Andrea's faith did not waver, not even when it seemed we had come so close to finding a cure for her, a cure she had researched, sought out, and prayed for. Sadly, I cannot say my faith was as strong. I was angry on the drive back home. Andrea wasn't angry at all. A few days later, that young doctor called Andrea and said, "I can't forget what you said to me. Regardless of what drugs you've taken, I will get you into the trial." Andrea had once again reminded me, above all else, to trust God no matter what.

For anyone who has lost someone or is separated from a loved one, you know how it feels to touch something they touched. Even the littlest things make you feel their presence in some small way. That is the feeling I have when I get in Andrea's old car, and it's the feeling I wanted Ginger and the kids to experience. In the summer of 2015, Ginger was speaking at a fund-raising event at the home of our dear friends Anne and Perry Schmidt. Country star Lee Brice was giving a private concert for about two hundred people to benefit Folds of Honor, a nonprofit organization dedicated to providing educational scholarships to the spouses and children of soldiers killed or disabled in service to the United States. Lee sang his hit "I Drive Your Truck," a song about the family member of a fallen soldier who deals with his loss by driving his old pick-up truck. Ginger told Lee how much music, and this song in particular, expressed what many families could not find the words to say. Ginger then went on to tell about a truck Troy owned and traded in about three months before he deployed. The truck first belonged to Troy's dad, who passed it down to Troy. It was a special truck, but it had gotten old, wasn't very reliable and most of all was impossible to put kids and multiple car seats in. They decided it was time to let it go. Later that year, Troy was killed in Iraq. Ginger said that at the time, she never imagined her very young children being old enough to drive. But years later, when she had two teenage boys driving, she expressed to Lee how much she wished she had that old truck back for her sons. It was a passing comment, but it was one that resonated with Lee, with his manager, Enzo, the Schmidts and a gentleman in the audience named Josh. But most of all, with me.

Troy with Boston and Greyson dove hunting in the
1992 Chevy Silverado truck, Arizona, 2005

Later that month, without Ginger knowing, the search for the truck began. I was able to get the vehicle identification number (VIN) from Troy's dad, and soon we were able to track the truck to an oil change station in Phoenix. I called the oil change facility and asked for the manager. Once I explained the situation, I asked if he could tell me who owned the truck. He looked it up in the system and surprisingly told me the truck's owner was a friend of the station's owner! I thought to myself, *This is the easiest detective work in the world.* He told me he would go talk to her and ask if she would be willing to sell the truck. When he called me back and described the truck, a 2002 blue Chevy, I was confused. I told him I was looking for a 1992 dark red Chevy. It turned out the VIN number did not match the one of the truck I was looking for. Someone typed in the wrong license plate number, and the system had mixed up the VINs. I was crushed at this dead end and thought we would never find the truck. I began to wonder, even if I did find it, what the odds were that it would still be drivable. It was probably in a junkyard or had been sold as scrap.

Five months later, Josh (the kind man at the event) called me and said he had a possible address in Phoenix for the truck. He was pretty sure this was Troy's truck. After getting my hopes up before, I was still a little skeptical. I called a friend in Phoenix, Kevin (Anne Schmidt's brother), to go drive by the address for me and see if there was a dark red Chevy truck at the house. Kevin called and told me there was a truck there and that the VIN matched. (We were all becoming detectives now!) I asked him to go back and see if the owners would sell it. It was in really rough condition but still ran. After confirming that it was, in fact, Troy's old truck, and after some serious weeks of negotiating, Perry Schmidt flew to Phoenix, went to the house with Kevin, and bought the truck.

I immediately called Lee Brice's manager, Enzo, and told him the good news. We began planning how to present the truck to Ginger and the kids. Enzo arranged a surprise presentation at the Academy of Country Music Awards, where Lee would be playing at an event called "Party for a Cause." I had planned on getting the truck restored first, but the event was only three weeks away. We decided to ship the truck to Vegas. Perry called a trucking company. When the people at the trucking company heard the story, they said they would ship the truck for free because they were veterans themselves. Ginger and the kids were still completely in the dark. I told her that she and the kids were all needed in Vegas to accept a donation check on behalf of Folds of Honor, the charity we have both been involved with for years. The plan was in place for the truck to be hidden way back behind the stage, covered with a tarp, and for Lee to bring Ginger and the kids up during his concert and give it to them.

When the day arrived, I did sneak out early to get a look at the truck myself. When I got inside it, I wept as I ran my hands over the steering wheel, much like I did when I would sit behind the wheel of Andrea's car. This time I wasn't crying for the wife and mother I lost; I was crying for the husband and father Ginger and the kids lost.

Lee Brice surprises Ginger and the kids with Troy's truck at the Academy of Country Music Awards, Las Vegas, 2016

Lee Brice, Ginger, and the kids with Troy's truck

As I watched the presentation of the truck from backstage, I could tell Ginger was barely able to process Lee's words. I watched as she and the kids were presented with the keys to the truck while 20,000 fans cheered from the audience, holding up American flags and cell phones lights, chanting, "USA! USA!" As the boys exited the stage, I asked them if they realized what had happened. They said, "He gave us a truck like our dad's." I said, "No, he gave you your dad's *actual truck*." It was so much for kids to process.

Lee, Ginger, the kids, a lot of paparazzi, and I walked behind the giant stage. I watched as my family got a small piece of their hearts back as they all climbed into the cab of that old beaten up truck. Greyson had just turned 16 years old and literally had just gotten his driver's license the day before. Earlier that day he told the Schmidts all he really wanted was an old truck. It was all they could do to not give away the big surprise he had ahead of him. Greyson was the first to sit behind the wheel, put the key in and crank up the engine. I watched Ginger cry and knew the sound reminded her of sweet days gone by.

News of the country singer giving a fallen soldier's family back their daddy's truck—all based on his famous song—spread like wildfire at the ACM's. Troy Bundy, who owns Iron Cross Automotive of Tulsa, Oklahoma, offered to restore the truck. In just three weeks, he not only restored the truck but also turned it into a memorial of Troy, complete with Troy's image and jet silhouetted on the tailgate, his call sign, "Trojan", welded into the dash, and his 555 fighter squadron patches stitched into the new leather seats. The dilapidated heap had become a super cool memory of Troy and a third-generation set of wheels. There couldn't have been a more perfect gift. On Memorial Day, Lee presented the pickup truck to Ginger and the kids live on Fox and Friends. As I watched Boston and Greyson drive off in the truck, I knew they felt closer to their Dad in that moment. The truck was finally back home, where it belonged. It was a Memorial Day no one would ever forget.

Ginger

I recently came across a blog post I had written years ago after I received the remnants of Troy's belongings that were scattered across a desert of Iraq the day after his crash. It took over 3 years after his accident for those things to find their way back to me. Here's an excerpt from that post dated March 13, 2009:

> Our Father, who art in heaven,
> hallowed be thy name.
> Thy Kingdom come,
> thy will be done,
> on earth as it is in heaven.
> Give us this day our daily bread.
> And forgive us our debts, as we forgive our debtors.
> And lead us not into temptation,
> but deliver us from evil.
> For thine is the kingdom,
> the power and the glory,
> for ever and ever.
> Amen.
> (Matthew 6:9–13 KJV)

That prayer was all I could think of as I laid my face on a part of Troy's flying gear taken from his crash site, my tears mixing with the dirt from the faraway deserts of Iraq still embedded in the fibers. The dirt is on my fingertips as I type this—the dirt from a farmer's field in a land far away. The dirt that clings to pieces of Troy's crumpled and burned helmet visor cover, the empty face of his watch, his Leatherman, his pilot's kneeboard, his flying notes, and his barely recognizable melted camera. None of it would ever come completely clean. Nor would I ever want it to. That dirt is part of the last things that he touched, which were a part of the last day he lived. I can wish it away. I can wish it all away. But in reality, that Iraqi soil will always be a part of our lives. I hate these things because they truly mark the last second he was alive on this earth. I love these things because they mark the first second he was made whole and joyfully met his Savior.

I'm so thankful for the gift of the efforts of those who hand-carried Troy's final belongings to me, General Rand and Chief Dearduff. They certainly could have shipped them to me but instead wanted to place them in my hands themselves. Kim Rand had a beautiful wooden box and cover made for the transport. It was all very reverent. By their example, I hope I will choose to go the extra mile to do something for someone who needs that mile more than I selfishly need my own. I do not know what I will do with those dirt-covered things found at the crash site, but I know I will hold, especially dear to my heart, the handwritten note that came with his things. It was from the pilot, a friend of Troy's, who searched for hours and found the belongings in the field the next day. I hope to meet this man someday, because his tenderness and kind words ministered to my aching heart. A stranger was there in that distant place, lovingly and carefully taking care of these precious things when I was unable to.

This is the note that I received:

Dear Ginger,

I was blessed to have known Troy and share his company at Balad before he was lost to us forever. I will always selfishly cherish the time I had with him. I was on the scene very early the morning after the crash, spending several hours on-site. My team and I found the special articles in this box, and I will tell you, finding each item was like discovering a treasure connecting us to Troy. Hundreds of soldiers and then marines had spent the previous night searching for Troy and securing the location. The morning was bright and sunny, and the gentle breeze floating across the quiet fields belied the true nature of the location. On that peaceful November morning in 2006, I came across the exact spot where Troy died. I knelt and prayed for him and for you and your beautiful children. I asked God to watch over Troy, to give you strength to deal with your enormous loss, and to be able to endure the difficult days, months, and years ahead. I think of Troy often and periodically visit section 60 [in Arlington National Cemetery] to have a word with Troy. I tell him that I hope he is well and how much we appreciate the sacrifice he made for us so we may live happy and free. Thank you for sharing him with us.

Love,
"Doc"

Only my Father in heaven knows what happened right after Troy's plane went down and his body was taken, probably rolled up in a carpet. However, Troy's family and I still ask for reaffirmation that the search for Troy continues. And each time we ask, the answer is the same. Always. Every lead is followed. No stone is left unturned. "No man left behind" is their motto. I have had to surrender this to our military's hands. I can't physically go to Iraq and hunt for my husband's body. But I can daily lay my requests to the Lord, who knows right where it lays. Those are the loving hands I actually surrender my desires to. Yes, my heart breaks over this. I never imagined having to sit my five children down and tell them their daddy wasn't returning from war. But, by God's strength, I did. Therefore, I know that by that same strength, someday I will explain to them what DNA is and how, for now, that is all we have. I either trust God with everything or trust Him with nothing. I pray every day I will finally see a flag-draped coffin with Troy inside being escorted from across the world by another brother-in-arms. I, like others from wars past, pray my airman will be returned home to this country's soil. I can't understand why God allowed this to ever happen. But I know He has a plan, even in this specific corner of my sorrow.

> Are not five sparrows sold for two pennies? Yet not one of them is forgotten by God. Indeed the very hairs of your head are numbered. Don't be afraid; you are worth more than many sparrows. (Luke 12:6–7 NIV)

Many years have passed since I wrote the blog post about receiving Troy's belongings recovered at the crash site. Many times I have pulled out that box and held those dirt-covered treasures. The feeling is always the same – there's that dirt that I love and hate. The term "losing someone" is very descriptive of what it's like when someone you love is gone. You turn around and look back, and they are suddenly missing. You feel the loss of who they were in your life in varying degrees, depending on your relationship to them. An acquaintance's death may bring pause or reflection. But the passing of a child, a spouse, or a parent leaves a gaping hole in your heart. Yet even in the earliest moments after the tragedy, when the search for Troy's body was going on 24/7, sadly unsuccessfully, I knew that Troy was not missing to God. God did not lose him. He was at the feet of Jesus and in his forever home.

Still, not having his body back always left an opening in the scar that just couldn't quite heal shut. As years passed, once the kids were old enough for me to explain the details of the kidnapping of Troy's body and the unexplainable injustice that befell our family, I could also say with confidence that who their dad was, the part of him we truly knew and loved, was not lost. Not in Iraq. Not anywhere at all. In the realm of heaven, he was found. Troy was Home. I remember singing these famous lyrics my whole life in church: "Amazing grace, how sweet the sound that saved a wretch like me. I once was lost but now am found. Was blind, but now I see."

What I didn't write about in that blog post in March 2009 I want to share here in this closing chapter of our book.

As I mentioned, one of the items I received from the crash site wreckage, was a melted camera Troy apparently had been flying with that fateful day. "Doc" Ellis explained to me that as he dusted off the badly burned and barely recognizable camera he noticed the edge of the memory card inside. He imagined it, too, would be melted into the body of the camera. But as he reached in and pulled it out, he was speechless. The card was completely unharmed and in pristine condition. How could that be? Still skeptical, he took it to the photo lab to see if any images could be pulled from it. There were – photos from the week before the crash. Doc printed them off and included them in the box for me. I carefully thumbed through them, barely able to see from the stinging tears in my eyes. Some I had indeed remembered seeing before – photos he had emailed me – mostly of his jet. But then I stopped. There was a new one. One that quite literally took my breath away. One I'd never seen before. It was a close-up of Troy in his battle gear. It looked as if he had taken it of himself inside the cargo of a plane. Besides how handsome he was, the striking thing was his eyes – a man at war but with total peace in his eyes. Indeed eyes are a window to the soul, and his soul was healthy and whole.

It's probably one of my favorite photos of all time. The fact that it came to me so many years after he was gone was such a gift. The fact that God quite literally saved it from the fire was such a miracle. There's no other explanation for it. Modern day miracles all around me. Over and over again, Christ was showing me He had not forgotten us.

Troy's selfie, taken 1 week before his crash, Iraq 2006

Early September 2016, Jim and I were in the late stages of finishing this book for submission to the publisher. All the while we were traveling for work, speaking as advocates for veteran families, raising a gaggle of kids, watching Greyson play high school football, trekking to Dallas to watch Boston play college soccer. Life was busy but blessedly normal.

It was October 1st, a Saturday morning, and I was at Bella's volleyball tournament. My cell phone rang. It was Jim. His voice sounded strange. I feared something had happened to Boston at college or to my parents. He said he needed to come pick me up. My mind raced with questions and worst-case scenarios. He finally told me that General Rand had called him and told him he needed to talk to me. In this setting, that could only mean one thing—news about Troy. I called General Rand back, and he told me the words we had all been waiting ten years to hear.

They found Troy.

Like so many times in the past, I realized how quickly life shifts from the mundane to the miraculous.

The day prior, September 30, 2016, a joint special operations task force fully recovered Troy's remains, flight suit, flight jacket, and harness.

I cried with stunned tears. I wasn't stunned at all that the Lord *could* do this impossible thing of finding Troy's body in a far away, war-torn country ten years later; I was stunned that the Lord *would* love us so extravagantly that he would allow this to happen at all. After all the ways the Lord provided for us, healing our broken hearts, binding up our wounds, pouring peace into our souls, and providing us with a new husband and father... it was all more than we deserved. Yet, God Himself gave us this final piece of closure. It was grace and mercy beyond understanding. I would later find out some details of the astonishing recovery mission but the one detail that stuck with me the most was to find out that the unit that recovered Troy's remains was the same unit that Troy saved all those years ago.

Ginger telling Greyson that Troy's remains
had been recovered, October 2016

I called Boston, who was away at college, and then called Troy's family to share the miraculous news. We all boarded flights to Dover, Delaware, the next day to meet the cargo plane that was bringing Troy all those miles home. On the runway, we sat in the family section, waiting to see our answered prayer – Troy back on American soil. The sun was quickly setting a beautiful shade of pinkish orange then majestic purple as the minutes passed. We then watched the flag-draped casket being carried out of the plane's cargo hold and down the ramp, carried on the shoulders of fellow soldiers Troy never knew. I was taken aback by how gently and respectfully they moved. Despite the downward slope of the ramp, the pallbearer soldiers shifted their own weight to carry Troy's casket perfectly level. Others in prominent positions in our Air Force; the Secretary of the Air Force, Deborah James, our friends; General Goldfein, Chief of Staff of the Air Force, General Rand, Colonel Pat Ryder, Colonel "Doc" Ellis, Brigadier General Ed Thomas and many others, all stood at attention saluting Troy one final time. Perhaps without the high-level leadership formation, but otherwise this is always how every US soldier who is killed overseas returns to our country. It's called a "dignified transfer." The casket was carefully loaded into the waiting vehicle. I looked over at the diverse group of troops standing at attention, not bound by anything other than the bond of service to our country. Whether or not they knew Troy personally wasn't a factor at all. Troy knew not one person he saved the day he died. That didn't matter either. All that mattered was that he showed up for them on that fateful November day in 2006. And for ten years, so many others showed up for him—faithfully searching, risking their own lives to pay a debt of gratitude. This wasn't the homecoming I planned for the day he deployed. That image was of me and our five little kids standing at the gate of the airport, the twins in their double stroller with a toddler, Bella, standing by, all in pretty red, white and blue dresses. Boston and Greyson holding balloons and handmade posters saying "Welcome Home from Iraq, Daddy!" We never got that homecoming. Now, I am with my almost-grown children on the tarmac of Dover AFB, behind the velvet-roped section for fallen families, looking at a flag-draped coffin instead.

Yet I had peace. I had many answered prayers. I had the assurance that despite Satan's attempts to destroy our family, I had experienced the Lord's healing powers. I had felt the Greatest Love rescue us all.

> "I remain confident of this. I will see the goodness
> of the lord in the land of the living."
> Psalm 27:13 (NIV)

Maj Troy Gilbert's dignified transfer at Dover AFB October 3, 2016

> Greater love hath no man than this; that a man lay
> down his life for his friends. (John 15:13 KJV)

That whole experience reminded me of an event that I witnessed many years ago. I was on a flight back from France, I noticed three small children who were apparently traveling from Africa. I watched as three middle-aged white American women, perhaps nurses or social workers cared for them. One tiny baby with a cleft palate and one with a severe mouth deformity were held in the women's arms. Another small boy looked weak, needing heart surgery. I inquired about the travelers and spoke with a woman who explained that the children were being transported by volunteers called airline ambassadors, who were helping them come to the United States to receive surgery before returning to their families. Many doctors in the United States donate their medical care, hospital, and surgical facilities. Host families house the children until they are well enough to return. France must have been only a stopping point on these travelers' long journey. The small boy, only twenty months old or so, would undergo heart surgery and then recuperate and rehabilitate for six months in the United States before returning to his home. I imagined his mother handing him over to strangers knowing she must trust her beloved to their hands, knowing she wouldn't be able to touch him, hold him, or help him in those moments he needed her. As a mother, she was willing to do whatever it took to help her precious son.

I watched people on the airplane offer to help the women. An older gentleman held the little African baby, walking him up and down the aisle to calm him, and rocking him to sleep. When the boy dropped his pacifier, a young Indian woman in front of me picked it up to hand it back to him. Different people from different corners of the world rallying to help these children. There is mercy left in the world. There is unselfish beauty. If our eyes are always fixed on ourselves or so tightly closed with despair and anger at our own pain, then we will miss these moments. I can't imagine how tired those workers were from the long journey and the heavy responsibility of caring for extremely sick children on a thirty-six-hour flight. The tiny boy woke up a little later. I watched him smiling and touching the man's face. Only hours before, the gentleman and tiny boy were strangers, but now they shared a special bond. I told his wife that I imagined the baby's mother would be very thankful if she knew what strong arms had taken care of her son on this part of the journey to his healing.

I knew how she would feel because I had felt the same—humbly grateful, the heartfelt thankfulness that comes because a stranger walked through a field in the middle of a war to find Troy's things for me. And years later, strangers who did not know Troy risked their lives to recover him and then carefully and respectfully carried him home to us. He was indeed my precious cargo. Love may tear your heart to pieces, but love also puts the pieces back together again.

On December 19, 2016, just days before this book went into editing at the publisher, my children and I once again returned to Arlington

National Cemetery to bury their father, for a final time. Troy is the only person in history to have had three burials at Arlington. It was the holidays yet again and I sat in the pew at the Ft. Myer Memorial Chapel next to my children – children who are now on the brink of adulthood. Children who are no longer small enough to sit in my lap or need to hold my hand, but whose shoulders were now big and strong enough for me to be able to cry on. Children who have overcome the greatest of heartaches and have carried on their father's good name with integrity, humility, gratitude and softly kind hearts. All I have ever wanted them to see is beauty *can* come from ashes. And that being better, *not* bitter, was the only option for us. It was the only outcome their Dad would have insisted on. Surrounded by many of the same beloved people who stood with us the two times before, we watched as his flag-draped casket was carried past our pew. Though surprisingly there were many, probably over one third of the attendees, who never even knew Troy. Ones who simply knew of him and who loved us, the family he left behind, with unexplainable devotion. People who love their country and all it stands for. Lee Brice came to the service, not as a country star but as our friend. He sang the beloved and bittersweet song "Go Rest High on that Mountain." As I listened, I felt waves of every emotion that had encompassed our 10-year journey; sorrow and joy, loss and gain, heartbreak and wholeness. The pew only physically held our five kids and me. There was no room for Jim so he sat directly behind me, but I could still feel his radiating love and support. My shoulders shook as I wept but Jim gently placed his hands on them. We all stood as the casket was carried out and we would begin our long walk behind the caisson back to Troy's final resting place in Section 60 of Arlington National Cemetery. As the children and I walked the winding path, surrounded by old sweeping trees and rolling hills covered in white tombstones laced with Christmas wreaths, I looked back and saw the literal sea of loving supporters following us; at least four hundred people if not more. Dignitaries, celebrities, world leaders, family, friends, and even strangers - all marching together to celebrate the life of one good and godly man. A man who didn't simply one day just decide to be selfless or in one moment opt to make an amazingly heroic decision. They came because Troy was a man who spent his entire adult life making the right, the noble, the kind and the unselfish harder choices in the day-to-day mundane. That's how legacies are made.

Photo Courtesy of M'Kate Photography
Ginger and the children at Troy's final service, Ft. Myer
Memorial Chapel, Arlington December 2016

The beautiful black horses pulling the old carriage came to halt. The skies were blue enough for the missing man F-16 fly-over but grey enough to remember the somberness of the occasion. I listened to Taps played by the uniformed bugler, heard the 21-gun salute so loud in the crisp winter air, felt the weight of the folded flag once again in my arms. But I didn't feel the despair, the hopelessness that encompassed me all those years before at this very same grave. I could look around and see how far God had brought not just us - me, my kids, but also Jim and his boys – both of our broken families. Once again the row in front of the casket only held five chairs. The kids and I sat just like we had twice before. Out of the corner of my eye I caught a glimpse of Jim standing and saluting Troy's casket as the uniformed pallbearers lowered it into the grave. Jim Ravella, Troy's ultimate wingman.

Photo Courtesy of M'Kate Photography

Col Jim Ravella salutes Maj Troy Gilbert at his final burial with Ginger's Dad standing by, Arlington National Cemetery, Dec 19, 2016

Later that night, after the burial, Boston would be handed the miraculously salvaged and meticulously cleaned flight jacket that Troy had been buried in for ten years. Boston slipped it on. It fit him perfectly. The small rips and tears representing untold stories of the time and miles we were separated from that handsome man I'd never stopped loving from that moment I met him in the college cafeteria.

Boston wearing Troy's flight jacket, Washington, DC, December 19, 2016

Every moment of that day had the dew of heaven sprinkled on it. It was a glimpse of Glory. When our time here on earth is over, how many more stories will be told, how many lives intersected, how many revelations, rescues and relationships will be unveiled. I was reminded of another line from "Amazing Grace:" "When we've been there ten thousand years, bright shining as the sun, we've no less days to sing Your praise than when we first begun."

Photo Courtesy of M'Kate Photography
Ginger and the kids' final goodbye to a beloved husband and father

I fully expect that the moment I meet my Savior and see Troy again, timelessness will begin. Troy and Andrea will have been singing for years, but when Jim and I join them, it will be as if no time has passed. The old dirt of this life will be long forgotten. Even when I look back now, I am able to see the hand of God a little more clearly. He was always working on our behalf, even when I thought that maybe He had forgotten us. Sometimes He spoke directly to my soul; other times he provided for me through family and friends. Often He met my needs through the kind acts of complete strangers. He always finds us, doesn't He? Whether we are in a hospital room, on our knees on the floor of our closet, or hidden in the depths of a remote and ravaged country. He's on both sides of the door – with the one who hears the knock and receives the tragic news, as well as with the one on the other side who is giving the news. He's there in the shadows and the valleys. We all feel lost at times, but by the grace of God, hope can be found.

Photo Courtesy of M'Kate Photography

Chapter 12 *Discussion Guide*

1. In the midst of our broken world, where do you see examples of God's love around you? How do you show love to others who are hurting?

2. Troy gave his life to save others. Despite Andrea's failing health, she still loved and served others. How will you view loving others differently after reading Hope Found?

3. How do you view the topics of hope and faith now that you've read about the Gilbert and Ravella families' struggles and stories?

4. What scripture(s) spoke to you about your own personal journey? Why? List them below?

Epilogue

Throughout our story, we have tried to show you our life with all its imperfections, along with our victories, our struggles, and our defeats. We did so because we want you to know that alone we do not have the strength to win any battle or overcome our losses. Tragedy quickly taught us how easily life can overwhelm us. But it also taught us how deep, how wide, and how high the love of God is for us.

Though our respective journeys to loss were different, the endings were the same. All the ups and downs, all the twists and turns, kept leading us back to the same conclusion: God is good and His ways can be trusted. Even though God was the one we wanted to blame and to push away in anger, we learned He was the very one we couldn't go through the fiery furnace without.

> Dear friends, do not be surprised at the fiery ordeal that has come on you to test you, as though something strange were happening to you. But rejoice in as much as you participate in the sufferings of Christ, so that you may be overjoyed when His glory is revealed. (1 Peter 4:12–13 NIV)

Prayers for Troy's safety. Prayers for Andrea's healing. Our prayers were heard, but they were not answered in the way we wanted. Though we still do not fully understand it, we believe that Troy's and Andrea's dying so young and in the ways they did was of eternal necessity.

Over the years, the Lord has proven Himself faithful to us in so many ways that we couldn't begin to recount them all here and now. He gave us tiny graces, gigantic miracles, clear protection, and direction when we needed it most. He is the God of the Universe, and that is all we need to know. Though He didn't need to prove Himself trustworthy, He chose to, out of His love for us.

We are still learning that this life is not about getting what we want but about getting what we need, and what we need is to become more Christ-like until we see Him face-to-face. That goes against what we call the "prosperity gospel," which claims that God will give us everything we want if we believe enough, pray enough, or serve enough.

Sometimes He simply says, "No, My child." How we respond holds the key to the rest of our days on earth.

> Man finds it hard to get what he wants because he does not want the best. God finds it hard to give because He would give the best and man will not take it. (George MacDonald)

We've learned that when life's trials come your way, you have choices. It's okay to get mad at God, feel cheated by God, or feel forgotten by God. He can handle your pouring all of those feelings out to Him. But you have to make a choice not to get stuck there. Choose to trust Him despite your feelings. All the modern-day medical advancements failed to stop that black spot on Andrea's x-ray that ultimately spread and took her life. All the most advanced military might failed to stop Troy's plane from crashing in the Iraq desert. But in the end, God did not let us down. He revealed Himself to us in ways we wouldn't have experienced otherwise. We just had to be willing to see Him through our pain and suffering. God was validated when Andrea and Troy left us with the greatest gift of all: their unwavering faith.

Sometimes you pray into the wee hours of the morning and write this:

> No light is as bright as one shown in total darkness.
> No voice is as loud as one spoken in total silence. (Jim Ravella, January 19, 2012)

Hope Found was written for those who are struggling to find their way out of total darkness and hoping to see a sliver of light, for those who feel God is silent and who long to hear His whisper. Both His light and His voice may seem faint and dim, but we promise that He is there and waiting to meet you in places you never thought possible.

> Are you asking one another what I meant when I said, 'In a little while you will see me no more, and then after a little while you will see me'? Very truly I tell you, you will weep and mourn while the world rejoices. You will grieve, but your grief will turn to joy. A woman giving birth to a child has pain because her time has come; but when her baby is born she forgets the anguish because of her joy that a child is born into the world. So with you: Now is your time of grief, but I will see you again and you will rejoice, and no one will take away your joy. (John 16:19–20 NIV)

There is a promise in this final scripture that has brought much comfort to us, and we offer a heartfelt prayer that it will do the same for you.

Col Jim Ravella USAF (ret) and Ginger Gilbert Ravella, both widows, faced the unthinkable; the loss of their spouses at a young age. Between them they were left with seven children to raise alone.

Jim's late wife Andrea was initially diagnosed with stage II breast cancer but tragically, later learned it had spread to her bones, liver and lungs. Andrea lost her fight with cancer but won her place in eternity. Jim was her primary caregiver and a F-15E fighter pilot in the United States Air Force (USAF).

Ginger was the mother of five young children married to Major Troy Gilbert a USAF F-16 fighter pilot. While Jim's loss was long suffering, Ginger's loss came with a sudden knock at the front door. She faced every military wife's greatest fear; her husband had been killed in combat.

Both families struggled to pick up the pieces of their shattered lives while reconciling their faith in God with the reality they faced. Ginger and Jim found each other and joined their two broken families. They quickly realized they had many shared experiences of God's faithfulness.

They started a blog to document their journeys and found numerous others were helped by their authenticity. This book grew out of their grief and from their desire to openly share what God so graciously taught them. It is about life and death and life after death. But always it is about God's unfailing love for us.

They met and married in 2008 and now reside in Franklin, Tennessee where they raise their blended family. They speak nationally sharing their story of loss and hope and have appeared on national television, radio and numerous publications.

Printed and bound by PG in the USA